Understanding
Abortion

Understanding Abortion

From Mixed Feelings to Rational Thought

Stephen D. Schwarz
With Kiki Latimer

LEXINGTON BOOKS
Lanham • Boulder • New York • Toronto • Plymouth, UK

Published by Lexington Books
A wholly owned subsidiary of The Rowman & Littlefield Publishing Group, Inc.
4501 Forbes Boulevard, Suite 200, Lanham, Maryland 20706
www.lexingtonbooks.com

Estover Road, Plymouth PL6 7PY, United Kingdom

British Library Cataloguing in Publication Information Available

Library of Congress Cataloging-in-Publication Data

Schwarz, Stephen D.
  Understanding abortion : from mixed feelings to rational thought / Stephen D.
Schwarz with Kiki Latimer.
      p. cm.
  ISBN 978-0-7391-6770-0 (cloth : alk. paper)—ISBN 978-0-7391-6771-7 (pbk. :
alk. paper)—ISBN 978-0-7391-6772-4 (electronic)
  1. Abortion—Moral and ethical aspects. 2. Pro-life movement. 3. Women's
rights. I. Latimer, Kiki. II. Title.
  HQ767.15 .S383
  179.7'6—dc23

                                                          2011042006

Printed in the United States of America

Contents

List of Tables and Figures   xi

1 **Introduction**   1
   "Oh My God, I'm Pregnant"   1
   Understanding the Abortion Issue   4
   The Moral Question and the Legal Question   5
   Is Abortion a Religious Issue?   6
   Neutral Terminology   7
   Is the Being in the Womb a Person?   7
   Points of Agreement between the Two Sides   7
   Facts about the Being in the Womb (BIW)   8

PART I: THE PRO-CHOICE MORAL POSITION   13

2 **The Feminist Quality of Life Argument**   15
   There are Many Reasons for Having an Abortion   15
   Women Themselves Must Be the Ones Who Make the
     Abortion Decision   16
   Pregnancy Has Profound Effects on Women's Lives   17
   Abortion Rights Are Basic Human Rights and Necessary for
     Gender Equality   17

3 **The General Quality of Life Argument**   19
   Every Child a Wanted Child   19
   Every Child a Healthy Child   20
   The Quality of Life of the Woman   20
   The Quality of Life of the Whole World: Overpopulation 20

4 **The Not-A-Person Argument**   21
   Human Beings and Persons   21
   A Fetus Has No Absolute Value   21
   Fetuses Are Not Persons   22
   Mary Anne Warren's Not-a-Person Argument   22
   Michael Tooley's Not-a-Person Argument   23
   Michael Tooley's Defense of Infanticide   24
   David Boonin's Not-a-Person Argument   25
   The Maguire-Morgan Not-a-Person Argument   28
   The Fetus Is a Potential Person, Not an Actual Person   29
   The Achievement View   30
   When Is Personhood Achieved?   31
   Summary Statement: The Fetus Is Not a Real Person, Only
      a Biological Organism   33
   Chapter Summary Statement: Basis and Implications of the
      Not-a-Person Thesis   33

5 **The No-Duty-to-Sustain Argument**   35
   A Woman's Right over Her Body   35
   Bolton's No-Duty-to-Sustain Argument   36
   Thomson's Violinist Argument   36
   Thomson's Violinist Argument and the Case of Rape   37
   Thomson's Intruder Argument   37
   Thomson on the Meaning of a Right to Life and the Right to
      an Abortion   38
   Thomson's Account Does Not Support an Absolute Right
      to Abortion   38
   Abortion Yes—Securing the Death of the Child No   39
   Standard Methods of Abortion   39
   Another Method: Dilation and Extraction   41
   A Controversy within the Pro-Choice Community   42
   The Question of Fetal Pain   43

PART II: THE PRO-LIFE MORAL POSITION   45

6 **The Reality of the Child in the Womb**   47
   First: The Continuum Argument   47
   Second: The SLED Argument   51
   Third: Being a Person and Functioning as a Person   55
   The Person-Human Being Distinction: Engineered to Try
      to Justify Abortion?   57
   Summary Statement: Being and Functioning   58
   Chapter Summary Statement: The Reality of the Child
      in the Womb   59

7 Abortion Means Killing This Child 61
Standard Methods of Abortion 61
Another Method: Dilation and Extraction or Partial-
Birth Abortion 63
"Partial-Birth Abortion" is not Really Abortion 64
What Are the Results of Abortion? 64
Abortion as Infanticide: The Kamchadal Practice 65
Abortion Kills the Child: The First Refutation of the Violinist
Argument 66
The Child's Right over His Body 69
Abortion Is Intentional Killing: A Second Refutation 70
A Mother's Duty to Sustain Her Child: A Third Refutation 70
The Violinist Argument and the Case of Rape 71
The Special Relation between a Woman and Her Child 72
Our General Duty to Help One Another: A Fourth Refutation 72
Summary of Refutations of the Violinist Argument 73
Objection and Reply: He Will Never Know the Difference 73

8 Abortion Causes Pain to the Child 75
Abortion Is Wrong because It Causes Horrible Pain to
the Child 75
The Special Horror of Partial-Birth Abortions 76
Controversy regarding Pain for the Child 77
The Risk Factor concerning Pain to the Child 78
Weighing Harms and Benefits 78
The Pain Argument Applies Even If the BIW Is Not a Person 79

9 The Dignity of the Human Person 81
A Reply to "Every Child a Wanted Child" 81
A Reply to "Every Child a Healthy Child" 82
A Reply to "The Quality of Life of the Woman" 82
A Reply to "The Quality of Life of the Whole World:
Overpopulation" 83
A Reply to "The Relative to Social Acceptance" View of Being
a Person 83
A Reply to Two Feminist Pro-Choice Arguments 84
The Question of Infanticide 84
Making Killing Seem Honorable 85

PART III: FURTHER MORAL CONSIDERATIONS 87

10 Some Pro-Choice Replies to Pro-Life Claims 89
Pro-Choice Replies to Pro-Life Claims regarding the
Continuum Argument 89
Pro-Choice Replies to Pro-Life Claims
regarding the SLED Argument 95

Pro-Choice Replies to Pro-Life Claims regarding the
  Being-Functioning Distinction   95
Pro-Choice Replies to Pro-Life Claims regarding the Violinist
  Argument: Active Killing   96
Pro-Choice Replies to Pro-Life Claims regarding the Violinist
  Argument: Intentional Killing   98
Pro-Choice Replies to Pro-Life Claims regarding the Violinist
  Argument: A Duty to the Child   100
Pro-Choice Replies to Pro-Life Claims regarding the Violinist
  Argument: A General Duty   101
Pro-Choice Replies to Pro-Life Claims regarding the Child's
  Right over His Body   102
Pro-Choice Replies to Pro-Life Claims regarding Pain to
  the Child   103
Pro-Choice Replies to Pro-Life Claims regarding the Dignity
  of the Human Person   103

11   **When Does a Person Begin to Exist?**   **105**
     Formulating the Question   105
     Some Main Lines Proposed as Marking the Beginning of
       a Person   105
     The Question of Infanticide   115
     An Objection to Almost All of These Lines   116
     The Achievement View, Being-Functioning, and the Lines   116

12   **Other Approaches**   **117**
     The Agnostic Position   117
     The Gradualist Position   118
     Early versus Late Abortion   119
     Pro-Life: The Don Marquis Future-Like-Ours Argument   120
     Pro-Choice: Some Replies to the Future-Like-Ours Argument   121

13   **What Should We Do If We Are in Doubt?**   **123**
     How Doubt May Arise   123
     The Pro-Life If-in-Doubt Argument   124
     The Pro-Choice If-in-Doubt Argument   125
     The Psychology of Pro-Choice and Pro-Life   126
     The Scope of Doubt: Early versus Late Abortions   127
     Which Way of Going Wrong Is Worse?   128

PART IV: THE LEGAL QUESTION   131

14   **The Legal Status: Pro-Choice and Pro-Life**   **133**
     Can We Legislate Morality?   133
     The Pro-Choice Legal Position   133
     The Pro-Life Legal Position   135

15 **The Role of Government**   137
    The Government Cannot Be Neutral: It Must Take a Stand   137
    The Government Cannot Be Neutral: It Must Draw the
        Line Somewhere   138
    "I'm Personally Opposed to Abortion, but I Think It Should
        Be Legal"   139

16 **Other Significant Legal Aspects**   143
    The Question of Discrimination   143
    The Question of Imposing   143
    The Question of Privacy   144
    The Question of Power-Freedom-Control for Women: A
        Pro-Choice View   145
    The Question of Power-Freedom-Control for Women: A
        Pro-Life View   146
    Which Way of Going Wrong Is Worse?   147

17 **The Hard Cases: Rape, Life of the Woman, Severe Deformities** 149
    Two Positions on the Hard Cases   149
    The Case of Rape: Protecting the Woman's Choice   150
    The Case of Rape: Protecting the Innocent Child   153
    The Case of Rape: The Testimony of a Person Conceived
        in Rape   156
    The Case of Rape: Some Final Thoughts   157
    The Life of the Woman   157
    The Child with Severe Deformities   159
    A General Analysis of the Pro-Life-With-Exceptions View 161

PART V: CONCLUDING TOPICS   163

18 **Safety Issues**   165
    Pro-Choice: Keep Abortion Safe and Legal   165
    Pro-Life: Legal Abortion Is Not Safe   167
    Pro-Choice: Back-Alley Abortions   169
    Pro-Life: Back-Alley Abortions   171
    Is Abortion Safer Than Childbirth?   173

19 **Going Beyond Abortion: The Unity Way**   177
    The Unity Way: Woman and Child Go Together   177
    The Unity Way: Abortion Is Harmful to Women   178
    Unwanted Pregnancy versus Unwanted Child   179
    Abortion Is about Family Relationships   179
    An Alternative to Abortion: Adoption   180
    A Final Note   181

20   Ultimate Issues   **183**
    First Set of Ultimate Issues: What Is Abortion?   183
    Second Set of Ultimate Issues: What Is a Human Person?   184
    Third Set of Ultimate Issues: Further Moral Considerations   190
    Fourth Set of Ultimate Issues: Other Items   192
    Final Set of Ultimate Issues: Identifying with Those Involved   193

Notes   195

Works Cited   205

Index   209

About the Author   215

List of Tables and Figures

Table 6.1   Summary Statement of the Continuum Argument   51
Table 6.2   SLED Argument   55
Table 11.1   Overview for Drawing Lines   106
Table 11.2   The "Conceived Question"   108
Table 14.1   PC: Keep Abortion Safe and Legal   134
Table 14.2   PL: The Child in the Womb Is a Real Person   136
Table 15.1   The Government Must Take a Stand   138
Table 15.2   The Government Must Draw a Line Somewhere   138
Table 17.1   Three Basic Views   161
Table 17.2   Total Pro-Choice and Total Pro-Life   161

Figure 13.1   The Moral Diagonals   129
Figure 16.1   The Legal Diagonals   148
Figure 18.1   Total Deaths   175

1

Introduction

 *có thai*

"OH MY GOD, I'M PREGNANT"

Jen was just about to pop the last tulip bulb into the ground when she heard Diana's car pull up with a screech. Diana rolled the passenger window down and yelled, "Why the hell aren't you answering your phone? For God's sake hurry up and get in the car!"

Jen looked up—"What?"

"Just get in!"

"I'm planting bulbs; what on earth is going on?"

"Just hurry and get in. I don't know what's going on. Lisa called a half hour ago, hysterical. For God's sake just get in. I've been trying to reach you! Where is your cell phone?"

Jen walked toward the car. "In the house." She hesitated. "I don't know . . . is this more of Lisa's drama with Mike?"

Diana looked more worried than usual. "I don't think so. She sounded really bad on the phone, crying, wouldn't say what the hell was wrong. Please just get in and go over with me."

Jen reluctantly pulled off her gardening gloves, tossed them on the lawn, brushed off her knees, and slid into the front seat. Diana pulled out as Jen said "Come on, we both know it's probably nothing. You know Lisa. It's probably just another tiff with Mike."

"Yeah, well, we can all handle the latest crisis I'm sure." Both girls laughed.

But when Lisa answered the door, Jen had her doubts. It was clear that Lisa had been crying, her eyes red and swollen.

Diana and Jen both enveloped Lisa with a hug. "What on earth is wrong, honey?" asked Diana gently.

Lisa stepped back and put her face in her hands. "Oh my God, I'm pregnant."

Neither friend spoke. All three young women stood in the raw silent aftermath of these words.

It was Lisa who finally broke the silence. "Well, for God's sake say something!"

Jen reached for Lisa. "Oh Lisa, I am so sorry!"

Diana spoke next. "Wow! Okay. I can't believe this. Okay, sit down. Everyone just sit down. Does Mike know?"

Lisa said "No, not yet. And, and well, I don't know if I want him to know. Does he have to know?"

"How far along?" asked Jen as they sat down in the circle of chairs.

"Oh God, I don't know, a few weeks, maybe longer; well, maybe six or seven weeks."

Diana nodded. "Okay, we can all deal with this. It's all going to be okay. You're going to be okay. We'll make an appointment today. It's still early enough for an abortion."

"What?" said Jen. "Are we talking about an abortion here?"

"Well what else? I doubt Lisa is going to have a baby when she's just started back to school." Diana looked at Lisa. "Right?"

"I don't know. I just don't know. I mean, of course, I'm thinking about it."

"Of course she doesn't know" countered Jen. "Maybe she wants to have the baby."

Diana shook her head. "For God's sake, it's not a baby yet; and she hardly knows what's-his-name." They both looked miserably at Lisa.

"I just don't know. I don't want to have a baby right now. Oh God! How did this happen to me? I can't have a baby! Not now. Oh not now!" Lisa bent over and began to cry again.

"Of course you can't," said Diana. "Go grab the phonebook Jen; we'll call right now and make the appointment and get this over with right away."

Jen didn't move. "I can't do this."

"Do what? Just get the phonebook!"

"I can't."

"What?" Diana looked confused.

"I can't do this," said Jen. "Be part of this abortion stuff; I mean, well, I just can't. It's just doesn't feel right, that's all."

"Feel right? Come on! Look at this mess. Look at Lisa! This is what doesn't feel right! Lisa has her whole life ahead of her, the college semester, graduation in a year. This is her life and her choice. It's a simple safe procedure and then it's all over with. This is no time to freak her out. Right?"

Lisa remained silent with her face in her hands.

Jen stood up. "Look, I'm not trying to freak her out. I'm not. But she's pregnant here. So that means something right? Like maybe a baby. Don't look at me like that! I just don't think abortion is necessarily the way to go."

"And why on earth not?" Diana stood up.

"I just don't. I can't explain how I feel. I just think it's a baby."

"Have you lost your mind? It's still just a tiny blob of cells. It's nothing yet! Nothing! For God's sake, now is the time to get rid of it!"

"Well, I think it is something. A baby. Or well, like a baby. Or something. It isn't just nothing! It's something."

Diana's voice jumped several notches. "Something? Oh yeah, it's something all right! Something horrible, and the sooner Lisa makes the appointment the sooner the terrible something will be nothing and she can put this behind her."

"What, by killing her baby, everything will be just fine, is that it? Good God, just run down the street and get an abortion like pulling a rotten tooth?"

"It's just not a baby yet. It's her choice. What part of choice do you not understand? And she sure isn't going to choose to have a baby right now. You know that as well as I do. Since when did you get so pro-life?"

"I'm not pro-life!" Jen raised her voice. "I just happen to not like the whole idea of abortion."

"Well, isn't that just nice for you. But you don't happen to be the one who's pregnant at the moment! Wake up. It's the twenty-first century and abortion is safe and legal."

"I just don't feel like that is all there is to it. I mean, well, she's pregnant!"

"Look, this is no time to confuse Lisa with all this emotional 'baby' talk."

"It's not just talk. It's just not that simple. I have mixed feelings about abortion."

"Yeah, well, so what? Don't we all. That's right, we all have mixed feelings. But when push comes to shove, you keep your mixed feelings to yourself and do what needs to be done."

That's when Lisa stood up. She walked between the two of them and opened the door.

"I need you two leave," she said.

"I'm sorry," said Jen.

"Me too. I'm sorry," said Diana.

"I just really need you both to leave" Lisa repeated. "Now."

"I need to be alone and I need to think."

Yes, Lisa thought; I need to really, really think.

UNDERSTANDING THE ABORTION ISSUE

In his Notre Dame address President Obama called for "open hearts, open minds and fair minded words" in the abortion debate. This book is written in the spirit of these words and provides tools for accomplishing their goals. It offers a guide to understanding a topic that is often confusing. It is intended for all people, both men and women, who want to really think about and come to truly understand what the abortion issue is all about. Some people are strongly on one side and wonder how anyone could hold the other side. The book will make plain that whatever this "other side" is, it has reasoned arguments that support it. As is often pointed out, you do not really understand your own position until you have understood the opposing position and the reasons for it. This means that the book will help you clarify your own position, be able to articulate it clearly and defend it when challenged. It means going beyond "gut feelings" to arrive at a reasoned position.

If you have mixed feelings—partly pro-life and partly pro-choice—and would like to sort them out and come to a clearer grasp; or if you tend to favor the one position or the other but are not quite sure why; or if you are simply interested in the topic as a moral, social, and political issue—then this book is for you.

As a guide to understanding the abortion issue it will address the basic questions. What does it mean to be pro-choice? What does it mean to be pro-life? Why are the two sides generally so far apart, each seemingly unable to see the other's point of view? We will try to provide answers to these questions, and thereby try to help each side see the other's point of view, "where they are coming from."

When properly articulated, the two sides, pro-choice and pro-life, are logically contradictory. They cannot both be correct. Which one is correct? Which one is the truth of the matter? The book is intended as a guide to help you to answer this question. It will focus on three key issues: (1) What are the logical grounds for adopting the pro-choice position? What reasons can be given in support of it? How can pro-life reply to these? (2) What are the logical grounds for adopting the pro-life position? What reasons can be given in support of it? How can pro-choice reply to these? (3) Which of the two positions is the more reasonable to hold?

This book is written to help each person arrive at his own position on this issue. One should not blindly follow others, or accept whatever position seems to fit in with one's previously adopted worldview. Perhaps those who hold "the other view" also hold views that one finds distasteful; but perhaps *on this issue* they are correct. This is something that my dear father, a philosopher and one of my teachers, so often stressed, and practiced in his own thinking. "Maybe *on this issue* they are correct."

This book grew out of my experience of some thirty or more years of teaching this topic in my ethics class as a professor of philosophy at the University of Rhode Island. It was always the most popular topic, and the students were always virtually unanimous in their reaction that it had helped them clarify this crucial issue and come to their own position based on their own understanding of it. The book hopes to share this experience with a larger audience.

It is a book intended both for beginners and those already familiar with the issue; both for laypersons and scholars. While not a "scholarly book" in style and in terms of what is assumed, it is scholarly in that it contains all the major classic arguments and approaches on both sides. It is written with the aim of providing an easy access to what can be a forbidding topic for many people. It includes some of the significant recent work on this issue, but does not try to provide an in-depth analysis of all recent developments. Most if not all of this recent work rests on the classic, traditional arguments that are developed here.

THE MORAL QUESTION AND THE LEGAL QUESTION

We usually think of "pro-choice versus pro-life" as if it were a single issue. In reality there are two issues, or two questions: the *moral* and the *legal*:

- Is abortion morally justified/neutral/right?
- Should abortion be legal?

An action or a practice may be morally justified or neutral or right and still be illegal in some legal system. An example would be holding a political meeting in one's home in a country where this is forbidden by a tyrannical government. Conversely, something may be morally wrong and yet legal by some legal code. Slavery is always wrong, and yet it was legal in America for many years. On the abortion question there are four possible positions:

1. Abortion is morally neutral and should be legal.
2. Abortion is morally justified and should be legal.
3. Abortion is morally wrong and should be illegal.
4. Abortion is morally wrong, but it should still be legal.

We will discuss the moral question in parts I, II, and III, chapters 2 through 13. Then in part IV, chapters 14 through 17, we will examine the legal question. The moral question is doubly important. First, it is important in itself: if abortion is morally right or neutral one should be free to have one, period; if it is morally wrong one should not have one, nor assist others in having one, even if the law allows them. Second, the moral question is important because it provides the basis for answering the legal question. Most laws, or at least the most important ones, are based on moral principles, and they are expressions of moral principles. Murder is illegal because it is, first and foremost, a terrible moral evil; so too, slavery. Our question then is: given a particular moral stand on abortion as neutral, justified, or wrong, what should be the corresponding legal stand? What legal stand does justice to a particular moral stand?

A word about the current legal situation in America today. Abortion is basically legal throughout the whole time of pregnancy, up until birth. This is the famous ruling of the Supreme Court in *Roe v. Wade*, January 22, 1973. It expressed its agreement with "the view that life does not begin until live birth"; and stated that "the unborn have never been recognized in the law as persons in the whole sense."[1] This means that abortion is de facto allowed until birth, when the "fetus" becomes a "person in the whole sense." We will return to this important ruling in later chapters.

IS ABORTION A RELIGIOUS ISSUE?

It is sometimes said that the abortion question is a religious issue. In some ways this is certainly true. Being pro-life is an essential part of many religious traditions. But there are also religions that do not include this. And some who say they are religious claim there are religious reasons to be pro-choice; for example, Constance Robertson in her book, *The Religious Case for Abortion* (1983). On the other side, many nonreligious people are pro-choice and see this as part of their nonreligious way of life. But there are also a significant number of people who are strongly pro-life and nonreligious. They see pro-life as a civil rights issue: the unborn should be respected and protected in the same way as every other human being.

In this book the abortion issue will be discussed in a strictly philosophical way, with neither an appeal to any religious faith nor any negation of such a faith. The case for each position will be made strictly by appeal to reason. You are then left to consider: Which side has the better arguments? In which direction does the evidence point? What squares best with your experience?

NEUTRAL TERMINOLOGY

To ensure a fair and balanced discussion of this important issue, it is crucial that the terms used not favor the one side or the other. Those who are pro-choice usually speak of the "fetus"; those who are pro-life speak of the "child" or the "baby." When presenting a particular side I shall use the term favored by that side. In other contexts, to assure objectivity, I shall use a neutral term, *the being in the womb* (BIW), an expression that leaves open its status. The term *being* is used here in a broad and very general philosophical sense, as referring to a concrete substance, such as a rock, a plant, or an animal.

IS THE BEING IN THE WOMB A PERSON?

A fundamental question in the whole abortion issue is the question: is the BIW a merely biological organism or a person? A biological organism is something that has the typical characteristics of a living thing such as growth and adaptation to environment; an example would be a microorganism such as bacteria or a plant. In contrast, a person is a being who is "one of us," who is owed the deep respect due to all human beings as persons; a being with the right to life, the right to not be killed. So, a fundamental question is whether the BIW is a mere biological organism; or a person just like the rest of us. As we shall see, pro-choice and pro-life are sharply divided on this question. Though perhaps the most fundamental question, the personhood question is not the only important question. Other very important questions concern the nature and significance of a woman's right over her body and her life, and how this affects the moral and the legal status of abortion. Each position on these and all other questions will be presented as if from a proponent of that position.

POINTS OF AGREEMENT BETWEEN THE TWO SIDES

A major point of contention between the pro-life (PL) side and some on the pro-choice (PC) side is the status of the being in the womb (BIW). Before we examine the opposing ways in which each side views the BIW, it is important to see the ways in which the PL and PC side agree on this issue. Both sides agree:

1. The BIW is human in the biological sense; it has forty-six chromosomes, and it is a member of the species "homo sapiens."

2. The BIW is alive and growing.
3. The BIW is the same *physical* organism from the moment of conception, all through pregnancy, and for the time after birth.
4. The BIW is not part of the woman's body. This was sometimes included in pro-choice arguments in earlier times but is no longer held due to advancements in scientific knowledge. It is a point of some significance, so let us look at it further.

There are several important aspects:

First, the BIW has its own gender (half are male) and its own genetic code. Second, the fact that the BIW is *in* the woman's body does not mean that it is *part of it*. Being in an MRI machine does not make you part of it. Third, neither birth nor abortion is considered an amputation, which is what it would have to be if the BIW were part of the woman's body. Fourth, as we shall again see later, the BIW and the woman do not exchange blood; the BIW has a separate and complete vascular system. Fifth, the woman's body initially tends to reject the BIW as a foreign entity, just as any human body rejects what it perceives as a foreign entity. This being said, both sides recognize the intimacy of the situation of the BIW being inside, but not part of, the woman's body.

FACTS ABOUT THE BEING IN THE WOMB (BIW)

To begin our investigation let us look at the scientific facts about the development of the being in the womb. This will also confirm the four points just made. But it should be noted that biological development alone does not suffice to determine the matter of personhood.

From the moment of conception there is a complex, dynamic, and rapidly growing biologically human organism. It starts out as a single cell, called a zygote. By a natural and continuous process, it will develop and be born with trillions of cells, in about nine months. This new human being, though it receives one half of its chromosomes from each parent, has its own unique genetic code, and is therefore unlike either parent. It should not be called "a fertilized ovum" because it is its own being, not an ovum or a sperm that is modified. Here is a chronology of the life of this being in the womb:[2]

4 days: The gender of the BIW is already determined and can be noted under a special microscope.

7–9 days: There are already several hundred cells formed; contact with the uterus is made and implantation begins.

17–18 days: Blood cells appear and a heartbeat begins.

18 days: Developmental emphasis is now on the nervous system; such early development is necessary since the nervous system integrates the action of all other systems; other vital organs such as the heart also begin development.

19 days: Eyes begin to form.

20 days: Foundation of brain, spinal cord, and entire nervous system established.

28 days: Building blocks are in place for forty pairs of muscles from the base of the skull to the lower end of the spinal column.

30 days: By the end of the first month the foundation of the brain, spinal cord, nerves, and sense organs is completely formed; the primary brain is present. Although the heart is still incomplete, it is beating regularly and pumping blood cells through a closed vascular blood system. The BIW and woman do not exchange blood, the BIW having from a very early point in its development a separate and complete vascular system.

30 days: Only about ¼ inch in length. By this time the BIW has completed the period of greatest increase in size and physical change of its entire lifetime. It is ten thousand times larger than the zygote which came into being when the egg was fertilized; it will increase in weight six billion times by birth, having in only the first month gone from a one-cell state to millions of cells.

33 days: The cerebral cortex, the part of the central nervous system that governs motor activity as well as intellect, may be seen.

39 days: Heartbeat is essentially similar to that of an adult.

42 days or 6 weeks: Earliest reflexes begin; it is about ½ inch long; cartilage begins to develop; the male penis begins to form.

43 days or 6 weeks: Brain waves have been noted at this time.

45 days or 6 ½ weeks: Electroencephalographic waves have been noted at this time, and so conscious experience is possible after this date.

6 weeks: The primitive skeletal system has completely developed by this time. This marks the end of the embryonic period (from Greek, to swell or team within). From this point on, the BIW is medically referred to as a fetus (Latin, young one or offspring).

7 weeks: The BIW now has the familiar external features and all the internal organs of the adult human, even though it is less than an inch long and weighs only $^1/_{30}$ of an ounce. The heart is functionally complete. The body has become nicely rounded, padded with muscles and covered by a thick skin. The arms have hands with fingers and thumbs. The slower growing legs have recognizable knees, ankles, and toes. Shettles and Rugh describe the BIW at this point of its development as a one-inch miniature doll with a large head, but formed arms and legs and a human face.[3]

7 weeks: Brain configuration is already like the adult brain; it sends out impulses that coordinate the functions of the other organs; the heart beats sturdily; the stomach produces digestive juices; the liver manufactures blood cells; the kidneys function by extracting uric acid from the blood. The muscles of the arms and body can already be set in motion.

8 weeks: After this time no further primordial will form. Everything is already present that will be found at full term.

9 and 10 weeks: The BIW's activity increases dramatically. If the forehead is touched, it turns its head away, puckers up its brow and frowns. It has full use of its arms and can bend its elbow and wrist independently. The entire body becomes sensitive to touch.

13 weeks: In the third month, the BIW becomes very active. By the end of the month it can kick its legs, turn its feet, curl and fan its toes, make a fist, move its thumb, bend its wrist, turn its head, squint, frown, open his mouth, and press its lips tightly together. The BIW can swallow and drinks the amniotic fluid that surrounds it. Thumb sucking is first noted at this age. The first respiratory motions move fluid in and out of its lungs with inhaling and exhaling respiratory movements.

12–16 weeks: During this period, the BIW grows very rapidly, to eight to ten inches in length; weight increases six times. For this incredible growth spurt it needs oxygen and food. It receives this through the placental attach-ment. The placenta is biologically part of the BIW, not the woman, as was previously thought.

In the fifth month, the BIW gains two inches in height and ten ounces in weight. By the end of the month it will be about one foot long and will weigh one pound. Fine hair begins to grow on its eyebrows and head and a fringe of eyelashes appears. Most of the skeleton hardens. The BIW's muscles become much stronger, and the woman finally perceives its many activities. The woman comes to recognize the movement and can feel the BIW's head, arms, and legs. She may even perceive a rhythmic jolting move-ment, fifteen to thirty per minute. This is due to the BIW hiccoughing. The heartbeat can be heard with a stethoscope.

The BIW sleeps and wakes. When it sleeps, it invariably settles into its favorite position called his "lie." Each being has a characteristic lie. When it awakens, it moves about freely in the buoyant fluid turning from side to side, and frequently head over heel. Sometimes the head will be up, and sometimes it will be down. It may sometimes be aroused from sleep by external vibrations. Movements of the woman, including her heartbeat and breathing, are communicated to the BIW.

In the sixth month, the BIW grows about two inches, to become fourteen inches long. It accumulates a little fat under the skin, and its weight in-creases to a pound and three-quarters. The permanent teeth buds come in high in the gums behind the milk teeth. Eyelids open and close and the eyes look up and down and sideways. It may perceive light through the abdominal wall.

The BIW develops a strong muscular grip with its hands. It starts to breathe regularly and can maintain respiratory response for twenty-four hours if born prematurely; it may have a chance of surviving in an incubator. The youngest ones known to survive by 2009 were twenty weeks old. The concept of viability (the ability to survive outside the womb) is not a static one, but one that changes with available technology.

I

THE PRO-CHOICE
MORAL POSITION

The pro-choice position in a nutshell. Pro-choice is basically three main points:

- Abortion is necessary for and morally justified by *quality of life* considerations, both for the pregnant woman herself and for society in general.
- The fetus is *not a person,* and so it does not have a right to life; therefore abortion is morally neutral or justified.
- But even if the fetus is a person abortion is justified because the woman has *no duty to sustain* it and may therefore free herself from it by having an abortion.

These are the points that will be developed in the next four chapters. The first is the theme of chapters 2 and 3. The second is taken up in chapter 4; the third in chapter 5.

The not-a-person argument in chapter 4 and the no-duty-to-sustain argument in chapter 5 are the two basic philosophical arguments for the pro-choice moral position. They are logically independent in that the pro-choice moral position is shown to be correct if either one is successful. The two quality-of-life arguments in chapter 2 and chapter 3 are often used in conjunction with either of the other two arguments, or both.

2

The Feminist Quality of Life Argument

The basic idea here is that abortion is often the best course of action for a woman in terms of protecting and furthering the quality of her life in all its dimensions. The woman herself is in the best position to make this decision. Pro-Choice asks us to *identify with the woman! Focus on the reality of the woman in the world.*

THERE ARE MANY REASONS FOR HAVING AN ABORTION

Speaking for the feminist perspective, Susan Sherwin points out that "feminists recognize that women have abortions for a wide variety of compelling reasons."

1. Some women, for instance, find themselves seriously ill and incapacitated throughout pregnancy.
2. They cannot continue in their jobs and may face insurmountable difficulties in fulfilling their responsibilities at home.
3. Many employers and schools will not tolerate pregnancy in their employees or students, and not every woman is able to put her job, career, or studies on hold.
4. Women of limited means may be unable to take adequate care of children they have already borne, and they may know that another mouth to feed will reduce their ability to provide for their existing children.
5. Women who suffer from chronic disease, who believe themselves too young or too old to have children, or who are unable to maintain lasting relationships may recognize that they will not be able to care properly for a child when they face the decision.

6. Some who are homeless, addicted to drugs, or diagnosed as carrying the AIDS virus may be unwilling to allow a child to enter the world with the handicaps that would result from the mother's condition.

7. If the fetus is a result of rape or incest, then the psychological pain of carrying it may be unbearable.

8. And the woman [in such a situation] may recognize that her attitude to the child after birth will be tinged with bitterness.

9. Some women learn that the fetuses that they carry have serious chromosomal anomalies and consider it best to prevent them from being born with a condition that is bound to cause them to suffer.

10. Others, knowing the father to be brutal and violent, may be unwilling to subject a child to the beatings or incestuous attacks they anticipate; some may have no other realistic way to remove the child (or themselves) from the relationship.

11. A woman may simply believe that bearing a child is incompatible with her present life plans at the time. Continuing a pregnancy may have devastating repercussions throughout a woman's life.

12. If the woman is young, then a pregnancy will likely reduce her chances of pursuing an education and hence limit her career and life opportunities.

13. In many circumstances, having a child will exacerbate the social and economic forces already stacked against a woman by virtue of her sex (and her race, class, age, sexual orientation, disabilities, and so forth).

14. Access to abortion is necessary for many women if they are to escape the oppressive conditions of poverty.[1]

WOMEN THEMSELVES MUST BE THE ONES WHO MAKE THE ABORTION DECISION

Whatever the reason, it is the pregnant woman herself who is in the best position to judge whether abortion is the appropriate response in her given circumstances. She is the only one who is able to weigh all the relevant factors, and there are no general rules for determining when abortion is, or is not, morally justified. A woman's personal deliberations about her abortion decision occur in the context of her commitments to the needs and interests of everyone concerned, including herself, her child, and other members of her household. Since there is no single formula available for balancing these complex factors through all possible cases, it is vital that a woman's right to come to her own conclusions always be respected and protected. By their very nature, abortion decisions are dependent on the specific features of a woman's own individual experience. No one should expect to set the agenda for these considerations in any universal way. Women are full moral agents, with the responsibility for making moral decisions about their own pregnancies.[2]

This is closely related to the fact that when a woman bears a child, this is a very important event in her life, because it involves very significant physical, emotional, social, and economic changes for her. And so her ability to exert control over the incidence, the timing, and the frequency of her childbearing is of the greatest importance for her, and is always significantly related to her ability to control the other things she values in her life.[3]

PREGNANCY HAS PROFOUND EFFECTS ON WOMEN'S LIVES

Pregnancy takes place in women's bodies and has profound effects on women's lives. This is a central feature of pregnancy; its moral significance cannot be emphasized enough. Accounts of pregnancy that attempt to be gender-neutral are not available. Pregnancy is explicitly a condition associated with women, and so policies about abortion affect women uniquely.[4] Clearly, many pregnancies occur to women who place a very high value on the lives of the particular fetuses they carry, and choose to see their pregnancies through to term despite the risks and costs involved. It would clearly be wrong to force such women to terminate their pregnancy under such circumstances. Other women, or perhaps some of these same women at other times, value other things more highly and choose not to continue their pregnancies. They also should be free to act on their own individual, personal decisions. In short, the value that women ascribe to individual fetuses varies dramatically from case to case, and may well change over the course of any particular pregnancy.[5]

Susan Sherwin's argument appeals not only to the importance of preserving and furthering the quality of life of women but also to the claim that the fetus is not a person. Indeed her quality of life argument rests in part on this claim, a theme we will take up in chapter 4.

ABORTION RIGHTS ARE BASIC HUMAN RIGHTS AND NECESSARY FOR GENDER EQUALITY

The right to choose abortion is essential not only for quality of life in terms of the individual woman but also for women in general. Alison Jaggar argues that this right is a basic human right, that:

> sexual and reproductive rights elaborate the most fundamental and generally accepted rights to life, health, and bodily integrity. Specifically the right to

abortion is implied by the rights to "life, liberty and the security of persons," which were asserted in the UDHR [the 1948 *Universal Declaration of Human Rights*] and the *International Covenant on Economic, Social and Cultural Rights* (ICESR 1967) as well as various regional human rights conventions[6]

Jaggar argues further that the right to abortion is necessary to ensure equality between men and women. We can call this the feminist egalitarian argument:

At its simplest abortion is an essential health care service. According to the Committee on the Elimination of Discrimination against Women (CEDAW), neglecting to provide health services that only women need is a form of discrimination against women that governments are obliged to remedy.

In addition to depriving women of equality in health care, a number of philosophers have argued that banning abortion selects women for forms of service that are not required of others. . . . By contrast [to military service], the sex-specific nature of pregnancy means that this service can presently be required only of women. Moreover, pregnancy is a service whose burdens have little parallel; certainly they are quite unlike those of military service or of fathers' obligations to provide financial support for their children. . . . Forced pregnancy requires a service that is especially problematic because it "involves direct invasions of the body or the imposition of physical pain or extreme physical discomfort. . . . The burdens imposed by pregnancy and birth should be considered in the broader context of women's and children's lives. In the real world, many pregnancies are regarded as shameful and may be punished by social humiliation or worse. Even when this does not occur, Anita Allen argues that the burdens of sexuality, pregnancy, and childrearing are overwhelmingly borne by women, though shared to an extent by men, and that laws restricting access to abortion make it more difficult for women to avoid these burdens. . . . Frequently, adoption is not a real possibility and, even when adoption opportunities are available, most women find it extraordinarily traumatic to consider giving away their babies. In the real world, the extra service that pregnancy demands of women usually lasts far longer than nine months.

This service is not only burdensome in itself; it also undermines women's equality in other areas. The social assignments of caretaking and often financial responsibility for their children to mothers means that the birth of a child, especially an unwanted child, often severely disrupts women's life plans. Anita Allen argues that abortion rights are a precondition of full or "first-class" citizenship for women. . . . Siegel argues that restrictions on abortion offend U.S. constitutional guarantees of equal protection because they inflict status-based injuries on women, such as compromising their opportunities for education and employment. . . . Given existing systems of social arrangements, gender equality is impossible without abortion rights.[7]

3

The General Quality of Life Argument

Abortion is often justified for the sake of the general quality of human life. Perhaps in an ideal world, all human beings should be allowed to continue to exist. But in the real world, with all its pain and suffering for so many people, in so many ways, this is surely not so. Let us look at some types of cases where this applies in regard to the abortion issue, where it is better if the fetus is killed than allowed to continue to live; and where an argument can therefore be made to justify abortion. Below are four main types of cases where this argument applies.

EVERY CHILD A WANTED CHILD

Abortion is morally justified in those cases where the child will not be wanted. We should not bring an unwanted child into the world. Because unwanted children often suffer neglect and feel unloved, it would be better to spare them that pain by ending their lives through abortion.

In the words of Margaret Sanger, "The first right of every child is to be wanted, to be desired, to be planned with an intensity of love that gives it its title to being."[1]

Another appeal in the same direction comes from Constance Robertson:

To stop the pregnancy and prevent the birth of a child who cannot properly be cared for shows wisdom—and understanding of the realities of life. The only life in an embryo is the woman's life within it. Until it can live a separate life, it is *not* a separate life.[2]

EVERY CHILD A HEALTHY CHILD

Abortion is also morally justified if the child will have severe physical defects. We should not bring a severely defective child into the world. The abortion would prevent a life of suffering for that child and would spare his parents the great burden of having to take care of him. This is the importance of doctors like the late Dr. Tiller who are willing to do late term abortions, up to the due date, on medically deformed infants.

Peter Singer is a well-known advocate of terminating the lives of infants who have a prospect of a poor quality of life. In the passage below he speaks of born infants, but his position applies equally to those not yet born.

> When the life of an infant will be so miserable as not to be worth living, from the internal perspective of the being who will lead that life . . . [then] if there are no "extrinsic" reasons for keeping the infant alive—like the feelings of the parents—it is better that the child should be helped to die without further suffering.[3]

THE QUALITY OF LIFE OF THE WOMAN

Abortion would also be morally justified if it is necessary to ensure the quality of life of the woman. A woman should not continue her pregnancy if she is not yet ready to receive and care for her child. Furthermore, giving birth is painful and can be dangerous for women and therefore should not be forced upon the woman.

THE QUALITY OF LIFE OF
THE WHOLE WORLD: OVERPOPULATION

Abortion is morally justified whenever it is needed in order to prevent the threat of *overpopulation*. In a utilitarian spirit, abortion is defended by saying that we need to consider the greatest happiness of the greatest number of people, and especially, the avoidance of misery for the masses of people. Therefore we must take measures, including abortion, to ensure that we do not have an overpopulated world. K. B. Welton speaks to this point:

> Millions of families, and the many children that result from unregulated procreation, are becoming dependent on public assistance in cities throughout the world. Millions now grow up in poverty and miss an equal chance in life. And the sad fact is they are likely to repeat the mistakes of their parents at an even earlier age, thus intensifying the pace of irresponsible demands upon their community and the world.[4]

4

The Not-a-Person Argument

HUMAN BEINGS AND PERSONS

We turn now to the claim that the fetus should not be counted as a person with a right to life. This claim is based on the not-a-person argument, the idea that what is morally significant for the wrongness of killing is the question of personhood, whether or not the being that is killed is a person. It claims that *the fetus is not a real person*, but only a biological organism (like bacteria), with no more right to life than any other merely biological organism, such as a clump of cells. It claims that the fetus is not an actual person, not a real person, but merely a potential person. It grants that the fetus is biologically human, but claims that this is not enough. We should note the clear distinction it makes in regard to the term *human being*:

- Human Being as a *biological organism*. It is a member of the species *Homo sapiens*. There are forty-six chromosomes and it grows like a plant. But there is no conscious self, there is no "you" there.
- Human Being as a *person*. There is a "you" there, a soul, spirit, or mind; there is a conscious self; or at least a potentially conscious self.

A FETUS HAS NO ABSOLUTE VALUE

As a support for her pro-choice quality of life argument, Susan Sherwin argues that there is no absolute value that attaches to fetuses. This means that their value does not reside in them objectively and intrinsically, and because of the nature of their being. Rather their value is determined by

their relational status, their acceptance by others and their ability to inter-
act with others, and by the context of their particular development. This is
taken to be part of the general point that human beings are fundamentally
relational beings. Fetuses are significantly limited in the relationships in
which they can participate. But after birth, human beings are capable of a
very wide range of relationships with those around them. Until birth, the
fetus is defined in its essential being as an entity entirely within the woman
on whom it is dependent.[1]

FETUSES ARE NOT PERSONS

Continuing with Susan Sherwin, the reason a fetus has no absolute value
is that it is not a person. Fetuses are not persons because they have not yet
developed sufficiently to be capable of social relationships with others, and
their entire existence is defined in terms of their relationship to the woman
in whom they exist. It is this development for social relationships that de-
fine persons in the morally significant sense. In contrast, newborn babies,
although they are just beginning their development into persons, are now
subject to social relationships, for they are capable of communication and
interaction with other persons.[2]

The basic idea of the not-a-person argument is the claim that the fetus is
not a real person since it cannot think rationally, has no sense of self, and
has no desire to continue existing. It cannot communicate intentionally
by talking or any other means. Therefore it does not have the right to life
proper to the being of a person. Various forms of this argument have been
proposed by several philosophers, most notably Mary Anne Warren and
Michael Tooley, and more recently David Boonin. We will now examine
their arguments, as well as another somewhat different argument for the
same conclusion.

MARY ANNE WARREN'S NOT-A-PERSON ARGUMENT

She asks: "What characteristics entitle an entity to be a person?"[3] Her reply:

I suggest that the traits which are most central to the concept of personhood,
or humanity in the moral sense, are, very roughly the following:

1. Consciousness (of objects and events external and/or internal to the being),
   and in particular the capacity to feel pain
2. Reasoning (the *developed* capacity to solve new and relatively complex
   problems)

3. Self-motivated activity (activity which is relatively independent of either genetic or direct external control)
4. The capacity to communicate, by whatever means, messages of an indefinite variety of types, that is, not just with an indefinite number of possible contents, but on indefinitely many possible topics
5. The presence of self-concepts, and self-awareness, either individual or racial, or both

Admittedly, there are apt to be a great many problems involved in formulating precise definitions of these criteria, let alone in developing universally valid behavioral criteria for deciding when they apply. . . . [However] All we need to claim, to demonstrate that a fetus is not a person, is that any being which satisfies *none* of (1)–(5) is certainly not a person.[4]

MICHAEL TOOLEY'S NOT-A-PERSON ARGUMENT

An essentially similar argument is advanced by Michael Tooley. He frames it in terms of the question of a person's right to life. When does a being have a right to life?

1. An entity cannot have a right to life unless it is capable of having an interest in its own continued existence.
2. An entity is not capable of having an interest in its own continued existence unless it possesses, at some time, the concept of a continuing self, or subject of experiences and other mental states.
3. The fact that an entity will, if not destroyed, come to have properties that would give it a right to life does not in itself make it seriously wrong to destroy it.[5]

Tooley then applies this reasoning to human beings:

If these philosophical contentions are correct, the crucial question is a factual one: At what point does a developing human being acquire the concept of a continuing self, and at what point is it capable of having an interest in its own continued existence? I have . . . suggested that careful scientific studies of human development . . . strongly support the view that even newborn humans do not have the capacities in question.[6]

In a more recent formulation he argues as follows:

First, a person is not merely a potential subject of experiences: a person is an entity that has had, or that is now having, actual experiences. Second, a person is not a momentary subject of experiences that can only exist for a moment: a person is a persisting subject of experiences that can exist at different times. Third, the experiences and other mental states of a person at different times must be psychologically connected. Otherwise, what would exist would not be a person, but simply a sequence of isolated, momentary subjects of consciousness. Fourth, the psychological connections cannot be based only on unconscious mental states: at least some of the connections must involve conscious thoughts at one time about experiences and other mental states at other times.[7]

In addition to these four points that are required for being a person in what Tooley calls the minimal sense, there are "two other characteristics [that] are also necessary if an entity is to have the right to continued existence."[8] This right is of course crucial in the present context, where the question is whether or not the fetus may be denied continued existence by being aborted. Tooley explains these two other characteristics:

First, I think that an entity cannot have a right to continued existence—or, indeed, any rights at all—unless it either has, or has had, conscious desires, since it seems to me both that something can have rights at a given time only if there can be things that are in its interest at that time, and that the morally relevant concept of interest presupposes the existence of desires. Second, I think that the thoughts that serve to tie together mental states at different times in a conscious way need to involve the idea that an experience or other mental state that existed at some other time was *one's own*. Self-consciousness, then . . . is needed for a right to continued existence.[9]

MICHAEL TOOLEY'S DEFENSE OF INFANTICIDE

Referring to his argument in terms of the concept of a continuing self and that being's consequent interest in its own continued existence (the earlier argument above), Tooley draws his conclusion about the moral question of infanticide.

If this is right, then it would seem that infanticide during a time interval shortly after birth must be viewed as morally acceptable.

But where is the line to be drawn? What is the precise cutoff point? Since it seems clear that an infant at this point in its development is not capable of possessing the concept of a continuing subject of experiences and other mental states, and so is incapable of having an interest in its own continued existence, infanticide will be morally permissible in the vast majority of cases in which it is, for one reason or another, desirable. The practical moral problem can thus be satisfactorily handled by choosing some short period of time, such as a week after birth, as the interval during which infanticide will be permitted.[10]

In a more recent work he again asserts that newborn infants are not persons, with the implication that killing them is morally permissible. He argues as follows:

In the first place, the behavior of newborn humans provides no ground for attributing higher mental capacities to them. In particular, it provides no reason at all for believing that newborn humans possess a capacity for thought, or for self-consciousness, or for rational deliberation. All the behavioural evidence indicates that such capacities emerge only later in the individual's development.

The neurophysiological data point to the same conclusion. The neuronal circuitry in the human brain undergoes, in general, tremendous development during the postnatal period. What is crucial, however, is that those networks, located in the upper areas of the cerebral cortex, that are thought to underlie higher mental functions, are not present at birth; their emergence takes place only over an extended period of postnatal development.

Finally, there is the bioelectrical evidence. This evidence is less direct, and its significance not yet fully understood. The bioelectrical changes taking place postnatally do, however, cohere very well with the behavioural and neurophysiological data, and thus lend additional support to the conclusions based upon those data. (1983: 407)[11]

DAVID BOONIN'S NOT-A-PERSON ARGUMENT

David Boonin's approach is best seen as addressing the question, why one would think that the fetus is a person; or more specifically in his case, why it should be treated as a person and given the same moral standing as a normal adult human being, especially the right to life. After all, the fetus is very different from the normal adult human or even a newly born human. So if the fetus is to be accorded the same moral standing, what are the grounds for this? What arguments can pro-life give to show this? In chapter 2 of his book he examines several arguments that might show this.[12] He finds all of them wanting and concludes that the fetus does not have the moral standing that you and I have, especially that it does not have the right to life. Three of these arguments are particularly noteworthy, as Boonin's replies to them can be seen as constituting his version of the not-a-person argument. Let us now look at these three arguments and see how Boonin replies to them to develop his not-a-person argument.[13]

The Common Species Membership Argument

The pro-life argument is that every human fetus is a member of the same species *homo sapiens* as you and I and so should be accorded the same moral status that you and I have.

Boonin's reply is this. The fact that the fetus is of the same biological species as a normal adult human being does not show that it should be treated as a person. Species membership is not a satisfactory reason for acknowledging personhood. An alien from another planet who showed all the marks of intelligence of a human person would be recognized as a person despite his being nonhuman; this shows that species membership is not a necessary condition for acknowledging personhood. It is also not a sufficient condition. Consider a human being who suffers "the permanent destruction of the higher regions of his brain but who was nonetheless able to be kept alive on a life-support machine." Boonin says of such a person, "surely the claim that he would continue to have the same right to life as you or I would be extremely controversial at best."[14] The conclusion he draws from this seems to be that such a person does not in fact have the same moral standing you and I have, especially not the right to life.

It could be argued by pro-life that in one sense species membership is morally significant. Boonin calls this "The species essence argument"; namely,

> that it is an essential property of every living member of the species *homo sapiens* that it has the capacity to function as a person. If this is so, and if the capacity to function as a person confers on one a right to life, then being a member of *homo sapiens* does ensure that one has a right to life.[15]

He replies that this capacity will be exercised only in the future; and the fact that a being has a capacity to do person-like things in *the future* does not grant it the moral standing to be treated as a person *now*.[16]

Another pro-life attempt to salvage the species membership argument would be to point out that *homo sapiens* is our own species. Boonin calls this "The kindred species argument." Do we not have greater duties to our family and friends than to strangers? Do we not likewise have greater duties of respect to our own species than to others? Shouldn't the BIW be shown respect just for this reason?

Boonin's reply is that even granting the major premise of this argument, that we have greater duties to our own than to strangers, it does not follow that "our own" have greater rights than strangers. And the "special duties we have to [our own] . . . certainly need not correspond to any difference in terms of their right to life."[17]

The Slippery Slope Argument

The pro-life argument is that there is a gradual and continuous development, hence a continuity of similarity, between the fetus at any stage of its existence and every later stage. This begins at conception when the fetus is called a zygote, and continues through all its stages, including being a newborn baby, being a child later, and finally being an adult. If we deny personal status to the zygote, we will have to deny it to the fetus at the next stage, since it is not significantly different at this stage; and then also the next stage after that, until we finally come to the adult human being. And then the logic of the argument will force us to deny personhood to him and her as well. Clearly this is absurd. To escape this absurdity we will have to accord personhood to the zygote, and of course to every stage following this.

Boonin replies that this is a logical fallacy. After a lengthy and detailed analysis he concludes:

> Finally, and I think most decisively, the slippery slope argument is subject to a commonly noted but not commonly appreciated rebuttal by *reductio ad absurdum*. As one writer has put it, the development from acorn to oak tree is equally continuous but "it does not follow that acorns are oak trees, or that we better say they are" (Thomson 1971: 131).[18]

The Potentiality Argument

The pro-life argument here is that the fetus is a being that has the potential to develop into an individual person just like us. The fetus eventually becomes a person with a right to life. This is because it already has the essential property of being a person. This potentiality, corresponding to the essential property, implies that the fetus will develop into an actual person. In view of this it should already now be accorded the status of a person, especially the right to life.

Boonin's basic reply is that potentiality does not imply actuality. "The fact that I now have the right to own property, or to watch anything I want on television, does not mean that I had the right when I was a small child."[19] And the essential property that the fetus now has is not that of actually being a person, since it cannot think rationally, it cannot communicate intentionally, and it has no concept of itself as an enduring subject of experiences. It has only the potential for these, and as we saw potentiality does not mean actuality. The fetus is not already a person in its nature; it is only a biological organism. And the reason that it is not a person in its nature, that it does not have the essential property of being a person, is that it has not yet achieved what it takes to actually be a person, a being who can say "I" and think rationally and talk to other persons. That is, being a person, an actual person, with the same moral standing you and I have, especially the right to life, is not something the fetus has in its nature; it is an achievement that will be attained only later with sufficient development and interaction with other persons in various social contexts. In its nature, in its essential being, the fetus is only a member of the species *homo sapiens*. And this is not enough to give it the same moral standing that a real actual person has, especially the same right to life that you and I have.[20]

THE MAGUIRE-MORGAN NOT-A-PERSON ARGUMENT

So far we have considered three forms of the not-a-person argument, those of Mary Anne Warren, Michael Tooley, and David Boonin. They all have at least one feature in common: they all seek to find an intrinsic and objective criterion for what it means to be a person. That is, they seek to discover what it means to be a person in the real nature of the person, not in any relation a being may have to social context, acceptance by other persons or other extrinsic and nonobjective factors. On each of their views if you meet the criteria they set forth, you are a person. That is, you are a person period, whether society accepts you or not. But there are also theories that make being a person relative to social acceptance. Let us now look at key passages from two writers who hold such a theory and who together may be seen as putting forth another version of the not-a-person argument, Marjorie Reiley Maguire and Lynn M. Morgan.[21] Let us begin with Maguire.

After remarking that "fetal personhood is important because underneath all the debates about abortion are conflicting beliefs about the personhood of the fetus" she says:

> Personhood is a concept that is incapable of empirical proof. It is not a biological judgment. It is a value judgment our society makes about a being. When we say a being is a person, we are saying it is a being like us, deserving of the rights, privileges, and respect to which we are entitled as members of the human community. There is no biological moment in human development, from the separate sperm and ovum to the octogenarian, that automatically signals the beginning of personhood.[22]
>
> In brief summary, my position is that what makes a being a person is membership in the human community. The touchstone of personhood is sociality. It is not our brain capacity, or the proper number of chromosomes, but our personal relatedness that makes us persons. To use the language of Martin Buber, it is when a being becomes a Thou, rather than an It, that it becomes a person.[23]
>
> I believe that the latest moment to mark the beginning of sociality is birth. I would argue, and I believe most people would agree with me, that at least birth marks the beginning of membership in the human community, even if no earlier moment in fetal development does. Birth puts into our midst a being that has come from a member of our species, that looks like us, and that elicits from us a certain sense of obligation.[24]
>
> My position is that the only way a fetus can become a member of the human community, and therefore a person, prior to birth, is if the woman in whose body it exists welcomes it into the human community by her consent to the pregnancy. It is the consent of the woman to continuing the pregnancy that marks the beginning of personhood, no matter how unwilling that consent is given. It is when she treats the biological reality within her as a Thou, that it

becomes a Thou rather than an It. And it is when she treats it as a Thou, that society also has an obligation to treat it as a Thou.[25]

Lynn M. Morgan adopts essentially the same position. It may be summarized in these five points:

1. Human life and personhood are culturally constructed.
2. Infanticide, then, with all the moral repugnance it evokes in the West, is a social construct rather than a universal moral edict.
3. The attribution of personhood is a collective social decision, for the legal and ethical boundaries of personhood can only be negotiated within social settings.
4. Personhood is contingent on social recognition, and a person is recognized using established sociocultural conventions.
5. What this means, in sum, is that "people are defined by people." There can be no absolute definition of personhood isolated from sociocultural context.[26]

In short, the Maguire-Morgan not-a-person argument claims that being a person is not something objective, something really there in the nature of things, and intrinsic to their being. Rather, being a person is contingent on something else; it is dependent on social recognition. A biologically human being is not as such a person, but only becomes a person when it is welcomed into the human community by other persons. Thus, whether or not a given being is a person is relative to social acceptance by others. The Maguire-Morgan view is a kind of ethical relativism. We may call it "The Relative to Social Acceptance" view of what counts as being a person.

THE FETUS IS A POTENTIAL PERSON, NOT AN ACTUAL PERSON

There are two features of the not-a-person argument in all its forms that are especially noteworthy: the notion of potential person and the achievement view. Let us now examine each of them, beginning with the notion of potential person.

The fetus is a biological organism that, after sufficient development, will become a person. It is therefore a potential person, somewhat like a medical student is a potential doctor. The medical student cannot legally practice medicine; being a potential doctor is not enough. Just as the medical student lacks the right to practice medicine, the fetus as a potential person lacks the moral right to life of an actual person. Even a late-term fetus lacks the right to life of an actual person, though he is fairly close to achieving the status of an actual person. Joel Feinberg brings this point out with two comparisons:

> In 1930, when he was six years old, Jimmy Carter didn't know it, but he was a potential president of the United States. That gave him no claim *then*, not even a very weak claim, to give commands to the U.S. Army and Navy. Franklin D. Roosevelt in 1930 was only two years away from the presidency, so he was a potential president in a much stronger way (the potentiality was much less remote) than was young Jimmy. Nevertheless, he was not actually president, and he had no more of a claim to the prerogatives of the office than did Carter.[27]

THE ACHIEVEMENT VIEW

All forms of the not-a-person argument, in particular those of Warren, Tooley, and Boonin, cite the obvious differences between the fetus and born babies. The argument basically claims that the fetus is too small, too undeveloped, and too much unlike the rest of us to be considered a real person. Pro-choice advocates also claim that abortion is justified by saying that if the fetus is killed by abortion, it will never know the difference. In short, the pro-choice position is that the fetus is an impersonal fetus, not a real baby, not a small person. It is only a potential person, not an actual person. It does not become an actual person until it achieves sufficient and significant development. The key idea here is *achieves*. And this points to the main theme of this section. Let us now carefully examine this.

Underlying the not-a-person argument is a basic idea about the nature of the human person that may be called the *Achievement View*. This is the claim that the fetus does not start out being a real person when it first comes into existence, but achieves this only when sufficient development has been reached or when other significant events occur. What this means is that being "human" or a "human being" does not guarantee being a "person." You become a person only when sufficient achievement has been accomplished. Warren's list of essential traits or meeting Tooley's criteria for the right to life are proposals as to what that something is; only when you achieve that do you become an actual person, or a person in the "whole sense."

In the case of Boonin it is particularly in his rejection of species membership and potentiality that the achievement view comes into play as a basic underlying assumption. Species membership is associated with being a person in the case of normal adult human beings. But this is because normal adult humans have achieved personhood, not because they are members of the species *homo sapiens*. And so species membership can be seen to be irrelevant; it does not entail having achieved being a person with the capacities this involves, such as thinking, talking and having a sense of self. The potentiality for these is there in the fetus, but as we saw, potentiality does not count as actuality. It is only when the fetus actually achieves these capacities that it is really a person. And to say "actually achieves" is precisely to express the achievement view. In sum, being a person, an actual person, with the same moral standing you and I have, especially the right to life, is not something the fetus has in its nature; it is an achievement that will be attained only later with sufficient development, or in some views, social acceptance.

WHEN IS PERSONHOOD ACHIEVED?

Those who hold the achievement view have made a variety of suggestions as to when personhood is achieved. Let us consider some examples. We will examine a more complete list in chapter 11.

Viability

This is when the fetus is capable of living outside the womb. The idea is that this capability gives it independence and that this independence is sufficient to give it the status of a person, or the achievement of personhood.

Organized Cortical Brain Activity

This is when the cerebral cortex is sufficiently developed to produce recognizable EEG readings. It occurs between the twenty-fifth and thirty-second week. It is the position advocated by David Boonin.[28]

Birth

This is the position of Mary Anne Warren. Her reason for adopting it may be summarized by saying that birth is the point at which the child is welcomed into the human community.[29] As noted above, it is suggested by Marjorie Reiley Maguire: "Birth marks the beginning of membership in the human community." It is also the position of U.S. Supreme Court in its *Roe v. Wade* decision, of January 22, 1973. It stated that unborn human beings are "not persons in the whole sense."

One Week after Birth

This is the earlier position of Michael Tooley noted above.

Three Months after Birth

This is the later position of Michael Tooley in his book, *Abortion and Infanticide,*[30] because there is sufficient brain development.

To be precise, Tooley does not actually say that personhood is achieved at three months. What he says is the following: Newborn infants are not persons. There is some reason to think that at three months humans become *quasi-persons.* A *quasi-person* is something that has the properties that make a being a person but not to the extent required for being an actual person. He summarizes the key parts of his position in this way:

> The general picture that emerges is as follows. New-born humans are neither persons nor even quasi-persons, and their destruction is in no way intrinsically wrong. At about the age of three months, however, they probably acquire properties that are morally significant, and that make it to some extent intrinsically wrong to destroy them. As they develop further, their destruction becomes more and more seriously wrong, until eventually it is comparable in seriousness to the destruction of a normal adult human being.[31]

When then does a human being achieve full personhood? When does what was merely a *quasi-person* become an actual person, with the full right to life of an actual person, or "a normal adult human being"? Tooley doesn't tell us in his book. The closest he comes to an answer is a kind of hint, when he suggests "that humans do not become persons until, say, about the age of one."[32]

Having defined a person as a being who has achieved a certain fairly high level of conscious thought, if it turns out that humans do not achieve this until about age one, then it follows logically that they are not persons until that time. Tooley seems extreme, but he is really only following his initial thesis about what it means to be a person to its logical conclusion.

Sometime after Birth

Another philosopher who takes Michael Tooley's position that newborn infants are not persons is Peter Singer. As with Tooley, Singer denies that a late-term fetus is a person, and asserts that birth does not mark a morally significant line. Thus if the late-term fetus is not a person, the newborn baby is not a person either. He tells us:

> I have argued that the life of a fetus (and even more plainly, of an embryo) is of no greater value than the life of a nonhuman animal at a similar level of rationality, self-consciousness, awareness, capacity to feel, etc., and that since no fetus is a person no fetus has the same claim to life as a person. Now it must be admitted that these arguments apply to the newborn baby as much as to the fetus.[33]

Singer also follows Tooley in holding that if killing the fetus in late-term abortion is morally justified and then so is killing a newborn infant. His position is that "the *intrinsic* wrongness of killing the late fetus and the *intrinsic* wrongness of killing the newborn infant are not markedly different."[34] Neither, he holds, is intrinsically wrong. The stress on "*intrinsic* wrongness" is in view of his remark earlier in the same paragraph that we should put restrictions on killing newborns, but only in terms of the effects of such killings on others, and not because such killings are wrong in themselves, in their very nature; that is *intrinsically* wrong.

SUMMARY STATEMENT: THE FETUS IS NOT A REAL PERSON, ONLY A BIOLOGICAL ORGANISM

This is because:

1. It is too small, too undeveloped, and too different from the rest of us.
2. It *cannot reason* in the sense of thinking rationally.
3. It *lacks self-consciousness*: it has no sense of self; it cannot think "I exist."
4. It is not a persisting subject of experiences.
5. It has no conscious desires.
6. It has no interest in its own continued existence.
7. It cannot communicate intentionally, as in talking to someone.
8. It is not a member of the human community.

CHAPTER SUMMARY STATEMENT: BASIS AND IMPLICATIONS OF THE NOT-A-PERSON THESIS

- The *Achievement View* is the basis for the not-a-person thesis and argument: the fetus has not yet achieved enough to be counted as a person.
- This means that it is not an actual, real person; it is only a *potential person*.
- And it means that destroying a potential person is not morally wrong. Such a being does not have the right to life of a real, actual person.
- Therefore abortion as the killing of the fetus is not morally wrong; it is morally neutral or justified.

5

The No-Duty-to-Sustain Argument

A WOMAN'S RIGHT OVER HER BODY

A woman has a right over her body. Clearly this includes her right to have an abortion. "After all it's my body. I have a right to control it. I have a right to determine what happens in it, and what doesn't happen. I have a right to reproductive freedom, to decide whether or not, or when, to become a mother. I may even grant that the fetus is or might be a person, a small child. But if there is a child in my body and I do not want him there I have the right to remove him. If he stays in me he draws his sustenance from me. He has no right to do this. And I have no duty to sustain him. I can expel him from my womb. This is what an abortion amounts to. If I perceive him as an intruder I can expel him. If he is a threat to my life I can defend myself against him by expelling him. In short, I have a right to control my body and this surely means that if I have an unwanted pregnancy I can terminate it by having an abortion."

There are three distinct claims here. (1) A woman has no duty to sustain the fetus/child. (2) She may expel the fetus as an intruder. And (3) she may defend herself against it if it is a threat to her life. The first two claims pertain directly to the general thesis that a woman has a right to an abortion because she has a right over her body. We will examine the case for these two claims in the present chapter, with the focus on the first claim. The third claim is more specific since it is limited to cases of threats to the life of the woman. It will be taken up later in chapter 17.

BOLTON'S NO-DUTY-TO-SUSTAIN ARGUMENT

The central feature of the woman's-right-over-her-body argument is the claim that the woman has no duty to sustain the life of the fetus, even on the assumption that it is or might be a child, a small person. Abortion is thus seen as essentially the exercise of the right of the pregnant woman to withdraw her support for the child, a support that the child is not entitled to. This argument has been proposed by Judith Jarvis Thomson and Martha Brandt Bolton. Bolton argues for a woman's right to abortion, and against the view that abortion is immoral:

> To see the incoherence in the anti-abortionists' argument, we need to look at the gaps in their account of what is at stake in an abortion. They emphasize the fetus's alleged right to life. They do not emphasize a matter that is equally important. This is that if a pregnant woman is obligated not to kill a fetus, then she is obligated to do a great deal more than that. She can meet the alleged obligation not to kill only if she takes on the various obligations involved in bearing and having a child. At the least, she must nurture the fetus, carry it to term, and give it birth; she must then care for the infant or make alternative arrangements for its care. It is relatively easy to live without deliberately killing someone; but it may require an indefinitely large commitment of time, energy, emotion, and physical resources to nurture and care for a child.[1]

THOMSON'S VIOLINIST ARGUMENT

Thomson argues in the same way, by appeal to an analogy that has become the classic statement of the no-duty-to-sustain argument.[2] She assumes for the sake of the argument that the fetus is a real person, a real child. She then asks us to imagine the following case. You wake up one morning and find that another person, a famous violinist, is "plugged into" you so that he can stay alive. You are attached to him, thereby sustaining his life. You did not agree to this; it was forced on you. But if you unplug yourself from him, he will die. It would not be proper to argue, Thomson says, in the following way: "All persons have a right to life, this violinist is a person, therefore he has a right to life, and so you may not detach yourself from him." On the contrary, you have no duty to sustain him, and therefore you may detach yourself from him. You have the right to do this, even though you foresee that the violinist will die as a result. This follows from the fact that the violinist has no right to be sustained by you. A pregnant woman is in essentially the same situation; she too may unplug herself from her "violinist," which means she may have an abortion.

The essential point of Thomson's argument can be summarized as follows:

1. A woman who carries the child to term is allowing the child to be in her body and she is providing him with sustenance.
2. She has no duty to do this. No one may force her to do it.
3. Therefore, she can expel the child by abortion. Abortion is the exercise of the right to refuse to sustain the child.
4. Therefore, abortion is morally justified as the exercise of the right to withdraw support.

THOMSON'S VIOLINIST ARGUMENT AND THE CASE OF RAPE

Thomson's analogy between a pregnant woman carrying a child and a person hooked up to a famous violinist seems to be closest in the case of pregnancy due to rape; both were coerced into the relationship. Does the analogy apply only then? Is it only the child conceived in rape and the violinist who do not have a right to be sustained? Thomson says no. She denies that her argument works only for rape cases.

> In this case, of course, you were kidnapped; you didn't volunteer for the operation that plugged the violinist into your kidneys. Can those who oppose abortion on the ground I mentioned make an exception for a pregnancy due to rape? Certainly. They can say that persons have a right to life only if they didn't come into existence because of rape; or they can say that all persons have a right to life, but that some have less of a right to life than others, in particular, that those who come into existence because of rape have less. But these statements have a rather unpleasant sound. Surely the question of whether you have a right to life at all, or how much of it you have, shouldn't turn on the question of whether or not you are the product of a rape. And in fact the people who oppose abortion on the ground I mentioned do not make this distinction, and hence do not make an exception in case of rape.[3]

Her key point here is this: *Surely the question of whether you have a right to life at all, or how much of it you have, shouldn't turn on the question of whether or not you are the product of a rape.* So, regardless of how or why you got connected up to the violinist, you have no duty to stay connected.

THOMSON'S INTRUDER ARGUMENT

Thomson offers us another analogy. She says that the child a pregnant woman is carrying in her body is an intruder. As with any intruder she has a right to expel him. The pregnant woman does this by getting an abortion.

> If the room is stuffy, and I therefore open a window to air it, and a burglar climbs in, it would be absurd to say, "Ah, now he can stay, she's given him a

right to the use of her house—for she is partially responsible for his presence there, having voluntarily done what enabled him to get in, in full knowledge that there are such things as burglars, and that burglars burgle." It would be still more absurd to say this if I had had bars installed outside my windows, precisely to prevent burglars from getting in, and a burglar got in only because of a defect in the bars. It remains equally absurd if we imagine it is not a burglar who climbs in, but an innocent person who blunders or falls in.[4]

THOMSON ON THE MEANING OF A RIGHT TO LIFE AND THE RIGHT TO AN ABORTION

How does Thomson see the relation between abortion and the right to life? What does it mean, on her account, to have a right to life?

> For we should now ask, at long last, what it comes to, to have a right to life. In some views having a right to life includes having a right to be given at least the bare minimum one needs for continued life. But suppose that what in fact is the bare minimum a man needs for continued life is something he has no right at all to be given? . . . To return to the story I told earlier, the fact that for continued life that violinist needs the continued use of your kidneys does not establish that he has a right to be given the continued use of your kidneys. He certainly has no right against you that *you* should give him continued use of your kidneys. For nobody has any right to use your kidneys unless you give him such as right; and nobody has the right against you that you shall give him this right—if you do allow him to go on using your kidneys, this is a kindness on your part, and not something he can claim from you as his due.[5]

Thomson is arguing that abortion is morally justified. She is not saying that human persons do not have a right to life.

> But I would stress that I am not arguing that people do not have a right to life—quite to the contrary, it seems to me that the primary control we must place on the acceptability of an account of rights is that it should turn out in that account to be a truth that all persons have a right to life. I am arguing only that having a right to life does not guarantee having either a right to be given the use of or a right to be allowed continued use of another person's body—even if one needs it for life itself. So the right to life will not serve the opponents of abortion in the very simple and clear way in which they seem to have thought it would.[6]

THOMSON'S ACCOUNT DOES NOT SUPPORT AN ABSOLUTE RIGHT TO ABORTION

> I do not argue that it [abortion] is always permissible. . . . I am inclined to think it a merit of my account precisely that it does *not* give a general yes or a

general no. It allows for and supports our sense that, for example, a sick and desperately frightened fourteen-year-old schoolgirl, pregnant due to rape, may *of course* choose abortion, and that any law which rules this out is an insane law. And it also allows for and supports our sense that in other cases resort to abortion is even positively indecent. It would be indecent in the woman to request an abortion, and indecent in a doctor to perform it, if she is in her seventh month, and wants the abortion just to avoid the nuisance of postponing a trip abroad.[7]

ABORTION YES—SECURING THE DEATH OF THE CHILD NO

While I am arguing for the permissibility of abortion in some cases, I am not arguing for the right to secure the death of the unborn child. It is easy to confuse these two things in that up to a certain point in the life of the fetus it is not able to survive outside the mother's body; hence removing it from her body guarantees its death. But they are importantly different. I have argued that you are not morally required to spend nine months in bed, sustaining the life of that violinist; but to say this is by no means to say that if, when you unplug yourself, there is a miracle and he survives, you then have a right to turn round and slit his throat. You may detach yourself even if this costs him his life; you have no right to be guaranteed his death, by some other means, if unplugging yourself does not kill him.[8]

STANDARD METHODS OF ABORTION

Before turning to the pro-life side let us look at the methods of abortion as seen from the pro-choice perspective.

Suction Aspiration

You will get medicine for pain. You may be offered sedation—a medicine that allows you to be awake but deeply relaxed. A speculum will be inserted into your vagina. Your health care provider may inject a numbing medication into or near your cervix. The opening of your cervix may be stretched with dilators—a series of increasingly thick rods. Or you may have absorbent dilators inserted a day or a few hours before the procedure. They will absorb fluid and get bigger. This slowly stretches open your cervix. Medication may also be used with or without the dilators to help open your cervix. You will be given antibiotics to prevent infection. A tube is inserted through the cervix into the uterus. Either a handheld suction device or a suction machine gently empties your uterus.

D&C: Dilation and Curettage

Sometimes, an instrument called a curette is used to remove any remaining tissue that lines the uterus. It may also be used to check that the uterus is empty.

D&E: Dilation and Evacuation

During a *D&E* your health care provider will examine you and check your uterus. You will get medication for pain. You may be offered sedation or IV medication to make you more comfortable. A speculum will be inserted into your vagina. Your cervix will be prepared for the procedure. You may be given medication or have absorbent dilators inserted a day or a few hours before the procedure. They will absorb fluid and grow bigger. This slowly stretches open your cervix. You will be given antibiotics to prevent infection. In later second-trimester procedures, you may also need a shot through your abdomen to make sure there is fetal demise before the procedure begins. Your health care provider will inject a numbing medication into or near your cervix. Medical instruments and a suction machine gently empty your uterus.

A D&E usually takes between ten and twenty minutes. But more time is needed to prepare your cervix. Time is also needed for talking with your provider about the procedure, a physical exam, reading and signing forms, and a recovery period of about one hour.

Mifepristone-Abortion Pill

The abortion pill is a medicine that ends an early pregnancy. In general, it can be used up to sixty-three days (nine weeks) after the first day of a woman's last period. The name for "the abortion pill" is mifepristone. It was called RU-486 when it was being developed. Medication abortion is a process that begins immediately after taking the abortion pill. There are three steps:

Step one—the abortion pill. Your health care provider will give you the abortion pill at the clinic. You will also be given some antibiotics to start taking after the abortion pill. The abortion pill works by blocking the hormone progesterone. Without progesterone, the lining of the uterus breaks down, and pregnancy cannot continue.

Step two—misoprostol. You will take a second medicine, misoprostol. It causes the uterus to empty. You and your health care provider will plan the timing and place for the second step. You'll take the second medicine up to three days after taking the abortion pill. Your health care provider will give you instructions on how and when to take the second medicine.

The second medicine, misoprostol, will cause you to have cramps and bleed heavily. Some women may begin bleeding before taking the second medicine. But for most, the bleeding and cramping begin after taking it. It usually lasts a few hours. You may see large blood clots or tissue at the time of the abortion.

More than half of women abort within four or five hours after taking the second medicine. For others, it takes longer. But most women abort within a few days.

It's normal to have some bleeding or spotting for up to four weeks after the abortion. You may use sanitary pads or tampons. But using pads makes it easier to keep track of your bleeding.

Step three—follow-up. You will need to follow up within two weeks. Follow-up is important to make sure your abortion is complete and that you are well. You will need an ultrasound or blood test.

In the unlikely event that you are still pregnant, your health care provider will discuss your options with you. It's likely you will need to have an aspiration abortion if the medication abortion did not end the pregnancy.[9]

ANOTHER METHOD: DILATION AND EXTRACTION

Another method of abortion has recently become controversial. Let us now examine it, again as seen from the pro-choice perspective.

D&X: Dilation and Extraction

This method is also called "Partial Birth Abortion," a term rejected as inaccurate by many pro-choicers, but used by the media and general public as well as the legislature. After several days of vaginal dilation, the surgeon uses ultrasound to get the exact location of the fetus for optimal viewing and removal of the fetus without dismemberment. Then while viewing the immediate ultrasound, the surgeon carefully uses forceps to pull the lower fetal extremities out through the dilated vaginal canal until the fetal skull is caught in the vaginal canal. At this point it is possible for the surgeon to feel for the back of the fetal skull and forcefully insert a closed scissor-like instrument into the cranium before opening the instrument to enlarge the opening enough to allow for suction removal of the brain and related materials. The intact fetal body and placenta are then removed from the vaginal canal. This method requires a great deal of surgical expertise, but once acquired, is a procedure that can be done with local anesthesia, without inducing labor, in a physician's office or outpatient facility. It is a far gentler procedure than fetal dismemberment with very low maternal complications.[10] It also reduces to zero the possibility of live birth, a complication of the earlier saline abortion method often used in the second and third trimester.

A CONTROVERSY WITHIN THE PRO-CHOICE COMMUNITY

Some people who are otherwise pro-choice condemn D&X or "Partial Birth" abortions as cruel and barbaric because it is so visually graphic in what it does to the fetus; a being that is now actually no longer in the womb but outside, except for its head. They claim it is therefore virtually equivalent to infanticide, the killing of a born baby.

They fear that approving such a visually graphic barbaric procedure in the name of defending women's right to choose gives the whole pro-choice movement a bad name. They realize most Americans reject this form of abortion because they can see that what is killed appears too much like a familiar baby.

On the other hand many in the pro-choice community, especially in executive positions, members of legislative bodies and in the judiciary, defend this procedure as one method among others that must remain available to women and doctors. They argue that doctors should be free to choose this method among others so that the best medical decision can be made in each particular case based on what is best for the woman. This is brought out in a report issued by a committee of the *American College of Obstetricians and Gynecologists* (ACOG) that thoroughly studied D&X procedures.

> They . . . determined that "an intact D&X . . . may be the best or most appropriate procedure in a particular circumstance to save the life or preserve the health of a woman, and only the doctor, in consultation with the patient, based upon the woman's particular circumstances can make this decision."[11]

They also argue that pro-choice must hold the line firmly to ensure that *all* forms of abortion remain legal. If we allow a ban on one method of abortion, others will surely follow, with the inevitable result that a woman's right to choose will gradually erode away. If D&X is banned, why not also D&E, which is often done at approximately the same gestational age? Both can be described as brutal and barbaric in what they do to the being that is destroyed. Both cause terrible pain to this being. It is hard to see how one can rationally allow one and ban the other. But if both are banned, this is tantamount to banning third and even some second trimester abortions. What's next? Other abortions, at ever earlier stages, will be banned. And the end result will be the loss of the right of a woman to choose to end her pregnancy. We cannot let this happen! We must hold the line firmly and courageously, even if it means holding onto a method of abortion that many people find repulsive.

THE QUESTION OF FETAL PAIN

An argument sometimes used by pro-lifers is that abortion is wrong because it causes pain to the fetus. Does this really constitute a valid reason against abortion?

> What of the claim by anti-choicers that even very early fetuses can feel pain? In fetal development, most major organs exist in rudimentary form by about 8 to 9 weeks. It takes several months for these organs to grow in size, complexity, and organization to the point they can function. For example, the myelin sheath—the insulating cover on nerve pathways that is required for efficient conduction of pain signals—does not begin forming around nervous system cells (neurons) in the spinal cord until about 24 weeks, and not till after birth in most of the cerebral cortex. Although sporadic brain waves can be detected by about 21 weeks gestation, genuine continuous brain waves do not begin until about 28 weeks, indicating that the nerve circuits needed to carry pain impulses to the brain are not connected till then.
>
> In short, the evidence indicates that fetuses do not feel pain until after the start of the third trimester—and even that evidence remains uncertain because it's impossible to know for sure that fetuses consciously experience pain in the same way that a person does.[12]

What this indicates is that the appeal to the possibility of fetal pain *does not* constitute a valid reason against abortion. It's really a distraction, a political ploy:

> Regardless, since virtually no abortions occur during the third trimester, it means anti-choicers are raising the issue of fetal pain as a political ploy—it's another possible way for them to restrict abortion. If a woman can be persuaded that an abortion will cause pain to her fetus, she might decide against having one. And if society can be convinced that fetuses feel pain, it might be easier to pass restrictions to abortion.[13]

Another point to keep in mind is that biologically instinctual movements that "look like pain" do not translate into actual pain, but are merely unconscious instinctual reactions. As to the question whether we should administer medications to prevent possible fetal pain, Richard Smith offers some thoughts:

> Evidence is imprecise, but the fetus is probably not capable of being aware before 16 weeks, and has the mechanisms necessary for awareness after 26 weeks. Administering fetal analgesia is not straightforward, and theoretical benefits for the fetus must be weighed against actual risks for the mother. Obstetricians should be aware of the issues to allow sensitive discussion with patients undergoing procedures where the subject of fetal awareness may arise.[14]

II

đạo đức

THE PRO-LIFE MORAL POSITION

The pro-life position in a nutshell. Pro-life is basically three main points:

- The reality of the child in the womb: the BIW is a small human person, one of us.
- Killing an innocent human person is wrong, a terrible moral evil. Abortion means killing this child, and is therefore basically an instance of killing innocent persons.
- It is an especially horrible moral evil because of the brutal methods it uses, such as cutting the child to pieces, and thereby causing her excruciating pain.

These are the points that will be developed in the next four chapters. The first is the theme of chapter 6, that abortion involves a real human person. The second is taken up in chapter 7; the third in chapter 8. All three are at least implicit in chapter 9.

The reality-of-the-child arguments in 6 and the wrong-to-kill arguments in 7 are closely connected; together they constitute the logical basis for the central pro-life moral position. The pain argument in 8 is independent of 6: causing such horrific pain to any being capable of suffering pain is a terrible moral evil, whether or not it is a person.

6

The Reality of the Child in the Womb

The central thesis, the most basic and fundamental claim, of the pro-life position is *the reality of the child in the womb*. Pro-life asks us to look at a pregnant woman and see, with the eye of our mind, and our heart, the reality of the child that she is carrying; the full reality of this child. It asks us not to let the fact that we can't see it or touch it, or that it is still very small, distract us from seeing and acknowledging his or her full reality.

Pro-life asks us to *identify with the child*. To make his or her interests our own. The paramount interest we all have is of course not to be killed. The same applies to this little child. "Don't let this child be killed."

The reality of the child in the womb means of course that this child is a member of the human community, that he or she is "one of us." This will be supported here by three basic, closely related, interlocking arguments:

FIRST: THE CONTINUUM ARGUMENT

The core idea behind this basic pro-life argument is that the life of a human person is a single continuum, which has different phases. Being a child in the womb, a pre-born baby, is the first of these phases. Later phases include being a newborn baby, a baby six months old, a toddler, a child at seven years, a teenager, a young adult, an older person. Life in the womb is part of life. A major part of what this means is:

I was once a tiny baby in my mother's womb. Small children have a perfectly clear understanding of this, remarking, "When I was in my mommy's tummy. . . ." The basic idea underlying this is the identity of persons. In other words:

The child in the womb is the same being, the same person, as the born child he will soon become, as the older child he will become later, and so forth. I am the *same person* as the child in the womb when my mother was pregnant with me. If I think back a few years ago I was obviously the same person then as I am now. I can think back still further, to when I was a small child, a newborn baby two minutes after birth, a pre-born baby two minutes before birth, that same baby four weeks before birth, eight weeks before birth, all the way back to the beginning: that was always me, the *same* person, the *same* I, at all these points. If I am clearly a person now, and I was the same being in my mother's womb, then clearly I was a person then.

Memory as a key to understanding the idea of being always the same person. I am now the same person I was ten years ago, even though I have changed. That "I have changed" means that I, *the same person*, have changed; that these changes happened to *me*. A good way to understand this is through memory. I remember not only events that occurred, say, ten years ago, but myself as experiencing these events. To remember an experience is to reach back, not only into the past, but into another phase of one's own existence, which means one's own existence as the same person one is now.

Memory of one's own past experiences presupposes oneself as experiencing them. I who now remember, and I who had those experiences, must be the same person. Memory can stretch no farther back than identity; I cannot remember an experience occurring before I came to be, for obviously such an experience was not my experience. But the converse is not true, for one's identity can, and does, stretch farther back than one's memory. That I cannot remember an experience does not mean it was not my experience. I cannot remember being born, nor any of the moments of my existence before birth. But each of these moments was a moment in my existence, a part of that continuum that is my life on earth.

The function of memory in the continuum argument is to provide a clear and vivid understanding of the meaning of personal identity. Suppose the being in the womb had mental capacities that were far more developed than they actually are. Then she could later say, "I now remember experiencing this while in the womb." That is—and this is the crucial point—I now remember myself, *the same person*, having these experiences. That means of course that I was already present then. The absence of such developed mental capacities means the absence of such (actual) memory experiences; it does not mean the absence of the real identity that links the person as she exists now and as she existed then, and that is made intelligible by this (supposed) memory experience.

What the continuum argument directly denies. The continuum argument is the direct antithesis to the idea that there is something in the womb—"a blob of tissue" or a mere biological organism—that is not a person but then turns into a person, a small child. Rather, the child is already there, the same child, the same person who will later be born. There are of course significant developmental changes, but these occur in the life of one and the same being who is present throughout; and who is the being to whom these changes occur. In short, the person is already there in the womb: nothing needs to be added to make him a person; indeed nothing can be added.

An important clarification: what the continuum argument is not. This argument is *not* the "slippery slope argument" dismissed by Boonin in chapter 4. That argument is indeed invalid. That is, the continuum argument being advanced here is *not* the claim, often heard, that one cannot find a clear cut-off point in the life of a human being from conception to birth and beyond, a point marking the line between nonperson and person, or merely potential person and actual person. If there is a spectrum, say from A to Z, the fact that no clear, nonarbitrary cut-off point can be found along the way does not mean that A and Z cannot be radically different. Think of such examples as the color spectrum from black to white, or night to day. In each case A shades off into B, B into C, etc. There are no clear dividing lines; there is continuity. But it is not the continuity of the continued existence of the same being; for example, a baby grows up to be a twenty-year-old, and always remains the same person.

If the continuum argument were merely that one can't find a clear cut-off point, it would indeed be invalid, and would not support the basic thesis, that the being in the womb is the same person who will later be born. Rejection of this argument does not touch the real continuum argument, the continuum of the same person. There is indeed no cut-off point, no line to be drawn. The reason for this is the continuum of human life. Continuum implies no line; no line by itself does not imply continuum.

Continuum and the stages of life. The child becomes an adult, and he is a child no longer. The fetus becomes the born child, and he is a fetus no longer. The stages, zygote, embryo, fetus, newborn baby, toddler, teenager, cease to be, but the person going through these stages continues to be, and continues as the same person. Being a fetus or BIW is merely one stage in the life of a person.

Continuum: just after-just before. Five minutes after birth, what do we have? A small baby. Five minutes before birth, what do we have? A small baby, the same baby who will soon be the five-minutes-after baby. If we now go back from this, an hour, a day, several days, or several weeks, what do we have? A small baby. It is a small baby all the way through. This is the continuum argument.

The child in the womb is already a unique individual person. He is the same unique individual he will be later on after birth. This is brought out by Dr. Arnold Gesell who suggests that by the first six months of life, the individuality of the human being in the womb is clear to all unbiased observers. He states:

> Our own repeated observation of a large group of fetal infants (an individual born and living at any time prior to forty weeks gestation) left us with no doubt that psychologically they were individuals. Just as no two looked alike, so no two behaved precisely alike. One was impassive when another was alert. Even among the youngest there were discernable differences in vividness, reactivity and responsiveness. These were genuine individual differences, already prophetic of the diversity which distinguishes the human family.[1]

The doctor treats the pre-born child just as he does any patient. When one views the present state of medical science, one finds that the distinction between born and pre-born has essentially vanished, that this is an artificial distinction.

There is a new specialty replacing fetology called *perinatology* which cares for its patients from conception to about one year after birth. For example, a child with severe anemia can now be given blood while he is still in the womb, using an unusual technique developed by Dr. A. Liley of New Zealand. This life-saving measure is carried out by using new image intensifier X-ray equipment. A needle is placed through the abdominal wall of the mother and into the abdominal cavity of the child. For this procedure the child must be sedated via maternal circulation and given pain relieving medication, since he would experience pain from the puncture and would move away from the needle if not sedated. As Dr. H. M. I. Liley states:

> When doctors first began invading the sanctuary of the womb, they did not know that the unborn baby would react to pain in the same fashion as a child would. But they soon learned that he would. By no means a 'vegetable' as he has so often been pictured, the unborn knows perfectly well when he has been hurt, and he will protest it just as violently as would a baby lying in a crib.[2]

The whole thrust of medicine is in support of the notion that the child in his mother's womb is a distinct individual in need of the most diligent study and care, and that he is also a patient whom science and medicine treat just as they do any other person.

Dr. Liley relates the experience of a doctor who injected an air bubble into the amniotic sac of a pre-born baby at eight months, in an attempt to locate the placenta on an X-ray. It so happened that the air bubble covered the pre-born baby's face. The moment the child had air to inhale, his vocal cords became operative and his crying became audible to all present, including the physician and technical help. The mother telephoned the doctor later to report that whenever she lay down to sleep, the air bubble got over the baby's face and he was crying so loudly he was keeping both her and her husband awake.

At seven weeks we see a well-proportioned small-scale baby. This is a very significant point that was made in the statement by the two hundred doctors presented earlier. It is the same baby who will soon be a newborn baby.

The child in the womb is an actual person, not a mere potential person. From all of the above it becomes clear that the child in the womb is a real person, a full, actual person, and not something on the way to becoming a person; as a medical student is on his way to becoming a doctor. He is just a small person.

Table 6.1. Summary Statement of the Continuum Argument

0	9	18	36			12	25	37	50	62	75	87	100
	WEEKS			Birth					YEARS				

1. Pick any two places: I was *the same person* in the earlier one and in the later one.
2. If I remember myself in the earlier place, I remember myself as *the same person.*
3. I am always the same person even though I undergo radical changes. These changes happen to me, *the same person*: I was once a pre-born baby.
4. I don't remember myself as a toddler, or as newborn baby, or as a pre-born baby; but in each case: that was me.
5. If I am now the same person as the pre-born baby, the BIW, I was a person in the womb.
6. Therefore, the BIW is a person.

SECOND: THE SLED ARGUMENT

The SLED argument is a pro-life argument that, like the continuum argument, stresses the essential personal continuity and morally significant similarity between the BIW and the rest of us. It is an answer to the question of the differences between born and pre-born human beings. The SLED argument is the claim that there are four and only four such differences, and that all of them are morally insignificant. The word "SLED" is a device that helps us remember these four differences between a born baby and a pre-born baby. These differences are:

S: Size
L: Level of development

E: Environment
D: Degree of dependency

Size

Recall what was noted above: at seven weeks we see a well-proportioned small-scale baby. The child in the womb at seven weeks is normally smaller than the new-born child. The latter is normally smaller than a one-year-old child, who is normally smaller than a five-year-old child. A 100-pound girl is smaller than a 250-pound football player. All this is of no moral significance. The larger person isn't any more a person, or more precious, than the smaller one. A small new-born baby is just as precious as an older child, or an adult. The child in the womb is simply a still smaller child.

Level of Development

A baby is less developed than a teenager. Is he or she less a person? Being less developed, as well as being smaller, represents earlier phases on the human life continuum. But he is equally a person; he is the same person at his earlier stage of development as at the later stages, or else it would not be his development.

The child at seven to eight weeks is less developed than later, but he is already very well developed. As noted earlier, "After the eighth week no further primordia will form: *everything* is already present that will be found in the full term baby."

Environment

If one person is in one environment and another person in another environment, nothing changes concerning the reality, or dignity and worth, of the two persons. Being inside his mother, nesting in her womb, represents being in a different environment than the familiar environment we know. But the being in the womb is as much a real person, a real child, at that time as after birth.

A child in an incubator is no less a real child than one in natural surroundings. The pre-born child is in the incubator of his mother's womb, a warm, protective nesting place. It is the necessary environment he needs while still small and fragile, what he needs for protection, nourishment, and growth. It is the environment he needs to develop into a being who can survive the rigors of life in the outside world. The difference between the pre-born and post-born child is one of needs, not of reality or worth and dignity.

mức độ
Sự phụ thuộc

Degree of dependency

We are all dependent on one another, physically and psychologically. Some of us are more dependent than others: children, the sick, the handicapped. A more dependent person—perhaps someone in an intensive care unit—is not less of a person than someone who is relatively more independent. To see clearly the moral irrelevance of degree of dependency for the reality, dignity, and preciousness of a person, consider the following:

1. Degree of dependency is relative. It is, precisely, a matter of degree, of more or less dependency. Everyone is dependent on others to some extent, physically and psychologically. At certain times each of us becomes, or can become, more dependent on others than usual: if we are lost, if we've had a serious accident, if we are blinded. Clearly these conditions do not affect our being as persons, our preciousness and dignity, our right to live.

2. Specifically, it is important to remember that when you are dependent on others, that is, more dependent than usual, you are the same person as you were before, and will be later. So too, the child in the womb. He is at this stage of his life the same person who will later be born and grow up to be less dependent.

3. Suppose you are now healthy and thus relatively independent. Then you have a serious accident that leaves you paralyzed and dependent on others. The continuation of your life depends on others for protection and nourishment, parallel to the child in the womb. You are still the same person. You have the same dignity and right to live.

   Suppose someone were to say to you, "You don't count: you are too dependent." This would be an outrage! If this were used as a reason for killing you—that you were perceived as being in the way—it would be regarded as a terrible injustice. But this is precisely what is said to the child in the womb by those who defend abortion on the grounds that the child is too dependent. The fact that the child can't hear and understand what is being said, or that it is not said in so many words, or out loud, surely is of no moral significance.

4. Physical dependency, as it applies to the child in the womb or to a person who is paralyzed, concerns a person's bodily dimension, and not the person as a person, or his right to live. I remain myself through the various changes, phases of growth and development, phases of relative dependency or independence that pertain to my body. I am not less me because my body may be in a state of greater dependency than at another time. Thus we see that dependency through connection to another person has nothing to do with being a person. It has only to do with how the body is sustained.

In short, to hold that a more dependent person—whether normally (in the womb) or not normally (as in paralysis)—is less of a person, less worthy of being treated like the rest of us is sheer prejudice, ungrounded in fact and reason. It is like the prejudice that asserts that certain people in distant lands, of different cultures and ethnic groups, are different in an odious sense, less human, not fully persons, whose death doesn't matter, or matters much less than the death of a familiar person. A person who is different, whether it is because he belongs to a different culture or because he is more dependent, is above all a person like you and me with the same right to live as we have. The class of pre-born persons is simply one instance of this. Such a person should be treated just like any other person, with respect for his dignity and right to live.

The fact that the child in the womb is dependent on another person, while the prematurely born child is dependent on an incubator, has nothing to do with the status of the being that is thus dependent. If person A is being sustained by, and thus dependent on, a direct blood transfusion from another person, while person B is similarly being sustained by a blood transfusion through a machine, then both are equally sustained, equally dependent; and they are equally persons. That is, the kind of dependency, whether it is on another person or on a machine, has nothing to do with the person's being and his moral status (his dignity and his right to life).

To kill a normal child sleeping in his crib is a terrible evil. Killing a child in an incubator, dependent on that incubator, is no less an evil. Abortion is killing a child in the incubator of his mother's womb. A more dependent child is simply a more fragile child, and therefore one who deserves more care and protection, not less. And so the fact of dependency implies a greater obligation towards the child, not less. Parents have greater obligations to their children when they are very young and very dependent, and lesser obligations as they get older.

Other Differences between Pre-born and Post-born Babies

Pre-born babies cannot be readily seen, they lack the mobility that we have; many have no name, and they are incapable of social interaction. These differences are likewise of no moral significance.

That pre-born babies cannot be readily seen really refers only to the fact that we cannot see them, not to anything about their being. A person enclosed in something, a closet or a womb, cannot be seen for obvious reasons. That says nothing about him as a person.

The child in the womb lacks the mobility that we have. First, this is only partly true. Beginning in the third month he becomes very active, and moves about in his amniotic sac. Second, in so far as it is true, it is due to his lack of development at the beginning; and later to his cramped quarters as he grows larger. Third, it is in any case morally irrelevant. A paralyzed person is as much a person as one who is fortunate enough not to be so afflicted. Mobility, to the extent that it pertains to the child in the womb, is a matter of development, environment, and degree of dependency.

That a pre-born child usually has no name says nothing about him as a person. An unnamed orphan is as much a baby as a named child. Actually some children are given a name before their birth.

Finally, no social interaction is an obvious consequence of the child's level of development and environment. Even if he were more developed, he couldn't very well carry on a conversation with us in his present position. But again, that says nothing about him as a person.

To summarize: the four features that differentiate pre-born persons and born persons can be put together and easily remembered by the acronym SLED:

Table 6.2. SLED Argument

	For the child is:
S: Size	Smaller;
L: Level of development	Less developed;
E: Environment	in a different Environment;
D: degree of Dependency	and more Dependent.

- These are *the only differences* between a pre-born and born baby.
- They are *all morally irrelevant.*

THIRD: BEING A PERSON AND FUNCTIONING AS A PERSON

In opposition to the not-a-person argument advanced in chapter 4, let me suggest as a counterargument the claim that the being in the womb really *is* a person and that all the not-a-person argument shows is that this being is not yet capable of *doing* the things we associate with persons. This is the distinction between *being* a person and *functioning* as a person. When we speak of functioning, we mean what you can *do* as a person. This includes rational thinking, intentional communication, having full consciousness, a sense of self, and the ability for self-reflection. In contrast, being a person refers to what you are as a person. It refers to your ontological and moral status as a person. The term *ontological* means what you are essentially as a person, your essence, what makes you a person and not some other type of being such as a plant. If you have the moral status of a person then it logically follows that you should have the legal status of a person and the full right to legal protection. Being a person distinguishes us from other living organisms such as dogs and trees.

Functioning as a person is not necessary for being a person. It is possible to be a person without having the ability to function as a person. Think of a person in a coma or a newborn baby. Clearly these have the being of a person even though they cannot function as a person. Exactly the same applies to the BIW: it is a person even though it does not function as a person. Once again, *functioning as a person is not necessary for being a person.* Think of a parallel case. A young cherry tree before it can bear fruit has the being of a cherry tree even though it cannot yet function as a cherry tree. Similarly, the BIW has the being of a person even though it doesn't yet have the capacity to function as a person. And if it has the being of a person, shouldn't it be afforded the same moral and legal rights as all persons?

Consider Warren's five characteristics of a person: consciousness, reasoning, self-motivated activity, the capacity to communicate, and the presence of self-concepts. Imagine a person in a deep, dreamless sleep. She is not conscious, she cannot reason, etc.; she lacks all five of these traits. She is not functioning as a person; that is part of what being asleep means. But of course she is a person, she retains fully her status of being a person, and killing her while asleep is just as wrong as killing her while she is awake and functioning as a person.

Functioning as a person refers to all the activities proper to persons as persons, to thinking in the broadest sense. It includes reasoning, deciding, imagining, talking, experiencing love and beauty, remembering, intending, and much more. The term *function* does not refer here to bodily functions, but rather to those of the mind, though certain bodily functions, especially those of the brain, are necessary conditions for functioning as a person.

When Warren points out that a fetus satisfies none of the five traits she mentions, she shows only that a fetus does not function as a person, not that it lacks the being of a person, which is the crucial thing. And it should be noted that not being able to function as a person is *perfectly normal* for a human being in his early stages in the womb. The ability to function as a person requires a degree of development that is still in process, hence not yet completed.

Let us now consider two objections that might be raised against this argument. First, the sleeping person will soon wake up and function as a person, while the BIW will not. In reply, neither the sleeping person nor the BIW now displays the qualities of a functioning person. Both will display them; it is only a matter of time. Why should the one count as a real person because the time is short, while the other does not display them simply because in her case the time is longer? In addition, as just noted, the BIW's inability to function is perfectly normal, just what we should expect for a human being at the beginning of her development.

Second, a sleeping person has the capacity to function as a person and therefore counts as being a person, even though this capacity is not now actualized. In contrast, the BIW lacks this capacity, and so it does not count as being a person. In reply, we need to make an important distinction within functioning as a person. The claim that the BIW lacks the capacity to function as a person is only partially true. It lacks what I call the *present immediate capacity* to function, where responses may be immediately elicited. Such a capacity means the capability of functioning, where such a capability varies enormously among people, and normally develops and grows as a result of learning and other experiences. But this capability of functioning as a person only exists because it is grounded in something deeper, in the very nature of the being of a person. I call this the *basic inherent capacity* to function as a person. This capacity is proper to the being of a person and it has a physical basis, in the brain and nervous system.

Thus the BIW, contrary to this objection, does not lack the capacity to function as a person in the only sense that is really important, the basic inherent capacity to function, which is proper to his being as a person; and indeed is part of what constitutes this being.

This basic inherent capacity may be *fully accessible*, as in a normal sleeping adult. It then exists in its present immediate form. It may also exist in other forms where it is *latent*, as in a coma, where the basic inherent capacity is present but damaged or blocked. In a small child, the basic inherent capacity is there but insufficiently developed for the child to function in the manner of a normal adult.

In short: all persons have the *basic inherent capacity* to function as a person. This then divides into three categories:

1. Actualized, when a person is awake and doing things that come under functioning as a person.
2. Not actualized, but there is the *present immediate capacity* to function, as during sleep.
3. Not actualized, but present in a *latent* form, either in a small child (born or pre-born) or someone in a coma.

THE PERSON-HUMAN BEING DISTINCTION: ENGINEERED TO TRY TO JUSTIFY ABORTION?

The contrast between the not-a-person view presented and defended in chapter 4 and the one presented and defended in this chapter should be clear. The former view is based on a radical distinction between persons and human beings, claiming that while the BIW is a human being (in a sense that carries no moral significance), it is not a person and so does not deserve the respect due to persons. The latter view, defended in this chapter, holds that the BIW *is* a person, just like the rest of us; he or she is truly and fully "one of us." He or she is of course a human being. And so we can say that he or she, with the rest of us, is a human person. Thus the radical "person-human being" distinction which forms the basis for the pro-choice claim that the BIW does not deserve the respect due to the rest of us—and so may be destroyed by abortion—finds no application in the present chapter.

This raises an interesting question. Does the "person-human being" distinction brought forth by writers such as Mary Anne Warren, Michael Tooley, and David Boonin find any other application, that is, one outside discussion of the abortion issue? Andrew Peach addressed this question. What did he find? And what conclusion did he draw?

> The first thing to note about the terms "human" and "person" is that, in everyday conversation, no one ever uses them in the way that Warren or any like-minded philosopher does. No expectant mother ever wonders whether her baby is merely a human being or actually a person. . . . And I would hazard to guess that few, if any, women who are wrestling with the question of whether or not to abort derive any consolation from the fact that the life inside them is merely a human being, not a person.[3]

Peach then points out that in questions concerning whether to continue or withdraw life support from comatose patients the issue is never whether the patient is or is not a person. The issues concern only matters such as brain activity, the possible usefulness of further treatment or lack thereof, and the prognosis for the future.[4]

He then draws his significant conclusion:

> *Indeed, there is not a single case of a human being outside the womb who is free to be killed because he or she is not a "person" in Warren's sense of the word; mere membership in the human race is a sufficient condition to be protected from harm.* Given this fact, there can be little doubt that the distinction between human and person has been engineered for no other reason than to justify abortion.[5]

SUMMARY STATEMENT: BEING AND FUNCTIONING

1. Functioning as a person means thinking rationally, saying "I," talking, etcetera.
2. Functioning as a person refers to all the items on the Warren list in chapter 4, pages 22–23.

3. The not-a-person argument confuses functioning and being. All it shows is that the BIW cannot function as a person, not that it lacks the being of a person.
4. What counts morally is only being a person.
5. A person in a coma, an unconscious person, a newborn baby, a baby in the womb: all these have the *being* of a person; they merely cannot *function* as persons.
6. What is wrong is to kill that which has the being of a person.

CHAPTER SUMMARY STATEMENT: THE REALITY OF THE CHILD IN THE WOMB

- The continuum argument: I was once a tiny baby in my mother's womb. The child in the womb is the *same* being, the *same* person, he will soon become.
- The child in the womb is a real person, an actual person, not a potential person.
- The differences between pre-born and post-born babies are SLED differences: size, level of development, environment, and degree of dependency. These are the only differences, and they are all morally irrelevant.
- The child in the womb has the *being* of a person; he cannot yet *function* as a person, because he has not yet achieved sufficient development. Achievement is relevant for functioning as a person, not for being a person.

7

Abortion Means Killing This Child

Abortion is wrong because it is the direct, deliberate, intentional killing of an innocent, defenseless small child, a member of our human community. Just as it is wrong, a terrible moral evil, to kill a *born* person, so too it is wrong, a terrible moral evil to kill a *pre-born* person. He too is "one of us."

Earlier, at the end of chapter 5, we looked at the methods of abortion as seen from the pro-choice viewpoint, described as the gentle emptying of the womb. "Either a handheld suction device or a suction machine gently empties your uterus." Now let us look at the methods of abortion as seen through the pro-life lens. A rather different picture emerges. Abortion as the killing of a small child is vividly brought out by looking at the methods of abortion from this perspective.

STANDARD METHODS OF ABORTION

Suction

Used between six and twelve weeks. About 95 percent of abortions are done in this way. The abortionist first paralyzes the cervix (womb opening). He then inserts a hollow plastic tube with a knife-like tip into the uterus. The tube is connected to a powerful pump with a suction force twenty-nine times more powerful than a home vacuum cleaner. The procedure tears the baby's body into pieces and the hose frequently jerks as pieces of the baby become lodged. The placenta is cut from the inner wall of the uterus and the scraps are sucked out into a bottle. Sometimes body parts are easily identified.

D&C: Dilation and Curettage

Used between seven and ten weeks. This method is similar to the suction method with the added insertion of a hook shaped knife (curette) which cuts the baby into pieces. The pieces are scraped out through the cervix and discarded [Note: This abortion method should not be confused with a therapeutic D&C done for reasons other than pregnancy.]

D&E: Dilation and Evacuation

Used between twelve and twenty-six weeks. This method uses a pliers-like instrument with a sharp tooth. The abortionist grasps a part of the baby's body, such as an arm or a leg, and tears it away. This dismemberment of the living baby continues until all the parts are removed. Body parts are removed and then reassembled to make sure the entire body has been removed so that no parts remain in the womb. Bleeding is profuse. No anesthesia is used for the baby.

Prostaglandin

This is a drug that causes the woman to go into labor at any stage of pregnancy. A hormone is used which produces a labor and delivery of whatever size baby the mother carries. The contractions are more violent than normal, natural contractions, so the baby is frequently killed by them, and some have been decapitated. If the baby survives this traumatic labor, it may be born alive.

RU-486

Used between two to three weeks and six to eight weeks. This is a drug that produces an abortion taken after the mother misses her period. Its effect is to block the use of an essential hormonal nutrient by the newly-implanted baby, who then dies, and drops off.

Hysterotomy

This method is usually used late in pregnancy and is likened to an "early" Caesarian section. The mother's abdomen and uterus are surgically opened and the baby is lifted out. Unfortunately, many of these babies are very much alive when removed. To kill the babies, some abortionists have been known to plunge them into buckets of water or smother them with the placentas. Still others cut the cord while the baby is still inside the uterus depriving the baby of oxygen.[1]

ANOTHER METHOD: DILATION AND EXTRACTION OR PARTIAL-BIRTH ABORTION

Five steps to a partial birth abortion:

1. Guided by ultrasound, the abortionist grabs the baby's legs with forceps.
2. The baby's legs are pulled out into the birth canal.
3. The abortionist delivers the baby's entire body, except for the head.
4. The abortionist jams scissors into the baby's skull. The scissors are then opened to enlarge the skull.
5. The scissors are removed and a suction catheter is inserted. The child's brains are sucked out, causing the skull to collapse. The dead baby is then removed. www.lifesitenews.com/abortiontypes/prolife.jpg (Accessed November 2001.)

D&X: Dilation and Extraction or Partial-Birth Abortion

Generally used between twenty and twenty-six weeks, but sometimes up to thirty-two weeks and even up to forty weeks, the end of pregnancy. The reason for steps one through three is not medical necessity, but to avoid actually birthing the baby; for if the baby were fully born, killing him would be murder. The entire procedure is performed on the baby without any anesthesia even though he is clearly capable of feeling pain. As we will see shortly in the next chapter, studies have shown that sensitivity to pain begins early, eight to thirteen-and-a-half weeks, and certainly by twenty weeks and beyond; in short, during the second and third trimester.

Proponents of D&X have asserted that it is rarely performed (approximately 450 to 500 hundred per year) and used only in extreme cases when a woman's life is at risk or the fetus had a condition incompatible with life. In actuality, one facility alone admitted to performing fifteen hundred of these procedures, the vast majority of which were carried out on healthy mothers with normal fetuses. One physician who had performed more than six hundred partial-birth abortions, stated that most of the abortions were elective. Another physician, James T. McMahon, MD, of Los Angeles, in detailing for Congress his experience with more than two thousand partial-birth abortion procedures stated that only 9 percent of those involved maternal health indications, of which the most common was depression. In addition, the insertion of instruments into the uterus is not without risks, since one out of six thousand of these kinds of procedures results in the death of the mother, while death from childbirth is one out of thirteen thousand.

Is the procedure ever medically necessary? First of all, the procedure itself requires several days to perform, since the cervix must be dilated first. This means that the procedure is *never* used in an emergency to save the life of the mother. And, as we saw, the procedure is medically risky to the mother. According to Drs. M. LeRoy Sprang and Mark G. Neerhof: "None of these risks are medically necessary because other procedures are available to physicians who deem it necessary to perform an abortion late in pregnancy. As ACOG policy states clearly, intact D&X is never the only procedure available."

In writing for the *Journal of the American Medical Association*, Drs. M. LeRoy Sprang and Mark G. Neerhof, conclude with the following statement:

> Intact D&X (partial-birth abortion) should not be performed because it is needlessly risky, inhumane, and ethically unacceptable. This procedure is closer to infanticide than it is to abortion.[2]

"PARTIAL-BIRTH ABORTION" IS NOT REALLY ABORTION

Perhaps what is called "partial-birth abortion" *is* really infanticide. This is essentially the claim of Samuel W. Calhoun in an article whose main title is "'Partial-Birth Abortion' Is Not Abortion." Referring to the *Roe v. Wade* U.S. Supreme Court decision of January 22, 1973, that legalized abortion, he writes:

> Despite the procedure's name, partial-birth abortion is not an "abortion" as that term was understood by the *Roe* Court. The Texas statute at issue in *Roe* defined "abortion" as destroying '"the life of the fetus or embryo . . . in the woman's womb.'" *Roe* is replete with language limiting its application to the duration of a pregnancy—a state's regulatory interests become compelling at some "point during pregnancy"; a state cannot criminalize abortion "without regard to pregnancy stage"; a state can regulate more as the pregnancy lengthens." At "live birth," all such constraints on a state's regulatory freedom disappear, as the fetus then becomes a person "in the whole sense." The Court thus thought of "abortion" only as an act that terminates a pregnancy at some point prior to live birth. Consequently, to kill a fetus during its live birth is not an abortion under *Roe*.[3]

WHAT ARE THE RESULTS OF ABORTION?

What do the results of abortion really look like? Before you make up your mind on whether abortion is morally right or wrong, wouldn't it be advisable to see for yourself what abortion really is? Either: "This is what I think is morally justified or neutral." Or: "This is what I think is morally wrong." The same will apply also to abortion as a legal issue. To find out, go to the following website: www.100abortionpictures.com. *photos*

The website includes these links: pictures of aborted babies; facts on abortion procedures; partial birth abortion; killing methods; killing tools; Black genocide; Nazis and abortion; see unborn babies.

ABORTION AS INFANTICIDE: THE KAMCHADAL PRACTICE

Abortion is wrong because it is actually a form of infanticide: the killing of a small child. We usually think of infanticide as the killing of a born child. But the killing of a pre-born child is not really different. He is hidden from view; he is smaller, more dependent, and more fragile. But he is a real person, just like the born child. He is simply at an earlier stage of his life and development. If it is wrong to kill him later (post-birth infanticide) it is equally wrong to kill him earlier (pre-birth infanticide).

The moral equivalence of infanticide (after birth) and abortion (before birth) is brought out by considering the Kamchadal practice: "The Kamchadal of northern Siberia have practitioners who specialize in killing a fetus through the wall of the abdomen, during the last stages of pregnancy. This may result in a stillbirth or in the birth of an injured but living infant that is killed forthwith."[4]

Is this abortion or infanticide? It is abortion because the child is killed while still in the womb. It is infanticide because a person aims a knife or dagger directly at a child in order to kill him, a child whose presence is obvious by the bulge in the mother's abdomen, and a child who could be seen and touched except for the abdominal wall that shields him. It is infanticide because it is killing a baby who is right there.

What this practice shows with unmistakable clarity is the practical moral identity of abortion and infanticide. It is not really one rather than the other. It is a form of abortion that vividly displays the moral equivalence of abortion and infanticide, and precludes any attempt to draw a line between them rationally.

What the Kamchadal practice amounts to is simply early infanticide: one doesn't even wait for the child to be born. What are called abortions, such as D&C, D&E, and D&X (partial birth abortion), are basically Kamchadal-like practices carried out earlier, and with different instruments. In D&C, for example, the knife has to be carefully inserted into the womb, because the baby is hidden away and not protruding as in the Kamchadal practice. In other words, it is easier to do a late Kamchadal because the baby is right there, protruding in his mother's abdomen; it is more difficult to do an early Kamchadal such as D&C or suction because the baby is more remote. But morally there is nothing that differentiates them.

Abortion is a form of infanticide. Whether the child is killed while still in the womb or after she has emerged from the womb is morally irrelevant. It is the same child before and after. If we recognize infanticide as a serious moral wrong, we must recognize abortion as an equally serious moral wrong. Let us keep the Kamchadal practice in mind, as well as its various modern forms (the methods of abortion) as we turn now to three refutations of the violinist argument presented in chapter 5 as a form of the no-duty-to-sustain argument.

Kamchadal and other *external* killings bother us; we see the killing with our own eyes. Shouldn't *internal* killings like abortion bother us equally? What difference does it make, morally, whether or not we see the child being killed with our own eyes? For the child it's the same thing: he or she is brutally, painfully killed.

Recall the case of Scott Peterson who murdered his wife Laci, December 24, 2002, in Modesto, California. He was convicted November 12, 2004, of two counts of murder. Why was it two? Because Laci was pregnant with their child, and so it was recognized that he killed two people. He killed his child, and so was convicted of second degree murder. The abortionist also kills the child, but many of us are not disturbed. Like Scott Peterson, the abortionist kills the child intentionally. But all this gets lost in the thick fog of "a woman's right to choose" and being "pro-choice."

ABORTION KILLS THE CHILD: THE FIRST REFUTATION OF THE VIOLINIST ARGUMENT

Let us recall Thomson's argument. She claims that a woman who carries the child to term is allowing the child to be in her body and is providing him with sustenance; that she has no duty to do this and may therefore expel the child; and that abortion is the exercise of the right to refuse to sustain the child, and is morally justified as the exercise of her right to withdraw support. She argues for her conclusion by an analogy. If you found yourself attached to a famous violinist who was plugged into you and who would die if you unplugged yourself from him, you would have a moral right to unplug yourself from him, even though he dies as a result. A pregnant woman is in essentially the same situation; she too may unplug herself from her "violinist," which means she may have an abortion. There are at least three things wrong with this argument; the first is the most important.

There are times when we may detach ourselves from another person, even though this results in his death. So far Thomson has a valid point.

Imagine a lifeguard trying to breathe life into a swimmer struggling between life and death. He does this for a long time, but the victim does not respond, nor does he die. He remains on the edge. At some point the exhausted lifeguard gives up and the victim dies. Suppose the lifeguard kept up his efforts for a reasonable length of time, and that he is then morally justified in giving up. When we say this, we are saying that at that point he no longer had a duty to sustain the life of the victim. It was morally right for him to withhold his support. So too, it might be argued that it would be right for Thomson to unplug herself from the violinist. This means she may withhold her support for his life; she need not sustain him and thus she may sever the link that ties her to him.

If this is correct, it means that Thomson may withhold support from the violinist as the lifeguard may withhold support from the drowning victim. *They may withhold life-sustaining measures—they may, however, not kill the other person.* This is the crucial distinction. Thomson's argument tries to justify abortion as an act of withholding support. But it is primarily an act of intentional killing. So even if it were justified under the heading of "withholding," it is not justified because it falls under the heading of intentional "killing."

Intentional killing refers to actions where (A) the intention is the death of another person, or (B) the intention is something else, but what is actually done is in fact killing. Thus (A) a killer shoots someone out of hatred because he wants him dead. Or (B) if you are trapped in a cave by someone stuck in the entrance of the cave and you intentionally blow him up with dynamite so you can get out, you may be said to intend his removal rather than his death; but clearly the act of dynamiting him is killing him. Thus killing, the deliberate bringing about of the death of an innocent person occurs (A) when the agent acts because he wants the person dead; or (B) when it is something else he wants but is obtained by an action that is in fact killing.

Withholding Support is morally justified only if two conditions are met. The first refers to the intention: it can only be to not sustain, or to not save the other person; it cannot be to cause her death. The lifeguard withholds support because he is exhausted, not because he wants the person dead. To withhold support because you want the person dead does not fall under morally justified withholding.

The second condition refers to the mode of implementation. Withholding can obviously take the form of an omission, as when the lifeguard ceases further support for the drowning victim; or you do not give a lifesaving medication to one person because you give it to another who needs it just as much. It can also take the form of an action, as when Thomson cuts the link connecting her to the violinist. But that action can only be the cutting of the link or something essentially similar. It cannot be an action that is in fact killing, even though the intention is only severing a link as the cessation of support. Thus if withholding takes the form of an action, it cannot be one that is in fact killing.

This is where Thomson's argument for abortion clearly fails. Assume that the woman has no duty to sustain the child. This means only that she has the right to withhold her support from him. It does not give her the right to kill the child, which is what abortion is. If Thomson's argument seems to have plausibility, it is because it views abortion only as an act of withholding support. But this is to overlook what abortion really is: intentionally killing the child—for example, by dismembering him. Thomson seizes on the withholding of support aspect of abortion, suppressing the deliberate killing aspect. The fact that an act may be right when viewed under one description does not mean that the act itself is right. For example, to describe an act as driving one's car on a public street is to offer a description of it under which it is perfectly all right. But if, in a particular case, that act includes running over a group of children who are playing there, then the act is quite obviously not right. What is clear from this example is that the latter description completely overrides the former one. Thus the act is clearly wrong because it is an act of killing, even if someone manages to find a description of it under which it is right. So too abortion is clearly wrong, even if Thomson manages to find a description of it under which it is, or might be, right.

Put another way, even if the child does not have the positive right to receive sustenance from her mother, she still has the negative right not to be killed. A beggar may not have the positive right to be fed by me; I may withhold that. But he surely has the negative right not to be intentionally killed by me. The same applies to the child.

"But," Thomson might argue, "if the only way I can exercise my right to withhold support for the child within me is by removing him, may I not do so even if this causes his death?" In reply consider a parallel case. I find a stranger in my house. He will die unless I take care of him. Assume I have no duty to do this, that I may rightly withhold support. Then I may do just that. But I cannot expel him if this means throwing him off a high cliff. That I throw him off in the name of withholding support does not mean that I don't also do something else: kill him. That the woman "throws the child out" in the name of withholding support does not mean that she does not also do something else: kill him. In both cases, the fact that the act is one of intentional killing makes it wrong, the other description (withholding support) notwithstanding.

Quite generally, I have the right to drive my car, to remove an impediment from the mouth of a cave where I'm trapped, and to free myself from another person to whom I'm attached. However I can exercise such a right only by intentionally killing an innocent person, I may not do so. Specifically, if the only way I can exercise my right to withhold support is to intentionally kill a person, I may not do it. My duty to not intentionally kill takes precedence over the exercise of my right to withhold support.

In summary, the no-duty-to-sustain argument fails. Even if there is no duty to sustain the child, *one may not kill the child!* Abortion is not merely a refusal to sustain, not merely a removal, of the pre-born baby; it is killing the baby. If it is seen as a removal it is a removal by killing. Recall the methods of abortion: suction, D&C, D&E, and D&X. In a parallel type of case, I may be justified in expelling an intruder from my house. But surely I cannot knife him to death or throw him off a high cliff to his death.

Thomson is correct when she holds that having a right to life does not always include having a right to be given all that one needs for continued life. That the violinist needs the continued use of my kidneys in order to stay alive does not establish that he has a right to be given the continued use of my kidneys. But he does have a right not to be actively killed. So too, the child has a right to not be actively killed by abortion, even in cases where removal may be morally justified as in an ectopic pregnancy. Thomson overlooks the fundamental moral distinction between:

- *Letting someone die* because one does not have the duty to take the extraordinary means necessary to keep him alive. The person's death is not intended. This is *not* a form of killing. An example of this is not sustaining the violinist.
- *Actively and intentionally killing him*. This *is* a form of killing. The death of the person being killed is intended, either as a means or as an end. An example of this is killing the child by one of the methods of abortion.

THE CHILD'S RIGHT OVER HIS BODY

If there is a right over one's body, two very significant features pertain to it. One, it is a right *everyone* has. Two, it includes the right to *not have one's body destroyed* (for example, by dismemberment), the right not to be killed. On both these counts the appeal to a woman's right over her body as a justification for abortion backfires, and provides an argument against abortion. Thus if a woman has a right over her body, then the child has that right too. Moreover, when did the woman's right over her own body begin? It began at conception when her body began; she was not given her body at birth. A woman therefore has a right to her body from the moment that she has a body; this right is not contingent on where her body is.

ABORTION IS INTENTIONAL
KILLING: A SECOND REFUTATION

The intention in the violinist case is clear: you disconnect in order to be free of the burden of sustaining the violinist. But is it a corresponding intention that is operative in a typical abortion? Patrick Lee argues that it is not; that in abortion

> what the parties involved desire is the absence of responsibility for a new child. Now, there are two ways of bringing it about that one is not responsible for a child. One is to arrange for someone else to fulfill those responsibilities, that is to put the child up for adoption. The other is to bring it about that there is no child. So, if the end is not-being-responsible for a child, and adoption is not chosen, then the abortion is a way of bringing it about that there is no child. The death of the child is the means chosen to end responsibility.[5]

This again makes it clear that abortion is not, as in the violinist case, a mere withholding of support, but in contrast, a case of deliberate, intentional killing. The first refutation of the violinist argument showed abortion is intentional killing by considering the way the child is killed: the brutal methods of abortion that tear the child to pieces. The second refutation showed abortion is intentional killing by considering why the child is killed: to avoid there being a child for whom one is responsible.

A MOTHER'S DUTY TO SUSTAIN HER CHILD:
A THIRD REFUTATION

The alleged parallel between the person plugged into the violinist and the woman with child fails in another very significant way. To see this, let us put aside the violinist argument for a moment and look at something else. We all recognize the obligation of parents to take care of their children: to provide shelter and protection, to feed them, to clothe them, to love them, and to support them emotionally. They have this obligation even when it costs them a great deal of effort and sacrifice, when it places great burdens on them. The reality and significance of this obligation becomes clear when considering its denial: child neglect.

The parents of a particular child have this obligation to him, and not someone else, because they are his biological parents, because they, and not someone else, begot and conceived the child. It is the biological bond that creates the obligation of parents to take care of their children, and also the rights that accompany this obligation. In bringing the child into existence they also brought into existence, by the same act, their obligation to nourish and protect him.

Parents have rights over their child, which other persons do not have; for example the right to discipline him. Rights and duties with regard to children go hand in hand. Parents have these rights because they first have the duties. Both the rights and the duties of natural parents toward their children come clearly into focus when the process of adoption is considered. Adoption is a legal transfer of rights and obligations to a new party. Only the natural mother can do this (or possibly the father). And she can do this because she is the mother. One can only give over what one already has. What is given over in adoption is precisely the relationship of obligations to the child (and the rights corresponding to them) stemming from the fact of conceiving the child. The woman can give her child for adoption because it is her child: her responsibility to sustain.

The violinist argument fails because the two cases are not parallel. The person hooked up to the violinist (we are assuming) has no duty to sustain him, for he is a total stranger, standing in a relation to the person that is most unnatural. This is exactly the opposite of the mother-child relation, which is most natural and proper. We may not have the obligation to sustain strangers artificially hooked up to us, but we do have the obligation to sustain our own children. So the very thing that makes it plausible to say that the person in bed with the violinist has no duty to sustain him; namely, that he is a stranger unnaturally hooked up to him, is precisely what is absent in the case of the mother and her child. She does have an obligation to take care of her child, to sustain her, to protect her, and especially to let her live in the only place where she can now be protected, nourished, and allowed to grow, namely the womb. If she ejects her from her womb, she is like a mother throwing her child out of her home, into the cold, refusing to take care of her. The pre-born child must be viewed, and treated, just like the born child.

If the mother has the duty to sustain the child, she may not unplug herself from him. Therefore abortion merely as unplugging is morally wrong. So the no-duty-to-sustain argument is false at its very core: the woman *does* have a duty to sustain her child, precisely because it is her child. The person with the violinist does not, correspondingly, have the duty to sustain him, for he is not her child. And with this we also see the invalidity of Thomson's intruder argument, which is refuted by the simple fact that the child is anything but an intruder; he or she is her very flesh and blood.

THE VIOLINIST ARGUMENT AND THE CASE OF RAPE

Suppose the woman has been raped. She still has a duty to sustain the life of the child. Despite the absolute horror of rape, the terrible injustice and violence of this most despicable act, the reality of the child must be kept in mind; he is absolutely innocent. The father is guilty of a terrible crime; the child is not. The child conceived in rape is a reminder to the woman of the horrible event that led to the child's coming into being. That is certainly a powerful psychological reality; it does not mean that the child partakes of the moral evil of this event. The child is real, and innocent, and she has the same preciousness and dignity as the rest of us, and the same right to life. That is, the same right not to be killed, and also, the same right to be sustained. She is still the child of her mother. What was noted above, that a parent has the obligation to take care of her own child, because she is her child, is something quite universal. It applies to all parents and all children. It does not cease to be true because the act of intercourse that led to the conception of the child was violent and forced upon the woman. The biological relation of mother to child is still there, unaffected by the circumstance of the rape.

It is interesting to note that Thomson herself does not press the rape argument for abortion in this context. She says, "Surely the question whether you have a right to life at all, or how much of it you have, shouldn't [doesn't?] turn on the question of whether or not you are the product of a rape."[6] This is a point well worth considering.

THE SPECIAL RELATION
BETWEEN A WOMAN AND HER CHILD

There is a special relation between a woman and her child: the child is entrusted to her, as she was entrusted to her mother when she was a child in the womb. The no-duty-to-sustain argument stems from a denial of this deep relationship of being entrusted or a refusal to accept it.

The claim to a right over one's body as a slogan for abortion is not a genuine claim to a right, as when a member of one group of persons claims the same rights as the members of another group. It is rather a refusal to acknowledge the relationship of being entrusted. And it expresses a determination to live one's own life even at the expense of utterly crushing that of another.

Abortion is a double evil: the killing of a helpless small child, in a most cruel way; and the denial of the special, profound relationship of entrustment. The woman who has an abortion destroys a child who is especially entrusted to her.

OUR GENERAL DUTY TO HELP ONE ANOTHER:
A FOURTH REFUTATION

Is it really so clear that I have no duty to sustain the violinist? Perhaps I do sometimes have such a duty. Consider some similar cases. Suppose I hear a person screaming for help. Do I not have a duty to help her, to save her life, to prevent her from being killed? Do I not have this duty even at a great sacrifice for myself? The *Carpathia* comes upon the *Titanic* disaster and says, "Sorry, we have no room." Can this be right? If I find you in the wilderness, should I not rescue you? In evaluating the duty to save the life of another person even at great cost to myself, I can apply the Golden Rule: if I were in need of being saved lest I die, would I not reasonably expect you to save me, even at great cost to yourself? If so, should I not save you, even at great cost to myself? Doesn't the same apply to the woman and her pre-born child?

SUMMARY OF REFUTATIONS OF THE VIOLINIST ARGUMENT

1. Abortion is not a mere withholding of support, not a mere "unplugging," but a deliberate intentional killing; recall the methods and Kamchadal. This is so even if its intention is bringing about the withholding of support (first refutation).
2. The argument about the right over one's body proves the wrongness of abortion: the child has the right not to have her body destroyed.
3. Abortion is intentional killing because it intends the destruction of the pre-born baby so that there is no child that one is responsible for (second refutation).
4. A pregnant woman is carrying a child who is her own child, entrusted to her. She has a special relation to this child, which implies an obligation to take care of him; failure to do so is child neglect. Hence unplugging is wrong already on the level of intending to withhold support (third refutation).
5. Do we not have a general obligation to come to the rescue of others, to save their lives, to sustain them if they need us to live? Perhaps we have such a duty even to the violinist; we certainly do so in cases that are significantly less in terms of the hardship they represent (fourth refutation).

OBJECTION AND REPLY:
HE WILL NEVER KNOW THE DIFFERENCE

A fundamental assumption underlying much of the support for abortion is the idea that the being in the womb may be aborted because he will never know the difference. "If I kill an adult or a child who realizes what is happening, that is of course terrible; but if I destroy the child in the womb, he will never know it. So what difference can it make to him? He just won't be born, and will never realize it. How can abortion be wrong?"

Let me offer three replies. First, if the being in the womb is indeed a child, a person, then whether or not he realizes he is being killed is irrelevant. Intentional killing is a terrible moral evil whether the victim is aware of it or not. If I kill a born person painlessly in his sleep, he will never wake up. He may never know the difference. But a terrible evil has been done nonetheless. If a pre-born child is killed in his sleep, his state in the womb, he will never wake up to be born; he may never know the difference. But again, a terrible evil has been committed nonetheless.

Second, the child in the womb has been wronged in the most serious way possible, since he has been denied his whole future. His being unaware of this is totally irrelevant. This is the future-like-ours argument that will be taken up in chapter 12.

Third, the objection assumes that the child in the womb is in a state like that of a deep sleep so that he will never know the difference. In the very early stages of his existence in the womb this is probably true. But in later stages there is sufficient development of the nerves and brain to make him sensitive to pain; to horrible pain when the abortionist's knife cuts him to pieces. He will then surely know the difference! This leads us directly to the next chapter, to a further argument against abortion.

8

Abortion Causes Pain to the Child

ABORTION IS WRONG BECAUSE IT
CAUSES HORRIBLE PAIN TO THE CHILD

A further pro-life argument against abortion is that it is an inhumane, barbaric procedure. Recall the methods; for example, a sharp instrument like a knife is inserted and the child is cut to pieces. Pain is certainly true for late abortions when the child is highly developed and hardly distinguishable from a born baby. Is it true also for earlier abortions? To answer this question, consider the testimony of Dr. Kanwaljeet Anand, of the University of Arkansas Medical Center. This leading specialist and researcher into medical issues dealing with pre-born children says he has no doubt that babies have the capacity to feel intense pain by the second trimester of pregnancy. In the third trimester the internal systems for feeling pain are completely developed and functional.[1] If a baby can feel intense pain at this time, it can certainly feel some pain earlier, perhaps much earlier. The second trimester is from thirteen to twenty-six weeks.

Other doctors have reached the same conclusion. Dr. Jean Wright, a specialist in Pediatric Critical Care Medicine, an anesthesiologist, confirmed the existence of pain in pre-born babies during Congressional testimony.

> [A]n unborn fetus after 20 weeks gestation has all the prerequisite anatomy, physiology, hormones, neurotransmitters, and electrical current to close the loop and create the conditions needed to perceive pain. In a fashion similar to explaining the electrical wiring to a new house, we would explain that the circuit is complete from skin to brain and back.[2]

Dr. Richard T. F. Schmidt, past president, American College of Obstetricians and Gynecologists, confirms this: "It can be clearly demonstrated that fetuses seek to evade certain stimuli in a manner which an infant or an adult would be interpreted as a reaction to pain."[3]

The testimony of these doctors confirms what earlier doctors had said about pain suffered by pre-born babies during abortion; their further research substantiates the work of the earlier doctors. Notable among these is Dr. Vincent Collins, professor of anesthesiology at Northwestern University, and author of a leading text on this topic. He says that the capacity to feel pain begins very early in the life of a pre-born child:

> Functioning neurological structures [nerves and brain centers] necessary for pain sensation are in place as early as 8 weeks (when most abortions are performed), but certainly by 13½ weeks of gestation. . . . The first detectable brain activity [relevant to pain] occurs in the thalamus between the 8th and the 10th weeks. . . . By 13½ weeks, the entire sensory nervous system functions as a whole in all parts of the body.[4]

"There are hundreds of studies which confirm the existence of fetal pain— overwhelmingly—by 20 weeks . . . with nearly 1,000 scholarly articles citing . . . comprehensive pain study."[5]

Some researchers say that a pre-born baby may actually feel *more* pain than a newborn baby.

> The last pathways in the nociceptive system are the inhibitory descending serotonin neurons, which can block the ascending pathways. These do not form until after birth, raising the possibility that the fetus may actually be more sensitive to noxious stimuli than the older child.[6]

The reality of the horrible pain inflicted on a baby by abortion is finally being given some public attention. In October 2010, the Nebraska fetal pain law went into effect. "The Abortion Pain Prevention Act" (LB 1103) bans abortion after twenty weeks on the basis that a pre-born child feels pain at that stage.[7]

At a conference, Life and Choice, held on the campus of Princeton University on October 15 and 16, 2010, at a session on fetal pain, Dr. Anand presented his research on this subject and restated his view that pre-born babies suffer pain from abortion.

THE SPECIAL HORROR OF PARTIAL-BIRTH ABORTIONS

The reality and the horror of excruciating pain apply in particular to partial-birth abortions. The U.S. Congress officially took notice of this:

The vast majority of babies killed during partial-birth abortion are alive until the end of the procedure. It is a medical fact, however, that unborn infants at this stage can feel pain when subjected to painful stimuli and that their perception of this pain is even more intense than that of newborn infants and older children when subjected to the same stimuli. Thus, during a partial-birth procedure, the child will fully experience the pain associated with piercing his or her skull and sucking out his or her brain.[8]

The same horrific picture is painted in a court ruling:

A D&X [partial-birth abortion] procedure may subject fetuses beyond twenty weeks gestational age to "prolonged and excruciating pain." Because the density of receptors is greater in the fetal skin at about twenty weeks of gestation, and because the mechanisms that inhibit and modulate the perception of pain do not develop until after thirty-two to thirty-four weeks gestation, there was testimony that fetus likely feels severe pain while the procedure is being performed. . . . The Court finds that the testimony at trial and before Congress establishes that D&X [partial-birth abortion] is a gruesome, brutal, barbaric, and uncivilized medical procedure.[9]

CONTROVERSY REGARDING PAIN FOR THE CHILD

As we saw, pro-choicers claim that the matter of fetal pain does not constitute a valid reason against abortion. They say that the evidence remains uncertain because it is impossible to know for sure that fetuses consciously experience pain in the same way that a person does. Further, that they do not feel pain until after the start of the third trimester; and that this is irrelevant since virtually no abortions occur during the third trimester. In reply to the latter point, to say "virtually no abortions" occur during this time is highly misleading. According to the Guttmacher Institute (which is pro-choice), about thirteen thousand abortions occur after twenty-one weeks. This is may be only 1.1 percent of the total—and probably the source of the "virtually no abortions" claim—but it is still a lot of abortions. If we hear of the terribly painful death of thirteen thousand people, or even animals, we would be shocked. In addition let us remember gruesome description (chapter 7, pages 63–64) of D&X or partial-birth abortions, performed late in pregnancy. For each of the babies subjected to this violent, excruciatingly painful death it is a cruel lie to be told "virtually no abortions occur during the third trimester."

The claim that "they do not feel pain until after the start of the third trimester" is directly contradicted by Dr. Anand. The start of the third trimester is twenty-six weeks; he says the baby can feel pain as early as twenty weeks, a significant difference. Further, other recent studies support the pro-life position that the BIW does feel pain.

The available scientific evidence makes it possible, even probable, that fetal pain perception occurs well before late gestation. Those attempting to deny or delay its occurrence must offer conclusive evidence for the absence of fetal pain at given levels of maturity.[10]

THE RISK FACTOR CONCERNING PAIN TO THE CHILD

Both sides often speak of what is "probable." This would mean that we are not sure whether abortion causes pain to the child. Or more precisely, from what point on does it cause pain, since even pro-choice admits the reality or at least the high likelihood of pain at the later stages. If we are not sure whether abortion causes pain to the child, there is at least a terrible risk that it does so. If we are not certain that it will cause pain, we should ask ourselves some questions. Would you put your dog or cat in a position where it *might* suffer that amount of pain? If you knew there was a situation where your pet *might* feel the kind of pain that abortion methods produce, would you risk getting it into that situation? Would you send a loved one into a situation where you knew there is a significant chance that he or she *might* suffer that kind of pain? If the answer to these questions is *no*, then isn't it clearly wrong to force abortion on a small, defenseless child, where the child is made vulnerable to that risk of pain? Let us apply the Golden Rule. *Do unto others as you would want others to do unto you.* Put yourself in the place of the child. Don't make another suffer pain that you yourself would avoid.

It might be useful at this point to review the website indicated above, that shows pictures of the results of abortion: www.100abortionpictures.com

WEIGHING HARMS AND BENEFITS

There is an important general moral principle that it is wrong to greatly harm one person in order to benefit another. I cannot cause serious pain and death to one person in order to alleviate the suffering of another. This means that we cannot directly kill the child in the womb in order to benefit the woman. The rightful claim of the child not to be subject to the terrible pain of death by abortion outweighs the claim of the woman to any benefits that having an abortion might provide. Our duty to not cause terrible pain and death to another is more urgent than any duty we may have to grant a woman a right to better her life and alleviate her pain, even if this gain is substantial.

THE PAIN ARGUMENT APPLIES
EVEN IF THE BIW IS NOT A PERSON

Suppose the pro-choice not-a-person argument is valid, and consequently the Warren-Tooley position that the BIW is not a person is correct. The pain argument still holds. It is wrong to inflict such pain on any creature that can feel it. Causing such pain to a cat or a dog, a chicken or a pig, a cow or an elephant, would be a horrible evil. Surely the same applies to the being in the womb, whatever his or her status as an actual or potential person. As Bentham remarked concerning animals, "The question is not, Can they *reason*? Nor can they *talk*? But, *Can they suffer?*"

9

The Dignity of the Human Person

There are several pro-choice arguments that can be brought together in terms of the pro-life replies to them. They are the feminist quality of life argument and the feminist egalitarian argument of chapter 2, the general quality of human life argument of chapter 3, and the Maguire-Morgan not-a-person argument, the relative-to-social-acceptance view of what counts as being a person, of chapter 4. The common pro-life theme here is the defense of human dignity. It is the claim that these pro-choice arguments treat some human beings as if they were disposable for the sake of securing a greater "quality of life" or similar goods for other human beings. This is an affront to the dignity of the persons. The following replies are all intended to develop and support the idea of human dignity as a moral imperative binding on all of us. Let us begin with the general quality of human life argument developed in chapter 3.

A REPLY TO "EVERY CHILD A WANTED CHILD"

1. That is certainly a noble ideal. Every child should be wanted. It is terribly sad when this is not the case. But does this mean that if a child is unwanted it should be killed? "Every grandmother a wanted grandmother." What if you were not wanted? Lots of people in the world are not wanted—should we kill them? If a child is now unwanted, does this mean that she will never be wanted? If you are unwanted when you are two years old, does this mean you will be unwanted when you are ten years old? Is being wanted what gives you your

dignity as a person? Does a woman derive her value and dignity as a person from being wanted by another person? Surely not.
2. To those who propose abortion in such a case: would you kill a *born* child for this reason? If not a born child, why a *pre-born* child? What's the difference?
3. We are told: "Don't bring an unwanted child into the world." But the pre-born child *is already* in the world. The mother is part of the world, her womb is part of the world, and what is inside her womb is part of the world. The child is already here; he or she is just not visible to us.

A REPLY TO "EVERY CHILD A HEALTHY CHILD"

The same three points apply here as well. A wonderful ideal, but should we kill those who fall short of it? Would we kill a born child who had a similar severe handicap?

To those who propose abortion in the case of severe physical handicap: why not wait until the child is born and then kill him? That is, kill him then when you can do so *painlessly* and thereby spare him the horrible pain of abortion.

There is a further point along the same line. If a handicapped child is to be killed, one should kill him only if one *knows* he has the handicap. Before birth sometimes one does not know this, one cannot always be certain. Often there is only a prediction that the child will be born with a handicap, and such a prediction can turn out to be mistaken. What a horrible mistake!

If killing the child after birth sounds shocking, we must ask if there really is any morally relevant difference between killing him before birth or after birth. Or is it rather simply a case of "out of sight, out of mind?" The word "abortion" is easier to say than the phrase, "kill the child after birth." This is a psychological difference, but hardly a moral difference.

Finally, let us remember that the handicapped child is already in the world.

A REPLY TO "THE QUALITY OF LIFE OF THE WOMAN"

As long as the reality of the child is denied or overlooked, the argument sounds plausible. But once one realizes that there is a child present, a real person, an innocent small human person, who is directly and intentionally killed, the picture changes dramatically. Can we kill one person to benefit another? No one would dream of suggesting that we kill the women to further the quality of life of the child (if that were possible). Is it any different in the other direction?

This assumes that abortion benefits the woman. Does it? Later we shall see that there are reasons given by some to doubt this.

A REPLY TO "THE QUALITY OF LIFE OF THE WHOLE WORLD: OVERPOPULATION"

1. Is killing innocent persons the way to solve this problem?
2. If one does resort to killing innocent persons, why should it be the very young, who have their whole life ahead of them, and not the old who have already had most of their life?
3. As in all these quality-of-life arguments, if one overlooks the reality of the child and the reality of abortion as the direct, intentional killing of this child and the horrible pain abortion causes the child, the argument may sound plausible. But if we shift our perspective and focus on the reality of the child and the reality of abortion as killing this child and causing her pain, this argument and all the other quality-of-life arguments lose their plausibility; and we can see that from this perspective they fail in their attempt at providing a moral justification for abortion.
4. It is interesting that it is always born persons who advance this argument, and recommend that someone else be sacrificed. They do not offer their own lives for this cause. Perhaps it is easier to volunteer others to be sacrificed than to offer yourself?

A REPLY TO "THE RELATIVE TO SOCIAL ACCEPTANCE" VIEW OF BEING A PERSON

Let us turn now to the Maguire-Morgan not-a-person argument discussed in chapter 4. Those who advance this argument—based on the relative-to-social-acceptance view, the idea that a human being is not really a person unless, and until, he or she is welcomed into the human community—should remember the fate of African-Americans in America prior to the enactment of civil rights laws. These persons were, precisely, *not* "welcomed into the human community." They were explicitly kept outside. The logical consequence of the relative-to-social-acceptance view is that they were not persons. And that is in fact how they were treated. Or they were at least not treated as full persons, with fully equal human rights and dignity. No one wants to adopt such an idea today. But proposing the Maguire-Morgan not-a-person argument is precisely to adopt such an idea, that being a person is relative to social acceptance, to being "welcomed into the human community."

If this view is adopted, no one is safe. What happened to Jews in Nazi Germany can happen anywhere if this view is adopted and put into practice. America is not exempt as we saw in the case of African-Americans. And, as we all know, there are also other groups that were, or still are, not "welcomed into the human community" and seen as being "non-persons" or "not persons in the full sense."

In short, those who advance the relative-to-social-acceptance view, which is at the core of the Maguire-Morgan not-a-person argument, should carefully consider where this view leads them; what it implies when taken to its logical conclusion. They surely do not want to say that African-Americans were not persons before they were "welcomed into the human community." They had their reality and dignity as persons before this; they had it in their very nature, independent of any social acceptance. Exactly the same thing applies to pre-born human beings.

A REPLY TO TWO FEMINIST PRO-CHOICE ARGUMENTS

The feminist pro-choice quality-of-life argument of Susan Sherwin claims that abortion is often the best course of action for a woman in terms of protecting and furthering the quality of her life in all its dimensions. The feminist pro-choice egalitarian argument of Alison Jaggar claims that the right to abortion is necessary to ensure equality between men and women. Both these arguments were developed in chapter 2. The pro-life reply is short and simple. No doubt these are worthy goals that should be pursued by all legitimate means. They cannot be achieved by killing another human being, a small child in the womb. It is also important to understand that a woman's quality of life and its protection begin in the womb. A woman's life begins as a small baby girl in utero. And in regard to egalitarian concerns, worldwide far more baby girls than baby boys are killed by abortion for cultural reasons. This alone shows that "the right to abortion" ensures not equality but inequality between men and women.

THE QUESTION OF INFANTICIDE

It should be noted that many of the pro-choice general quality-of-life arguments, if taken to their logical conclusion, would if accepted justify infanticide as well as abortion. There is a division here. There are pro-choice advocates who explicitly accept infanticide as morally justified. Peter Singer, Michael Tooley, and Lynn M. Morgan are examples. But most pro-choicers draw a clear and explicit line: abortion yes, infanticide no.

Each of these is beset with serious problems. If we accept infanticide, we are saying that it is right for some human beings to kill others, if they judge their lives not worth living, or if they are seen as being "in the way"; and if they have the power. Once we go down this route no one is safe. Those who advocate killing young human beings today may end up on the other side of this crucial fence when they are older, and judged in the same way that they now judge those for whom they recommend an early death. It is the doctrine of might makes right, the stuff of which the worst tyrannies are made.

It is surely for this reason, understood clearly if only implicitly, that most people who advocate the pro-choice position reject infanticide. But they should be careful where their arguments lead when thought through carefully. There are two key points here.

First there is the point just noted that some general quality-of-life arguments if taken to their logical conclusion naturally lead to infanticide. That is, it is hard to see how one can argue that a pre-born child may be killed by abortion for reason x (such as severe handicap), and then not also agree that if this, same factor x applies to a born child it too should be killed. But if one does this one is agreeing to infanticide as well.

Second, can the pro-choicer who rejects infanticide give a logically sound reason for drawing the line at birth? If he or she accepts the no-duty-to-sustain argument, the way is clear: birth marks the end of the time the pregnant woman is sustaining the BIW in her body. But the not-a-person argument runs into trouble here. As noted, it rests on the achievement view: the BIW does not become a person until it achieves certain things, generally defined in terms of the physical development necessary to function as a person. This development is not completed at birth. Why then choose birth as the cut-off point? As we shall see in chapter 11, one writer explicitly acknowledges this; and argues that the not-a-person argument when taken to its logical conclusion can justify abortion only if it is also taken as justifying infanticide. The writer is Michael Tooley.

MAKING KILLING SEEM HONORABLE

One of first acts of war is to make the killing of persons seem honorable. A newspaper article makes this point:

> The language of war discourages soldiers from seeing the enemy as individuals capable of suffering. An American soldier refers to an Iraqi prisoner as "it." A general speaks not of "Iraqi fighters" but of "the enemy." A weapons manufacturer doesn't talk about people but about "targets.". . . Under normal conditions, most people find it very difficult to kill. But in war, military recruits

must be persuaded that killing other people is not only acceptable but even honorable.[1]

Is this happening in the case of abortion? Is abortion made to seem honorable because it is labeled as "the removal of the fetus," rather than what it really is, the killing of a small child? John Finnis, Oxford University, addressed this question at the October 2010 Princeton University Conference, Life and Choice:

About the moral status of the phrase "the fetus," I will just say this. As used in the conference program and website, which are not medical contexts, it is offensive, dehumanizing, prejudicial, and manipulative. Used in this context, exclusively and in preference to the alternatives, it is an F-word, to go with the J-word, and other such words we know of, which have or had an acceptable meaning in a proper context but became in wider use the symbol of subjection to the prejudices and preferences of the more powerful. It's not a fair word, and it does not suggest an open heart. Those of you who have an open mind or a fair heart may wish to listen to every speaker at this conference, and see whether they are willing to speak, at least sometimes, of the unborn child or unborn baby, and to do so without scare quotes or irony.

III

FURTHER MORAL CONSIDERATIONS

10

Some Pro-Choice Replies
to Pro-Life Claims

We have examined some basic pro-choice arguments and some basic pro-life arguments. Which set best represents the truth of the matter? To help the reader decide, two things will hopefully be helpful. First, since pro-choice was presented before pro-life, giving pro-life up to now "the last word," it would be helpful to have pro-choice give some replies to these pro-life arguments. This will be our theme in this chapter. Second, it will be useful to compare the most basic theses on each side in order to come to an understanding of what are the ultimate issues in this debate. Later this will be our theme in chapter 20.

PRO-CHOICE REPLIES TO PRO-LIFE CLAIMS
REGARDING THE CONTINUUM ARGUMENT

The pro-life continuum argument claims that the life of a human person is a single continuum which has different phases. Being a child in the womb, a pre-born baby, is the first of these phases; later phases include being a newborn baby, a child at seven years, a young adult, and an older person. A major part of what this means is: *The child in the womb is the same being,* the same person, *as the born child he will soon become,* as the older child he will become later. I am the same person as the child in the womb when my mother was pregnant with me. If I am clearly a person now, and I was the same being in my mother's womb, then clearly I was a person then.

I am now the same person I was ten years ago, even though I have changed. That "I have changed" means that I, the same person, have changed; that these changes happened to me. A good way to understand this is through memory. I remember not only events that occurred, say, ten years ago, but *myself* as experiencing these events. To remember an experience is to reach back, not only into the past, but into another phase of one's own existence, which means one's own existence as the same person one is now.

Thus the central claim of the continuum argument is that child is already there in the womb; the *same* child, the *same person* who will later be born. The significant developmental changes that occur do so in the life of one and the same being who is present throughout.

Pro-choice can reply to this by pointing out that the continuum argument relies on a particular view of personal identity which can be denied and replaced by another view. On this other view, if it is true, the basis of the continuum argument collapses, and with it the argument itself as a defense of the pro-life position.

Let us now examine this other view as developed by Derek Parfit in his book, *Reasons and Persons*, and see how it attempts to undermine the pro-life continuum argument. Parfit's view stands in direct antithesis to what we can call the Strong Personal Identity View. The Strong Personal Identity View is the view assumed in the pro-life continuum argument. On this view whether a given future person is me or not me is an all-or-nothing affair: any future person is either me or he is not me, there is no in-between or gray area. The Strong Personal Identity View is expressed by Thomas Reid:

> The identity of a person is a perfect identity; wherever it is real, it admits of no degrees; and it is impossible that a person should be in part the same, and in part different; because a person . . . is not divisible into parts. The evidence of identity in other persons does admit of all degrees, from what we account certainty, to the least degree of probability. But it is still true, that the same person is perfectly the same, and cannot be so in part, or in some degree only.[1]

Parfit denies this. His argument begins with the following observation:

> Human beings have a lower brain and two upper hemispheres, which are connected by a bundle of fibres. In treating a few people with severe epilepsy, surgeons have cut these fibres. The aim was to reduce the severity of the epileptic fits, by combining their causes to a single hemisphere. This aim was achieved. But the operations had another unintended consequence. The effect . . . was the creation of "two separate spheres of consciousness."[2]

Let us take this further. Suppose "that I am one of three identical triplets." Then:

> *My Division.* My body is fatally injured, as are the brains of my two brothers. My brain is divided, and each half is successfully implanted into the body of one of my brothers. Each of the resulting people believes that he is me, seems

to remember living my life, has my character, and is in every other way psychologically continuous with me. And he has a body that is very like mine.[3]

The big question of course is "What happens to me?" Parfit says "There are only four possibilities: (1) I do not survive; (2) I survive as one of the two people; (3) I survive as the other; (4) I survive as both."[4] He considers all four possibilities, none of which are really satisfying or convincing. The conclusion that he suggests from this case is that we adopt what he calls the Reductionist View, the view in direct opposition to the Strong Personal Identity View. On the Reductionist View there is no personal identity as we commonly assume it in daily life. There is no "me" who exists now and also at a future time as the very same "me," which would be the Strong Personal Identity View. In contrast:

> On the Reductionist View, each person's existence just involves the existence of a brain and body, the doing of certain deeds, the thinking of certain thoughts, the occurrence of certain experiences, and so on.[5]
>
> What a Reductionist denies is that the subject of experiences is a *separately existing entity*, distinct from a brain and a body, and a series of physical and mental events.
>
> Is it true that, in memory, we are aware of what the Reductionist denies? Is each of us aware that he is a persisting subject of experiences, a separately existing entity that is not his brain and body?
>
> This is not a point that can be argued. I do not believe that *I* am directly aware that I am such an entity. And I assume that I am not unusual. I believe that no one is directly aware of such a fact. . . .
>
> [Even assuming such an entity] I could not know that this entity continued to exist . . . [for] there might be a series of such entities that were psychologically continuous. Memories might be passed from one to the next like a baton in a relay race. So might all other psychological features. Given the resulting psychological continuity, we would not be aware that one of these entities had been replaced by another. We therefore cannot know that such entities continue to exist.[6]
>
> There is no evidence that the carrier of psychological continuity is something whose existence . . . must be all-or-nothing. And there is much evidence that the carrier of this continuity is the brain. There is much evidence that our psychological features depend upon states and events in our brain. A brain's continued existence need not be all-or-nothing. Physical connectedness can be a matter of degree. And there are countless actual cases in which psychological connectedness holds only in certain ways, or to some reduced degree.[7]

The Strong Personal Identity View holds that we *are* "separately existing entities," that our being as persons, though intimately related to our bodies and brains, is not simply the body and brain and its activities. When I say that I am now the same person as I was when I was five, I do not mean merely that there is some physical and psychological continuity between my brain and body then and now. I mean that the same person, "me," existed at both times.

The brain division case provides one example of what Parfit claims undermines personal identity as we commonly assume it. Another is where a surgeon tampers with my brain and alters it, at first slightly and then more extensively, so that at the end there is a radical change from what existed at the beginning. Given that "our psychological features depend upon states and events in our brain," what happens to me? Parfit's reply is three-fold: at the near end of this spectrum, where the changes are slight we can use the language of personal identity and say it will be me; at the far end it will not be me but someone else; in the middle there is a gray area, with no clear answer to the question, "Will this still be me?" And that is the crucial point: personal identity is a matter of degree. It is not an all-or-nothing reality; rather I can be a tenth me, a quarter me, a half me, or some other degree of me that is not fully me at any given time.

Consider a club. It meets for a time, then disbands. Later some of the original members form a club with the same name and the same rules. Is it the same club? Or a different one which happens to have some features in common with the first? Parfit's reply is in effect: take your pick, it doesn't matter, the facts of the case are the same either way. A club has no true identity, but only one of convenience, or a manner of speaking; or perhaps a matter of degree. The same essential point, Parfit claims, applies to persons.

> If we are Reductionists about personal identity, we . . . can describe cases where, between me now and some future person, the physical and psychological connections hold only to reduced degrees. If I imagine myself in such a case, I can always ask, "Am I about to die?" Will the resulting person be me? On the Reductionist view, in some cases there would be no answer. My question would be *empty*. The claim that I was about to die would be neither true nor false.[8]

Parfit denies personal identity in the way we commonly assume it, and as it is held by the Strong Personal Identity View. What does he offer in its place? What is it that relates the person I am now and past persons and future persons that I assume are all "me," that (usually) have the same first name, often the same last name, and are considered by others to be the same person?

> The rival view is that *personal identity is not what matters*. I claim
> *What matters is Relation R*: psychological connectedness and/or continuity, with the right kind of cause.[9]
> *Psychological connectedness* is the holding of particular direct psychological connections.
> *Psychological continuity* is the holding of overlapping chains of *strong* connectedness.[10]

Psychological *connectedness* is a direct relation found largely in memories and intentions. If I remember an experience I had yesterday, that constitutes a psychological connection. If I now form the intention of leaving for my vacation tomorrow that too constitutes a psychological connection. Psychological *continuity* is not a direct relation but one constituted by overlapping chains of relations. For example, at age forty I remember x at age twenty; at age twenty I remember y at age ten; but at age forty I do not remember y. In the latter case there is no direct psychological connection between me at forty and y at ten, hence no *connectedness*. But because there are overlapping memories, there is *continuity* between me at forty and me at ten.

But doesn't Parfit presuppose personal identity in describing these things? He would say no. He may be using the language of personal identity but what he means is something else, what he calls Relation R. This is a suitable combination of psychological connectedness and continuity that does not (like strong personal identity) have the character of absoluteness, of being all-or-nothing; meaning that any future person will either be me or not be me, with no in-between. On the contrary, Relation R precisely admits of degrees, gray areas, unanswerable questions, especially, "Will this future person be me or someone else?"

In the short term, say from yesterday to today, where there are direct psychological connections, we may see our usual notions of personal identity and Parfit's Relation R as coinciding; but only in a practical sense, and only relatively and to a great extent, not absolutely. When the time span is long, or when the psychological differences are great, then personal identity as we know it breaks down on Parfit's view. Consider a telling example. A person is a victim of a brutally sadistic Nazi guard in a concentration camp. Forty years later he meets a kind elderly gentleman who bears a striking resemblance to the man he knew as the guard. Could it be the same person? Perhaps he has had a deep conversion. Or is it a different person, possibly his identical twin, who only looks like him? What is important for us is the stark contrast between the two theories about personal identity as they apply to this case.

On the Strong Personal Identity View which we assume in our daily lives, the question, "Is it the same person?" has overwhelming force. It is an absolute yes or no, an all-or-nothing. The kind elderly gentleman either is or isn't the same person as the brutal guard. If he *isn't* we have two separate persons, each with his own personal identity and separate life history. Neither is morally responsible for what the other did. The other possibility is that, however much his personality has changed, the elderly man *is* the same person; and is therefore morally responsible for the terrible crimes he committed in his past.

In contrast, on Parfit's view where personal identity in the strong sense is replaced by Relation R, which is merely certain psychological connections or continuities, the question loses its original force. If there are not two distinct persons, there is one individual manifesting radical changes. Is it *the same* person?" This otherwise dramatic question now becomes an empty question. The second older person is partly the same person as the first younger one but also partly a different person. It is like a club which evolves over the years; some things remain the same, some things change. Is it the same club? Or a different one? Take your pick; there is no really correct answer. The identity of a club or a person is merely a matter of degree.

The stark contrast between the two views comes out also when we consider survival as opposed to death. Going back to the brain division case, Parfit says:

> The best description is that I shall be neither person. But this does not imply that I should regard division nearly as bad as death. As I argued, I should regard it as about as good as ordinary survival. . . . Since I cannot be one and the same person as the two resulting people, but my relation to each of these people contains what fundamentally matters in ordinary survival, the case shows that identity is not what matters. What matters is Relation R: psychological connectedness and/or psychological continuity.[11]

Let us note Parfit's key points:

- Identity is not what matters.
- What matters is Relation R: psychological connectedness and/or psychological continuity.
- I should regard division, where I am neither of the two future persons resulting from this division, as about as good as ordinary survival.

We can now see how Parfit's view—in its denial of strong personal identity, identity as commonly understood and assumed in daily life—can provide a pro-choice reply to counter the pro-life continuum argument. On Parfit's view the BIW and a born person are not one and the same person. The born person cannot say "I was once a baby in my mother's womb," for this expresses personal identity in the strong sense. Only this strong sense can ground moral rights, so that if the born person has the right to life, and the BIW is the same person, then he too has the right to life. On Parfit's view a born person and the BIW are not "the same being" in the strong sense that can ground such a right. Except in a loose and informal sense, they are not "the same being." Nor are you now the same person as the person who had "your" experiences as a young child. The expression, "that was me" has no real meaning in the strong sense in which it is commonly, but according to Parfit, mistakenly, used.

Based on his denial of personal identity as we normally understand it, Parfit has an explicit view on the moral question of abortion. It is a form of the Gradualist Position, which we will examine later in chapter 12.

PRO-CHOICE REPLIES TO PRO-LIFE
CLAIMS REGARDING THE SLED ARGUMENT

The pro-life SLED argument stresses the essential personal continuity and the morally significant similarity between the BIW and the rest of us. It is an answer to the question of the differences between born and pre-born human beings. It is the claim that there are four and only four such differences, and that all of them are morally insignificant. The acronym SLED can help us remember these four differences: Size, Level of development, Environment, and Degree of dependency.

Pro-choice can counter this argument by claiming that two of these four features are indeed morally significant. Level of development is precisely what matters in the growth of the fetus from being merely a biological organism to being a person worthy of moral respect; from being merely a potential person to being an actual person. This was the point extensively developed by Mary Anne Warren, Michael Tooley, David Boonin, and others in chapter 4.

Degree of dependency is also morally significant. Pro-choice claims that there is no legitimate comparison between the fetus, inside the woman's body and utterly dependent on her for its very existence and survival—and a person in the world, the woman, or a born baby. It is only when the child emerges at birth, as its own being, independent of the woman; and welcomed into the world as a member of the human community, that it can be said to acquire the status of a person, worthy of moral respect. This was the point, also made in chapter 4, by Mary Anne Warren and Marjorie Reiley Maguire: "Birth marks the beginning of membership in the human community."

PRO-CHOICE REPLIES TO PRO-LIFE CLAIMS
REGARDING THE BEING-FUNCTIONING DISTINCTION

Pro-life claims that there is a morally significant distinction between *being* a person and *functioning* as a person. Functioning refers to what one can *do* as a person, especially rational thinking, intentional communication, and having a sense of self, while being a person refers to what one essentially *is* as a person. Being a person distinguishes us from other living organisms such as dogs and trees. The key pro-life claim is that *functioning as a person is not necessary for being a person,* for it is possible to *be* a person without having the ability to *function* as a person. A person in a coma or a newborn baby has the *being* of a person even though he cannot *function* as a person. And the same thing applies to the BIW: it has the *being* of a person even though it does not yet have the capacity to *function* as a person. But if it has the being of a person, it should be afforded the same moral and legal rights as all persons.

Pro-choice can agree that being a person is what matters, but it then goes on to ask what this means. And the answer can only be in terms of functioning. A person is a being who either now functions as a person or now has the present and immediate capacity to do so, as we see in the case of a person in deep sleep or under total anesthesia. It does not include a being which merely has the potential to develop this capacity. As Tooley puts it in an earlier quote, "a person is not merely a potential subject of experiences: a person is an entity that has had, or that is now having, actual experiences." Having actual experiences is of course functioning as a person. Thus pro-choice holds that, while this distinction is basically valid, it will not serve pro-life in establishing the real personhood of the BIW. Only those who now *function* as persons or have done so in the past have the *being* of a person, and with this are due the respect owed to persons.

PRO-CHOICE REPLIES TO PRO-LIFE CLAIMS REGARDING THE VIOLINIST ARGUMENT: ACTIVE KILLING

This was the claim that abortion is not a mere withholding of support, not a mere "unplugging," not a mere "letting die"; but a deliberate active killing. We can see this if we recall the methods of abortion and the comparison of these methods to the Kamchadal practice of killing the BIW by a sword through the woman's abdomen. Abortion, pro-life claims, is deliberate active killing.

The focus here is on the contrast between *killing* and *letting die*; on the difference between doing something and merely allowing something to happen. The next pro-life claim and pro-choice reply will focus on the contrast between intending something to happen and merely foreseeing that it will happen.

Turning to the contrast between *killing* and *letting die*, David Boonin offers a defense of the Violinist Argument on this score. Let us examine its essential features; the argument in its entirety is too long and complex to be included here. To begin with Boonin claims:

> that even if one accepts the moral relevance of the distinction between killing and letting die, there is at least one method of abortion, hysterotomy, that is more plausibly described as a case of letting die rather than a case of killing. Hysterotomy involves removing the living fetus through an abdominal incision of the uterus and then allowing it to die. This procedure is more invasive and more dangerous to the woman than are the other procedures, and for this reason is typically reserved for later stages of pregnancy when other techniques are no longer feasible. But there is no reason in principle why it could not be

performed much earlier, if other methods were thought for some reason to be morally impermissible.[12]

To defend the Violinist Argument against the pro-life claim that it would justify at most only "letting die" and not the "active killing" of the standard methods of abortion, Boonin asks us to imagine the following case. You are driving a trolley with a steering wheel heading for a hospital. There is a fork, where you can go either left or right; the two branches of the fork reunite later. On the left branch, which is considerably longer and thus takes much more time, there are five dying people you can save by bringing them to the hospital. But before you get to the fork there is a section of track with one dying person, trapped by being stuck to the track. There are also noxious fumes in that area. If you stop to rescue the dying trapped person and then go left to save the five, he will die since he must be taken to the hospital immediately (by going right) in order to be saved. Boonin holds that "there are three salient options":

1. stop and free the trapped person, exposing yourself to the noxious fumes, then turn left at the fork, thus saving the five and allowing the (formerly) trapped person to die;
2. run over the trapped person, avoiding exposure to the noxious fumes, then turn left at the fork, thus saving the five and killing the trapped person;
3. stop and free the trapped person, exposing yourself to the noxious fumes, then turn right at the fork, thus saving the (formerly) trapped person and allowing the five to die.[13]

Boonin's claim is that this case "parallels the structure of the choice a woman faces when she considers ending an unwanted pregnancy." Such a woman can:

- have the fetus removed by hysterotomy while exposing herself to higher costs and risks than if she had an abortion by some other method, thus avoiding the burdens of an unwanted pregnancy and allowing the fetus to die;
- have an abortion by some other method, thus sparing herself the higher costs and risks of hysterotomy, killing the fetus and avoiding the burdens of an unwanted pregnancy;
- carry the pregnancy to term, thus sparing the fetus and incurring the burdens of an unwanted pregnancy.[14]

Boonin defends "the claim that it would be morally permissible for you to run over the dying person." He concludes from this that the Violinist

Argument "justifies all methods of abortion even if killing is substantially worse than letting die." To substantiate this claim he asks us to consider the following:

> But given that it would be permissible for you to let the currently trapped person die if you were to free him first [since he will die while you take the longer branch to save the five people], it is difficult to believe that it would be morally *required* for you to first expose yourself to the fumes in order to free him, given that in doing so you would then turn left and allow him to die anyway. And if you are not morally required to free him, then you are morally permitted to run over him, since stopping to free him and running over him are your only two options.[15]

Running over the dying person lying on the tracks is actively and directly killing him. Abortion by the standard methods is actively and directly killing the BIW. If the active killing of running over can be morally justified by the circumstances of the situation in the trolley case, then, Boonin argues, so can the active killing of the BIW by the standard methods of abortion.

This counters the pro-life claim that the Violinist Argument can justify at most only letting die and is therefore not parallel to abortion, which is not a mere letting die of the BIW but an active and direct killing. It shows that the Violinist Argument, when suitably expanded by the use of the trolley case that allows you to choose to run over the man on the track, justifies not only hysterotomy (letting die) but the standard methods of abortion (active and direct killing).

This case leaves you the reader first to decide whether or not Boonin is correct in his assessment that it is in fact justified to run over the man tied to the tracks. If he is not, this defense of the Violinist Argument fails. If he is morally justified in running the man over, there is the further question whether or not the trolley driver analogy fits the case of pregnancy.

PRO-CHOICE REPLIES TO PRO-LIFE CLAIMS REGARDING THE VIOLINIST ARGUMENT: INTENTIONAL KILLING

We turn now to the pro-life claim and pro-choice reply where the focus is on the contrast between *intending* something to happen and *merely foreseeing* that it will happen. The pro-life claim is that there is a significant moral difference between:

- *Merely foreseeing death.* Someone withholds support for a person who would need it in order to stay alive because he does not have the duty to provide it, since this would amount to taking extraordinary means to keep the person alive. The person's death is not intended but merely

foreseen, as a side-effect. This is not a form of killing. An example of this is not sustaining the violinist by unplugging yourself from him.
- *Intentionally killing a person.* The death of the person is intended, either as a means or as an end. An example of this is killing the child by one of the methods of abortion.

Boonin's reply to this pro-life claim is that one can grant that this difference is morally significant and that it is often crucial; but that the pro-choice violinist argument can still be defended. He considers two hypothetical cases which he calls Bomber I and Bomber II:

- *Bomber I* drops a single bomb on the enemy's munitions plant, foreseeing but not intending that nearby innocent civilians will be killed.
- *Bomber II* drops a single bomb to destroy the munitions plant and deliberately kill innocent civilians in order to destroy enemy morale as well as weapons. "The good ending of the war suffices to outweigh the evil of killing them."[16]

Boonin's assessment of these two cases is "that what Bomber I and Bomber II *do* are different and, in particular, that what Bomber I does is permissible, whereas what Bomber II does is impermissible."[17]

We saw in the Bomber I case that it is permissible in a just war to bomb the enemy's ammunitions plant if what one intends is its destruction, even though one also foresees that innocent civilians will be killed as a side-effect. But Boonin, recognizing this distinction, goes on to claim that there are cases where, if death as merely foreseen is morally permissible, then intentionally killing is also morally permissible. He asks us to suppose the following, which he calls Bomber V. In order to destroy the plant I can use either one of two types of bombs:

For reasons peculiar to its design . . . Bomb A cannot be successfully detonated if there are living human beings on the roof of the building. So in order to use Bomb A, I will first have to fly over the plant and kill all the sleeping civilians with a lethal gas. Then, after they are dead, I can return and drop Bomb A. The alternative is to drop Bomb B. It has a special guidance system that will allow it to enter from the side of the plant, allowing the civilians to continue their sleep without disturbance until the bomb detonates. They will then die as a result of the plant being blown up. But Bomb B also releases a dangerous form of radiation that will reach as far as my cockpit, making this method more dangerous and potentially fatal to me.[18]

Boonin now claims that if Bomb B is morally permissible, then so too is Bomb A. In using Bomb A he intentionally kills the innocent civilians. Boonin justifies this by saying, "The civilians will be killed by his actions in either case, and so it is not their dying rather than not dying."[19] that is crucial. And of course the advantage of using Bomb A is that it avoids the release of the lethal gas.

With this Boonin provides a defense of the Violinist Argument against the pro-life charge that it is invalid, based on the distinction between intending death (not permissible) and merely foreseeing it (permissible in some cases). Boonin's claim is that even if there is a morally significant difference between bombing where one *merely foresees* that innocent civilians will be killed but does not intend their death and bombing where one *intends* their death, there are still cases where the latter is permissible, as shown by the example of Bomber V. He argues:

> And so one can agree that there is morally important difference between Bomber I and Bomber II and still maintain that if it is permissible for a woman to have an abortion by hysterotomy, then it is also permissible for her to instead have an abortion by a less risky and invasive method that involves killing the fetus before or in the process of removing it.[20]

This case leaves you the reader to decide whether or not Bomber V is in fact morally justified in his intentionally killing the innocent civilians on the roof by gassing them. If he is not, this defense of the Violinist Argument fails. If he is morally justified, there is the further question whether or not the bomber analogy fits the case of pregnancy.

PRO-CHOICE REPLIES TO PRO-LIFE CLAIMS REGARDING THE VIOLINIST ARGUMENT: A DUTY TO THE CHILD

The pro-life argument is that a pregnant woman is carrying a child who is her own child, entrusted to her. She has a special relation to this child, which implies an obligation to take care of him or her; failure to do so is child neglect. Hence unplugging is wrong already on the level of withholding support. She has this obligation to her child because she is his biological mother; because she, and not someone else, begot and conceived the child. It is the biological bond that creates the obligation of a mother to take care of her children. Thus the violinist argument fails because the two cases are not parallel. The person hooked up to the violinist (we are assuming) has no duty to sustain him, for he is a total stranger, standing in a relation to the person that is most unnatural. This is exactly the opposite of the mother-child relation, which is most natural and proper. We may not have the obligation to sustain strangers artificially hooked up to us, but we most certainly have the obligation to sustain our own children. So the very thing that makes it plausible to say that the person in bed with the violinist has no duty to sustain him; namely, that he is a stranger unnaturally hooked up to her, is precisely what is absent in the case of the mother and her child.

Boonin challenges this argument by asking why it should be thought that the woman carrying the child "has a special relation to this child," one "which implies an obligation to take care of him." It is presumably the biological relation. To this he says

> that it seems to be utterly mysterious how the mere fact of biological related-ness could, in and of itself, generate such a difference in moral obligations. It would not be mysterious if the claim turned on the fact that the woman did some voluntary action that led to the conception of the child, since the moral salience of the distinction between voluntary and involuntary actions is rela-tively straightforward.[21]

But perhaps the special relation of the woman to this child is based on the fact that the child is entrusted to her. Boonin considers this under the heading of being a guardian. It is the idea that a "woman has a stronger duty to assist her son or daughter than to assist a stranger not because she is the child's biological parent, but because she is the child's *guardian*."[22]

But why is she his guardian? Boonin argues that the only rational answer to this is that she has voluntarily accepted the role of guardian. He says that "it seems plausible to suppose that when a woman (or man) takes a newborn child home with her from the hospital, she tacitly accepts the role of guardian for the child."[23] Clearly this does not apply to the pregnant woman involuntarily hooked up to the BIW.

The reader must ask: what is indeed the relationship between the woman and the BIW? There is also the question of the nature of guardianship. Is it always voluntary? Or could one be forced into a position of guardianship and still have a moral obligation?

PRO-CHOICE REPLIES TO PRO-LIFE CLAIMS REGARDING THE VIOLINIST ARGUMENT: A GENERAL DUTY

Pro-life asks: is it really so clear that I have no duty to sustain the violinist? Perhaps I do sometimes have such a duty. If I hear a person screaming for help, do I not have a duty to save her life, to prevent her from being killed? Do I not have this duty even at a great sacrifice for myself? If I find you in the wilderness, should I not rescue you? In evaluating the duty to save the life of another person even at great cost to myself, I can apply the Golden Rule: if I were in need of being saved lest I die, would I not reasonably expect you to save me, even at considerable cost to yourself? If so, should I not save you, even at considerable cost to myself? Doesn't the same apply to the woman and her pre-born child for the relatively short duration of nine months when compared to a lifetime and a life?

Pro-choice replies that it is very difficult to assess how far this general duty to help one another applies. And so it is at least very debatable whether or not it does in fact apply to you and the violinist. The greater the burden and pain and hardship involved in coming to the help of another, the less clear it is that there is a real duty to do so. In the case of the extreme burden of the violinist case it is certainly very debatable. And so if the two cases (violinist and pregnant woman) are parallel and if you have no duty to sustain the violinist, then neither does the woman have a duty to sustain the BIW.

There is an important further point. Even if it is admitted that you have a duty to sustain the violinist, it does not follow from this that he has a *right* to your providing this sustenance. This would mean that if we accept the parallel between the two cases, the BIW would not have a right to be sustained by the woman. But this is of course precisely the pro-life claim, that the BIW has the right to life, hence the right to remain in the woman's body and to be sustained by her.

In general, duties do not always imply rights. I may have a *duty* to repay you for a big favor that you provided for me; it hardly follows that you have a *right* against me that I repay you for this big favor.[24]

PRO-CHOICE REPLIES TO PRO-LIFE CLAIMS REGARDING THE CHILD'S RIGHT OVER HIS BODY

Another pro-life argument related to all these points is this. If there is a right over one's body, two very significant features pertain to it. One, it is a right *everyone* has. Two, it includes the right to *not have one's body destroyed* (for example by dismemberment), the right not to be killed. On both these counts pro-life claims that the appeal to a woman's right over her body as a justification for abortion backfires, and provides an argument against abortion. Thus if a woman has a right over her body then the child has that right too. Moreover, when did the woman's right to her own body begin? It began at conception when her body began; she was not just given her body at birth. A woman therefore has a right to her body from the moment that she has a body; this right is not contingent on where her body is.

Pro-choice replies with the claim that this is an inappropriate application of the important principle that a woman has a right over her body. The principle is meant to apply to independent, mature women making their own reasoned and informed decisions about how to lead their lives. But pro-life attempts to apply it to a totally different type of case: a small, completely dependent being, absolutely incapable of making any kind of decisions, let alone her own reasoned and informed decisions about how to lead her life.

PRO-CHOICE REPLIES TO PRO-LIFE CLAIMS REGARDING PAIN TO THE CHILD

An important pro-life argument against abortion is the claim that it is an inhumane, barbaric procedure, as when a sharp, knife-like instrument is inserted and the child is cut to pieces. Pain is certainly true for late abortions when the child is highly developed and hardly distinguishable from a born baby. If the child can feel intense pain at this later time, it can certainly feel some pain earlier, perhaps much earlier. In addition, pro-life claims that our duty to not cause terrible pain to the child is more urgent than our duty to grant a woman the right over her body.

Pro-choice replies with the claim that the whole matter of fetal pain is still highly controversial and very speculative. We really don't know exactly what happens. If we place the two claims side by side—possible pain for a biological organism versus the real needs and the actual rights of the woman—it is clear that we must give the preference to the latter. Besides, even if there is some pain for the fetus in a procedure necessary to ensure basic personal rights for the woman, then that is the price we must pay. War is surely painful; yet it is sometimes necessary to protect ourselves from unjust attacks.

PRO-CHOICE REPLIES TO PRO-LIFE CLAIMS REGARDING THE DIGNITY OF THE HUMAN PERSON

Pro-life claims that the pro-choice arguments to allow abortion for the sake of the general quality of human life, the quality of life for women and to ensure genuine equality between men and women imply an affront to the dignity of the human person.

Pro-choice replies with the claim that human dignity is not the only thing that is important. Above all we must be concerned with the quality of human life. What good is dignity if life is miserable, and lacking in those qualities that make it worthwhile? The idea of respect for human dignity may actually be merely a code for the traditional "sanctity of human life" ethic. For this ethic is what really underlies the pro-life objections to allowing abortion in those cases where it furthers the quality of human life. We now need a more enlightened ethic to replace the old, traditional sanctity of human life ethic. Such an ethic is proposed by Peter Singer in his book, *Rethinking Life and Death: The Collapse of Our Traditional Ethics*. He compares the transition from the old ethic to the new ethic to the Copernican revolution in astronomy, where the earth was no longer seen as the center of the universe.

It is time for another Copernican revolution. It will be, once again, a revolution against a set of ideas we have inherited from the period in which the intellectual world was dominated by a religious outlook. Because it will change our tendency to see human beings as the center of the *ethical* universe, it will meet with fierce resistance from those who do not want to accept such a blow to human pride. At first, it will have its own problems, and we need to tread carefully over the new ground. For many of the ideas will be too shocking to take seriously. Yet eventually the change will come. The traditional view that all human life is sacrosanct is simply not able to cope with the array of issues that we face. The new view will offer a fresh and more promising approach.[25]

To give some indication of what this new, more enlightened ethic might look like, Singer suggests a "rewriting the commandments." Here are some of his proposed changes:

From *"Treat all human life as of equal worth"* to *"Recognize that the worth of human life varies."* From *"Never intentionally take innocent human life"* to *"Take responsibility for the consequences of your decisions."* From *"Be fruitful and multiply"* to *"Bring children into the world only if they are wanted."*[26]

11

When Does a Person Begin to Exist?

FORMULATING THE QUESTION

What, exactly, is the question? If we simply ask "when does human life begin?" we may be distracted from the real question. For *human life* is, in a sense, a continuum, passed on from one generation to the next. Sperm and ovum are, in this sense, "human life." That is not the crucial matter. Nor do we mean by *human life* merely a biological organism. Virtually everyone holds that human life in that sense begins at conception-fertilization. That is not where the issue lies. Rather, the crucial question is this: when did *I* begin to exist? When did the "I" that I am now, the human person that is me begin to exist? As I go back in my history as a person, to last year, to when I was a child, to when I was small newborn baby, to when I was a tiny being in my mother's womb, I can ask: when did this "I" begin to exist? When does a human person begin to exist?

SOME MAIN LINES PROPOSED AS MARKING THE BEGINNING OF A PERSON

When does a human person begin to exist? When did *I* begin to exist? Let us consider ten positions that have been suggested as an answer to this question:

1. *Conception-fertilization.*
2. *Segmentation:* After this, twinning is no longer possible; at one week.

3. *Basic organs in place,* including cerebral cortex, heart and eyes; at five weeks.
4. *A well-proportioned small-scale being that looks like a baby.* At seven weeks.
5. *Sentience:* Rudimentary consciousness, sensitivity to pain; from eight to thirteen weeks.
6. *Viability:* The ability to exist outside the womb. It is now at about twenty to twenty-three weeks. Premature babies born and survive after twenty weeks as of 2009.
7. *Organized cortical brain activity.* For functioning as a person; from twenty-five to thirty-two weeks.
8. *Birth.* Entrance into the human community. Mary Anne Warren.
9. *One week after birth.* This is the early position of Michael Tooley.
10. *Three months after birth.* This is the later position of Michael Tooley.

Table 11.1. Overview for Drawing Lines

WEEKS ...1......5...7.........13............20..........26.......32.........39			..1
MONTHS ....3.............................6...........................9			MONTHS 3
FIRST TRIMESTER	*SECOND TRIMESTER*	*THIRD TRIMESTER*	*AFTER BIRTH*

Let us now examine some arguments pro and con for some of these positions.

Conception-Fertilization

In Defense of Conception-Fertilization

There is a two-step argument to show that conception-fertilization marks the beginning of a person's existence. The first step is to point out that the coming together of sperm and egg represents *a radical break.* There are three reasons for this:

1. Sperm and egg are *two* distinct entities—the new human being is *one* entity.
2. Sperm and egg are each at the *end* of their existence—the new human being is at the *beginning* of his existence. A mature egg lives twenty-four hours; a sperm lives three to five days; a new human being can live one hundred years or more.
3. Sperm and egg have the genetic code, respectively, of the man and the woman—the new human being has *its own unique genetic code,* one

that is different from the parents; the new human being is a distinct entity with its own unique identity.

Second, because it is a radical break, conception-fertilization is the logical place where a real "line" can be drawn; a line that can be rationally defended as marking a real moral difference between what is not, and what is, an individual human person. All the other suggested "lines" do not mark a real difference. It is the same being before and after each one. The changes that characterize each of these other lines do not change a nonperson into a person. It is the same being before and after. The changes that occur are changes that happen to it, the same being. In each case, that being is only a little more developed after in comparison with before. Or, in the case of birth, it is the same being before and after, only in a new location. Each of these "lines" falls victim to the SLED argument (see chapter 6): the differences between before and after are only differences in size, level of development, (sometimes) environment, and degree of dependency; and these are all morally irrelevant. It is the same being all the way through, with no "lines" marking any morally relevant differences, which is the point of the continuum argument.

The standard, traditional, full pro-life position is that an individual human person begins his existence at conception-fertilization.

The Case against Conception-Fertilization

Several arguments have been advanced in opposition to this position. First, the result of conception-fertilization is a tiny being, called a zygote that is smaller than a period at the end of a sentence. In comparison with "real persons" as we know them from experience, including little babies, these tiny beings are simply too small to be taken seriously as persons equal in dignity to the rest of us.

Second, this tiny being is also too undeveloped to count as a real human person. None of the physical structures that underlie being a person are present. It is all a matter of potential, the potential for becoming a human person, not the actuality of an existing person. What we have is like a blueprint for a person, not the "finished product" of an actual person. Or we can see it on the analogy of an acorn: the acorn is to the oak tree as the zygote is to the actual human person.

Third, there is the possibility of twinning. Suppose a given zygote "splits" into two beings, resulting in twins. A person cannot be split in two; therefore what split into two beings cannot have been a person already.

Fourth, David Boonin argues that "the fact, if it is a fact, that conception is a radical discontinuity in one's developmental history means that this is where the line between having a right to life and not having a right to life can be drawn most clearly, but it does not mean that this is where it can be drawn most reasonably."[1] What matters is that this line "must be drawn in a manner that is relevant to such rights attributions."[2] That is, merely being a radical break does not yet establish that the result of this break is a person with the same right to life that you and I have.

Those who reject conception-fertilization include all those who are pro-choice, as well as some who consider themselves pro-life and draw the line very soon thereafter.

The "Conceived" Question

There is a striking way of "conceiving" the difference between the traditional, full pro-life position that an individual human person begins his existence at conception-fertilization, on the one hand—and, on the other hand, the various alternative positions that the beginning comes some time later, either at some line or gradually. And that is by asking which of these two statements is true:

- My parents conceived *me*.
- My parents conceived *an organism* that was not me; that only became me later on, after sufficient development had occurred.

Table 11.2.   The "Conceived Question"

Both Positions	A single biological reality in continuous development. The same being on the biological level all the way through.
Pro-Choice Some others.	My parents conceived a *biological organism*. Biological organism * * * * * * * * * Person. It changes from one to the other, from non-person-organism to a person.
Full Pro-Life	My parents conceived *me*. It's *me* all the way through. I was once a zygote, a tiny baby.

Segmentation

In Defense of Segmentation

Why might segmentation be selected as marking the beginning of a human person's existence? The answer has to do with the possibility of twinning. Identical twins develop from a single conceptus, formed at conception-fertilization by the union of sperm and ovum. If the conceptus divides twins result. This can occur up until the time of segmentation, about seven to eight days after conception. Hence segmentation marks a real line in human development.

The reasoning here is clear. A human person is essentially one, an absolute individual. A person cannot be split in two. Since the conceptus that divides to form two identical twins obviously does split, it cannot be an individual. Hence it cannot be a person, and a person cannot be said to exist prior to segmentation. Hence segmentation marks the beginning of a human person's existence.

The Case against Segmentation

It is certainly true that a person is an individual who cannot be split in any way. But does it follow from this that segmentation is the place to draw the line, that the individual human person does not exist prior to segmentation? There are clear and compelling reasons to answer this question in the negative.

First, consider the case where twinning does not and cannot occur. This is where the conceptus is and always will be an individual. Here the problem does not arise. For there is simply one conceptus who is one individual person. That another conceptus is different since it has the potential to split says nothing about the first single conceptus.

Second, consider the case where twinning does occur. There is no reason for saying that the individuals who result from the twinning process came into existence at that time and did not exist prior to it from the moment of conception-fertilization. Rather, they existed together in one conceptus, and at segmentation (or prior to it) they separated. It is possible for two individual persons to exist bodily joined together, especially at the very beginning of their physical development. To see this, consider Siamese twins, joined together at the head, or perhaps side to side. Just as each of the Siamese twins is an individual person, though joined to another person, so each of the two newly-conceived persons is an individual person, though joined—in this case much more closely—to another individual person. The two individuals joined together in one conceptus are an extreme case of what we see in a less extreme and very tragic form in Siamese twins: two individual persons joined together.

We may see human development as a matter of unfolding. The development of the child especially at the early stages up to eight weeks—after which "no further primordial will form; everything is already present that will be found at full term"—is a series of unfoldings. It is a moving from the potential to the actual, on the part of the being who is already an actual reality, whose actual reality underlies these unfoldings, in whom they occur, and of whom they are developments. The potential for the brain is already there at conception-fertilization; it only needs to unfold. Now this unfolding sometimes includes the unfolding of two separate bodies, in the case of identical twins. Potentially the two bodies are there all along; the actual separation takes some time. Segmentation represents, not the beginning of human existence, but a certain stage of development; when, in the case of identical twins, their bodies actually separate.

Viability

In Defense of Viability

Viability refers to the fetus's ability to live outside the womb. Three reasons may be given for selecting viability as the beginning of a person's existence. First the fetus in the early stages prior to viability is seen as part of his mother's body. In being viable it shows its independence, that it is a distinct being. Second, the pre-viability fetus is too intimately involved in the body of his mother to be a real person on his own. Third, the fetus after viability is very much like a born child and so it can be treated as a person, but this is not true of the fetus in the earlier stages.

As we will see immediately below, there is a strong case to be made against viability as marking the point at which a person's existence begins. But there is another way in which it can enter the picture. If one adopts the no-duty-to-sustain argument, one is saying that a woman has a right to unburden herself of the presence of the fetus in her body. If she does this prior to viability, she can do so only in ways that mean killing the fetus; removal is accomplished by methods of abortion that in fact kill the fetus. But after viability the picture changes. Boonin argues: "If the fetus is viable, and thus can be safely removed, then the woman has the right only to have it removed, not to have it killed."[3] On this approach viability marks the beginning of the BIW's right to life, not because it is a person after viability, and because of viability, while it is a non-person before—but rather, because only after viability can it be kept alive and thus respected as a person. Viability on this view represents a significant moment in the no-duty-to-sustain approach, which often admits the personhood of the fetus (as we saw in the case of Thomson, its most famous proponent). It does not represent anything significant in the debate between the not-a-person approach and those who maintain the personhood of the fetus.

The Case against Viability

In reply to these points: First, the child is not a part of his mother's body as was already noted in chapter 1. Second, the intimate involvement of the child in his mother's body reflects his dependency on her. Dependency does not affect personhood. He is dependent because he is small and fragile; he needs the protective nest of his mother's womb. This says something about his body, its state of development; it says nothing about his status as a person. Dependence on and involvement in his mother's body simply reflects the state of his development along the continuum of human life.

Third, long before viability the child already looks like a familiar baby. As was noted in chapter 6: *By the end of the seventh week [long before viability at present] we see a well-proportioned small-scale baby.* So this point does not establish viability as the place to draw the line. Much more important: it is irrelevant. The fact that the baby in his very early stages doesn't look familiar to us, that he doesn't resemble what we are used to seeing as a baby, says very little about him. He is what he is, regardless of resemblances. That he is noticeably different from the highly developed baby in middle and late pregnancy and at birth is hardly surprising: he is near the beginning of his development. Looking like a familiar baby means having the physical features of a familiar baby, and these take time to develop. Before this time elapses a less developed and therefore a less familiar-looking baby is just what we should expect.

The irrelevance of viability marking the beginning of a person's existence comes out even more clearly when we consider the following points.

1. Viability has nothing to do with whether a being is a person or not. Cats and dogs are "viable"; this does not make them persons. Viability has to do with the body and its environment. That is, a pre-viability child can live only in a certain environment, his mother's womb, while a post-viability child can live either in his mother's womb or outside it. For the pre-viability child this is simply an instance of a general truth: every organism needs its proper environment. A fish can live only in water, not in dry air. A cat can live only in dry air, not in the water. Each is nonviable in the other's proper environment. So too an adult human being would be nonviable inside a uterus, if we imagine one large enough to hold him. Human beings are not viable in most parts of the universe, because they are too hot, or too cold, or lack oxygen, etc. One class of human beings, those in the early stages of their development, are further restricted in regard to their viability. But this concerns the relation of their bodies to an environment, not the reality of their being as persons.

2. Viability is not a definite line. It can properly refer only to an extended period of time during which the probability of surviving outside the womb increases. Near the beginning of this time the child might have only a 25 percent chance of surviving, later 50 percent, then 75 percent, still later 90 percent. None of these is able to mark the point of viability and with it the alleged beginning of a person's existence.

3. Viability is not a real line because it is constantly changing. It is now about twenty to twenty-three weeks. As technology advances it will

be pushed further and further back; perhaps even to point zero with the creation of an artificial womb. That is, viability is a function of medical technology; it has nothing to do with the BIW as a person. It measures our ability to sustain human life, not the status of that life. The same BIW will be viable given one degree of medical technology, not viable given another. Viability, then, cannot be the determining factor for whether the BIW is a real person or not.

4. The arbitrariness, indeed the unfairness of making viability the line at which a person begins to exist is expressed by Blumenfeld. Referring to a certain determination of viability he asks:

> Why choose viability as the cut-off point? The human fetus is not viable before the twenty-fourth week merely because its lungs are not sufficiently developed for outside respiration. Nature decided that lung development could wait because it had nine full months in which to do its work. It gave priority to brain, neural, sensory, skeletal, digestive, and circulatory development before it completed its work on the lungs. So why penalize an unborn infant because nature decided to complete its kidneys before its lungs?[4]

Birth

In Defense of Birth

Four main reasons have been proposed to defend the view that birth marks the beginning of a human person's existence.

1. At birth the child becomes fully independent of his mother.
2. He can be seen and touched.
3. He becomes a member of society.
4. Age is marked from one's day of birth.

A somewhat qualified defense of birth as the place to draw the line is offered by Mary Anne Warren. In connection with point (1) above, she argues that:

> Birth is morally significant because it marks the end of one relationship and the beginning of others. It marks the end of pregnancy, a relationship so intimate that it is impossible to extend the equal protection of the law to fetuses without severely infringing woman's most basic rights. . . . We should not . . . seek to extend the same degree of protection to fetuses [as to newborn infants]. Both late-term fetuses and newborn infants are probably capable of sentience. . . . However, to extend equal legal rights to fetuses is necessarily to deprive pregnant women of the rights to personal autonomy, physical integrity, and sometimes life itself. *There is room for only one person with full and equal rights in-*

side a human skin. That is why it is birth, rather than sentience, viability, or some other prenatal milestone that must mark the beginning of legal personhood.[5]

In connection with point (3) she remarks that:

Birth also marks the beginning of the infant's existence as a socially responsive member of the human community. Although the infant is not instantly transformed into a person at the moment of birth, it does become a biologically separate human being. As such it can be known and cared for as a particular individual. It can also be vigorously protected without negating the basic rights of women.[6]

The infant at birth enters the human social world, where, if it lives, it becomes involved in social relationships with others, of kinds that can only be dimly foreshadowed before birth....The newborn is not yet self-aware, but it is already (rapidly becoming) a social being.

Thus, although the human newborn may have no intrinsic properties that can ground a moral right to life stronger than a fetus just before birth, its emergence into the social world makes it appropriate to treat it as if it had such a right. This, in effect, is what the law has done, through the doctrine that a person begins to exist at birth.[7]

The Case against Birth

Regarding point (1), the dependency of a child on his mother does not make him a nonperson. The dependency of the child on his mother before birth says something about the state of his body and his bodily needs. It says nothing about him as a person. Dependent persons are persons.

Regarding (2), a child inside an opaque protective shell cannot be seen, nor can any person for that matter. This indicates nothing about the status of his being.

Regarding (3), it is not true that a child in his mother's womb is not a member of society. For a long time preceding birth the mother knows the child is there; that the child is known to be there and is expected makes him, in a very real sense, a member of human society.

Further, through the instruments of modern technology, especially fetoscopy and hysteroscopy, we can literally see the child and perform diagnoses and surgery on him. Dr. Bernard Nathanson tells us, "With fetoscopy we are looking at the child eyeball to eyeball, seeing it in living color."[8] Surely anyone whom we can see, and perform surgery on, is a member of our society.

It is true of course that the child in the womb is not a direct participant in human society. He cannot be! Part of the evil of abortion is that it takes unfair advantage of this. He has no voice to defend himself. And so nonparticipation in society, far from being an argument for abortion, throws further light on its evil. Abortion is the killing of a small person that takes unfair advantage of his not being among us as a direct member, like a shut-in, ignored, out of sight and out of mind.

Regarding (4), no one would have a birthday unless he was already there to be born. A birthday is a day of entry. But a person must already be in order to enter into something. That we mark our age from our birthday is simply a social custom we have. The Chinese mark a person's age from conception. Ours is more convenient because one's birth date is easily known; one's conception date is not.

That birth should even be suggested as a line is incredible. For the baby just before birth and just after birth is obviously the same child, and hardly different in appearance. The baby just before birth is fully there, waiting to be born. The doctor monitors his heartbeat and determines his position. How could a change of location from inside the mother to outside change a nonperson into a person? There is also a change in how nourishment (oxygen, food, water) is taken, from direct input to the stomach via the umbilical cord to breathing, eating, and drinking through the mouth. Such a change can hardly transform a nonperson into a person.

If birth is so irrelevant as a line, why is it nevertheless so widely accepted? Clearly the reason is not the status of the child, which is the same before and after. Nor is it that the pre-born child is more dependent than the born child. These are often the reason given for selecting birth as the line. In reality there is a deeper reason; namely, the claim that a woman has "a right over her body" in the sense of "a right to an abortion." If one assumes this right, it becomes plausible to say that a woman may remove a being that is inside her and burdensome to her. But if such a removal is killing, and killing persons is wrong, it must be held that this being is not a person. Thus the impetus to make birth the line stems not from anything to do with the child, but from the desire to get rid of him. And so he must be labeled the sort of being who may justifiably be terminated. That is why birth is selected as the place to draw the line.

Some Reflections on Drawing the Line after Birth

Many people are shocked when they hear about Michael Tooley's thesis that a human person's existence begins only some time after birth; that a newborn baby, even a two-month old baby is not a person but merely a biological organism; and consequently that infanticide is morally permissible. He will reply that he is only being consistent, that he is merely following the argument to its logical conclusion. If a late-term BIW is not a person because it cannot think rationally, has no self-consciousness and no desire for its continued existence, then a newborn baby is not a person either, since it too lacks these features. Tooley and pro-life may be at opposite ends of a spectrum in their position on the morality of abortion; but they have one very significant thing in common: they both reject birth as being morally irrelevant. They agree that whatever the being is shortly before birth it is that same being in the time shortly after birth as well.

THE QUESTION OF INFANTICIDE

Those who defend infanticide do so for two essentially distinct reasons. The first was just noted, the claim that a newborn baby is not a person and may therefore be killed. The second appeals to quality of life. We saw this in chapter 3, in the words of Peter Singer: "When the life of an infant will be so miserable as not to be worth living, from the internal perspective of the being who will lead that life . . . it is better that the child should be helped to die without further suffering." Imagine a child suffering from constant, horrible pain, who will perhaps be bedridden for the rest of his life, unable to learn to talk and read, condemned to a life of utter misery. What should one do?

Some people recommend infanticide in such cases; not as a good option, but as the least objectionable. They reject trying to keep such a child alive as long as possible, because of the immense suffering this entails. They also reject doing nothing and simply letting the child die. A slow death by starvation and dehydration is horrible. And if the intention is to bring about the death of the child, why not do this quickly and painlessly? But this is of course infanticide, the course of action recommended by Singer.

Our hearts are deeply moved by such cases, our moral sentiments probably torn in different directions. We cannot and need not offer a solution to this vexing problem here. What we can do is examine how it relates to the pro-choice/pro-life abortion issue. The crucial point is that these are two separate matters; specifically that any arguments that support infanticide in extreme cases do not support the pro-choice position on abortion:

1. These are extreme cases. The abortion issue ranges over a wide variety of cases. Pro-choice means the right to terminate pregnancy for any reason that the woman deems appropriate, not just in extreme cases.
2. The vexing problem is part of the general issue of euthanasia, or mercy killing. It is not specific to infants (infanticide) or the BIW (abortion) but applies to all ages.
3. Supporting infanticide for such cases is not a type of "pro-choice" position. It means saying that such a child *should* be killed; not that the matter be left up to the judgment of a specific person, such as the woman considering abortion.

AN OBJECTION TO ALMOST ALL OF THESE LINES

Conception-fertilization is a radical break; we do not have the same being before and after. Rather, two beings, sperm and ovum, are transformed by their union into one being, a zygote. The zygote represents the first stage of a long continuous development, the development of the same being through all of pregnancy, and continuing after birth. The other lines seem to be nothing but milestones in this continuous development. That is, at each of the places suggested for drawing the line the BIW is essentially the same on either side of that line. It may be a little larger and a little more developed, but it is the same being before and after. It acquires nothing at any of these suggested places that would transform it from a nonperson into something else, a human person; as the fairy-tale frog is transformed into something else, a charming prince. This would be a radical break, a real place to draw a line. Nothing of this sort occurs at any of these places. Rather, what we have is like the tadpole developing into a mature frog, a development in the life of one and the same being.

THE ACHIEVEMENT VIEW,
BEING-FUNCTIONING, AND THE LINES

Let me suggest that the impetus for trying to find a line (other than #1) that marks the beginning of a person's existence stems from the achievement view, discussed in chapter 6. If the BIW is not a person from its very beginning at conception-fertilization but only achieves this at some later time, then it is natural to ask when that time is. The various places to draw a line after conception-fertilization are then offered as answers. On the other hand, if the achievement view is rejected, the various lines will be seen as irrelevant, because they are nothing but points in the continuous development of the same being, as was just noted.

In a similar way the lines (other than #1) are irrelevant because they apply only to *functioning* as a person and not to *being* a person. There is the same being all the way through, the lines representing stages of progress in functioning as a person or in the development of the physical basis for this.

If these suggestions are correct, the often-heard question, "At what point or stage in pregnancy does a human person begin to exist?" is a false question. That is, it rests on a false premise, that there is a point or stage during pregnancy—or at its end in birth or at some time after birth—at which a human person begins to exist. If there is no such point what shall we say? What alternatives are there? One is #1, conception-fertilization. Are there others? Let us see. This takes us to our next chapter.

12

Other Approaches

THE AGNOSTIC POSITION

The claim "No one knows when a human person begins to exist" is the typical expression of the agnostic position. But if it is true that conception-fertilization marks the beginning of a person's existence, then it may be possible to know when a person begins to exist. The same is true if it is correct to say that my parents conceived *me*, rather than a biological organism that became me only later. On the other hand, if conception-fertilization does not mark the beginning of a person's existence, and we turn to the list of other possible places to draw a line, such as viability or a developed brain, we may indeed be puzzled as to which of these suggested places is really the correct one, and how one would go about establishing this. It seems likely that none of these other lines are really convincing because each is seen as representing merely a development in a being who is already there, whose existence has been in place all along. At this point, the agnostic position may seem an attractive option.

What would follow for the abortion issue if one adopts the agnostic position? If for any stage in the development of the BIW we say that we don't know whether or not it is a person, we are also saying that it may well be a person. The further along in pregnancy, the more likely this is. And this means of course that abortion may well be the killing of a human person. This favors the pro-life position. We cannot kill a being that *may* be a person; we can only kill it if we *know* that it is *not* a person. And of course the agnostic position includes exactly that: we don't *know* that it is *not* a person.

The agnostic position makes sense when it is applied to *functioning* as a person. It is indeed difficult if not impossible to know when in the course of a human being's life a certain level of functioning as a person first comes into existence. It does not follow from this that *being* a person is also something beyond our ability to know; unless we identify being and functioning in the way that the achievement view does, when it essentially defines being a person as that which can now function as a person or could do so at some time in the past.

THE GRADUALIST POSITION

If none of the suggested places to draw a line seems appropriate, this is probably because there is a gradual process of growth and development, with no "line" marking any significant and morally relevant transition from nonperson to person. This leads many people to adopt the gradualist position: the BIW starts out as a nonperson and then gradually develops into a person. The change from nonperson to person is subtle and gradual, like the change from day to night and from child to adult. Proponents of this position may adopt one of two versions of this view:

- Abortion is justified in the early stages of pregnancy and wrong in the later stages, with a gray area in between.
- Abortion is wrong all the way through, but it is less wrong in the early stages and more seriously wrong in the late stages.

The first version of the gradualist position is proposed by Derek Parfit. As we saw in chapter 10, he adopts what he calls the Reductionist View of the way persons exist over time:

> On the Reductionist View, we do not believe that at every moment I either do or don't exist. We can now deny that a fertilized ovum is a person or a human being. This is like the plausible denial that an acorn is an oak-tree. Given the right conditions, an acorn slowly becomes an oak-tree. This transition takes time and is a matter of degree. There is no sharp borderline. We should claim the same about persons, and human beings. . . . We can believe that there is nothing wrong in an early abortion, but that it would be seriously wrong to abort a child near the end of pregnancy. Such a child, if unwanted, should be born and adopted. The cases in between we can treat as matters of degree. . . . After being in no way wrong, it becomes a minor wrong-doing . . . as the organism becomes fully a human being, or a person, the minor wrong-doing changes into an act that would be seriously wrong.[1]

Critics of the position argue that this confuses *being* a person and *functioning* as a person. It is surely true that acquiring the ability to function as a person is a gradual process; it does not follow that being a person is also a gradual process. On the contrary, it seems that a being is either a person or not a person; there is no in-between. It is absurd to say that halfway through the pregnancy you are half a person. What would this be? Perhaps you are thinking along the lines of a person who is half asleep and half awake; he or she is half *functioning* as a person but fully *is* a person. I cannot kill you just as you are waking up! In order to be "waking up," there must be someone there who is doing the waking up, someone who has the full being of a person.

The gradualist position rests on the achievement view. Given this view, the gradualist position makes sense: being a person is an achievement, and this is achieved gradually. The opposing view, that being a person is not an achievement but is our very nature and essence as humans, the core of our being, is not consistent with the gradualist position.

EARLY VERSUS LATE ABORTION

Despites its difficulties a gradualist approach seems to have wide intuitive appeal. Most people who approve very early abortions when the BIW is tiny and undeveloped are horrified by late-term abortions when it is obvious to them that one is killing a real baby. Perhaps there is something to this common intuition. Let us now see how each of the two positions, pro-life and pro-choice, can make use of what this intuition points to.

It must be stressed that for pro-life *all abortions* are wrong. They are all seriously wrong, terrible moral evils; no abortions are justified. Nevertheless, many on the pro-life side hold that some are still worse than others; late-term abortions are especially wrong, horrific moral evils. This implies that earlier abortions, though seriously wrong, are less wrong than later ones. Three reasons can be advanced for this idea:

1. Late abortions cause pain to the child, very early abortions do not. And the later the abortion the greater the pain. Where there is uncertainty as to whether abortion causes pain, the later the abortion the greater the chance of pain. As one goes to very late abortions where the child is virtually indistinguishable from a born baby, the reality of pain becomes an undeniable certainty. Therefore late pain-causing abortions are worse than very early abortions that are possibly without pain.
2. Late in pregnancy, after viability is reached, the child can live outside the womb. If a woman does not want to continue her pregnancy, she can have the child removed rather than have it killed. Therefore to kill the child at this point when there is an alternative which allows it to live is still worse than killing it when no such alternative exists.

3. Late in pregnancy it is clear that there is a real baby, a premature baby, or at least a being so much like a baby that it deserves to be treated like a baby, a small person. Ignorance of this is hard to excuse at this stage. But early in pregnancy, ignorance of the status of the BIW as a small person is much more understandable, and thus much easier to excuse. Once again, this time in terms of the intention and the condition of the agent (the doer of the action), late-term abortions are morally worse than early ones.[2]

For some versions of the pro-choice position—those that claim there is a morally significant difference between early and late abortions—there are two options here. The first is to say that early abortions are justified and later ones not justified and therefore wrong. The second is to say that early abortions are not as such justified but that they are easier to justify than later ones; that early abortions can be justified by lesser reasons while later ones need weightier reasons. All this, as noted, applies to some pro-choice views, those that are sometimes called moderate. Other versions of the pro-choice position make no difference among early and late abortions, claiming they are all justified until one line or another is reached, such as developed brain capacity, viability or birth; or in some cases such as Tooley and Singer, sometime after birth.

PRO-LIFE: THE DON MARQUIS
FUTURE-LIKE-OURS ARGUMENT

Let us now examine another argument in defense of the pro-life position, one that bypasses the question whether or not the BIW is a person; and thereby also the question, when does a human person begin to exist? All parties agree that the BIW is biologically continuous with what will become a person at some point. It is therefore at least a potential person already now. Can this be used to show that abortion is morally wrong? In an influential article, "Why Abortion Is Immoral,"[3] Don Marquis claims that it can be used to show this. His argument may be summarized as follows:

1. Even if the BIW is only a "potential person," it has a future as a person, a future like ours. If it is not killed, it will grow to be a newborn baby and later an adult.
2. Therefore to kill the BIW by abortion is to deprive it of this future as a person.
3. To deprive anyone of his future as a person is a terrible evil. If I kill you, I deprive you of your entire future. This is a major part of the wrongness of killing.

4. Therefore, abortion is wrong. *It deprives the BIW of its entire future as a person.*

When I die, I am deprived of my entire future; this is the greatest loss for me. Exactly the same thing applies to the BIW when it is killed by abortion.

An important clarification is called for. The Marquis future-like-ours argument applies to the being that results from the union of sperm and ovum, the zygote. It does not apply to the sperm alone, nor to the ovum alone. The difference is crucial:

1. The zygote is its own being, with its own unique genetic code, different from that of the father and that of the mother. In contrast, the sperm is not its own being but a part of the father, and the ovum is not its own being but a part of the mother. A sperm alone has no future; an egg alone has no future.
2. The zygote is continuous with the BIW in its later stages, as embryo, fetus and then newborn baby. It is the same individual organism all the way through. It is that at least on the biological level, even if we leave open the question whether it is a person all the way through. This does not apply to the sperm and the ovum, each of which, either by itself or in a union that brings forth a new being, comes to the end of its existence.
3. The zygote-embryo-fetus is a new, unique being, an *actual* human being. In contrast, sperm and ovum are only *potentials* for the coming into being of a zygote; each contains only ½ the DNA needed to form a human being. They have no future of their own and the future-like-ours argument cannot apply to them.

The Golden Rule. You would not want me to deprive you of your entire future as a person. Therefore, you should not deprive me of my future: you should not kill me when I am born; you should not kill me when I am pre-born.

PRO-CHOICE: SOME REPLIES
TO THE FUTURE-LIKE-OURS ARGUMENT

Let us now examine some opposing arguments that challenge the Don Marquis future-like-ours argument, and thereby provide support for the pro-choice position. One is an argument presented by Peter K. McInerney in his article, "Does a Fetus Already Have a Future-Like-Ours?"[4] He agrees that the BIW is biologically continuous with what will become a person at some point. That is, it is the same biological organism that will later be born. But it is not the same person as the later person. The BIW and the later person are not the same being. And this means that the BIW does not have a future of which it can be deprived.

A child of three is deprived of her entire future by being killed. This is because the child now and that same child later as an adult are the same being, the same person; they are connected by personal identity. "I was once that child of three." And the reason for this is that there is a real psychological continuity between earlier and later phases of this being; not just a biological continuity of being the same organism. This psychological continuity centers on the continuity of character, memory links and intentional actions. All this is absent in the relation between the BIW and the child later. As McInerney puts it:

> The situation of a fetus at an early stage of development is very different [from that of a young infant and his future]. A fetus at an early stage of development has neither a mental life of feelings, beliefs and desires nor a developed brain and nervous system. There are none of the main relations with a personal future which exist in persons. Although there is some biological continuity between them so that there is a sense in which the later person stages "are the future" of the fetus, the fetus is so little connected to the later personal life that it cannot be deprived of that personal life. At its time the fetus does not already "possess" that future personal life in the way that a normal adult human already "possesses" its future personal life.[5]

Another argument is that of Gerald H. Paske, "Abortion and the Neo-Natal Right to Life: A Critique of Marquis's Futurist Argument."[6] His basic thesis is that Marquis's argument only works if we assume that the being in question—who has a future like ours that should not be destroyed—is already a person. But if we do, the whole point of Marquis's argument is lost, since it was supposed to show that abortion as depriving the BIW of its entire future is wrong even if it is not a person. Why is it, Paske asks, that it is not wrong to destroy a pig or a cow? "The answer lies in the concept of personhood. . . . It is this personhood which makes a future-like-ours possible and it is, hence, personhood which underlies Marquis' right to life."[7] A pig or a cow doesn't have a future-like-ours because it is not a person. If it is wrong to destroy the BIW since it has such a future, it is because it is a person. Further evidence that it is personhood and not the loss of a future that is crucial is brought out when Paske points out that it is the loss of one's personhood "which makes the murder of a person even on their deathbed a serious harm."[8]

13

What Should We Do
If We Are in Doubt?

HOW DOUBT MAY ARISE

Doubt may arise in several ways. The first concerns whether the BIW is already a person. The pro-choice not-a-person/achievement view says no (chapter 4); the pro-life continuum/SLED view says yes (chapter 6). If we are in doubt about which side is correct, where should we give the benefit of doubt?

Second, we may be in doubt about the logical status of the pro-choice no-duty-to-sustain/violinist argument (chapter 5). Is pro-choice correct when it claims that it justifies abortion as being something other than the wrongful killing of an innocent person? Or is pro-life correct when it holds that abortion is wrong as the direct, intentional killing of an innocent person, by horrible methods (chapter 7)? And that abortion is especially wrong because of the terrible pain it causes to a living, sentient being (chapter 8)? What should we do if we are in doubt?

Third, we may be in doubt about the role of quality of life. Pro-choice says it can justify abortion, either for the woman herself (chapter 2), or more generally for society at large (chapter 3). Pro-life appeals to the dignity of the human person and says that killing a person for the sake of advancing quality of life is morally wrong (chapter 9).

Fourth, doubt may arise about when a person begins to exist (chapter 11). We looked at conception-fertilization as the place to mark this beginning. We saw that it represents a radical break, and is therefore a likely candidate for drawing the line. But perhaps we are not completely persuaded, as we also noted reasons for denying that this is the beginning of a person's existence. We then considered other possible lines, but each is apt to give rise to serious doubts, as each seemed to indicate nothing more than a greater development of one and the same being who is there both before and after. This led directly to the next topic.

Fifth, we examined the gradualist position (chapter 12). If true, what would it imply for the morality of abortion? It seems that no definite answer can be given to this question, so that we cannot confidently assert that abortion at any given stage of pregnancy when abortions are typically performed is justified. This is because the gradualist position by its very nature allows that the BIW at such a stage might already have reached a level of personal being that would make killing it by abortion immoral. That is to say doubt is written into the very fabric of the gradualist position; that position is essentially one of doubt.

Sixth, the same is true of the agnostic position (chapter 12). It is even more a position essentially of doubt, and expressing doubt in its very name.

Seventh, there is the attempt by Don Marquis (chapter 12) to bypass the entire question of when a person begins to exist, and whether or not the BIW is a person, by focusing on the future that this being has if it is not killed by abortion. What should we do if we are in doubt about whether or not his argument is successful?

Doubt may arise for any of these reasons, or for several of them, perhaps for all of them. What can the two main positions, pro-life and pro-choice, offer us here?

THE PRO-LIFE IF-IN-DOUBT ARGUMENT

First, we must always give the benefit of doubt to the presence of human life, the actual presence of a real human person. We all know this intuitively and with absolute certitude; and we consistently apply it in all areas of life. Consider some examples:

- A hunter hears a rustling in the bushes. He thinks, "It is probably a deer." Can he shoot? No! "It's almost certainly a deer." Not good enough! He must be *absolutely certain* that it is not a human person. There can be no doubt. If there is any doubt we must give the benefit of the doubt to the presence of human life.
- A person is lost at sea. Is he still alive? Perhaps. Continue the search! Give the benefit of doubt to the presence of human life.
- A person falls from window onto the pavement. Is he still alive? Perhaps. Treat him as one who is alive. Give the benefit of doubt to the presence of human life.

The case of the BIW is the same as all these cases. If there is any doubt about whether or not it is a human person—in general or at any particular stage where an abortion is considered—one must give it the benefit of the doubt and treat it as a human person. This means respecting it and not killing it by abortion. You can't just kill beings that "may or may not" be persons. You have to *know*; or if in doubt, assume that a person is present, as in the case of deer hunting.

A very important point: if there is even a small chance, a tiny chance, that human life is present, or that something will destroy a human life, we must give the benefit of doubt to life. There is a tiny, tiny chance that this food will poison the (newborn) baby. If so, don't feed her with it! This applies all the more if there is a fifty/fifty chance, or maybe a sixty/forty or greater chance. With the BIW the chance that it is a person is surely more like fifty/fifty than a tiny chance. And so the argument based on the three examples above, if it gives the benefit of doubt to life already in cases of tiny chances of life, it does so with immensely more force when the chances of life are so much greater, as with the BIW.

Second, we must consider the pain factor. We cannot risk the terrible pain that abortion causes to a being with sensitive nerves. For all the benefits expected from abortion, can it be justified in the terms of the terrible risk of such pain?

THE PRO-CHOICE IF-IN-DOUBT ARGUMENT

First, we should focus on the reality of the woman, and this means giving her the benefit of any doubt. She is clearly a person. We should acknowledge her moral right to choose what she believes is best in her situation. We should recognize her right to control her body. We should let her decide if the BIW is a person or not. She should draw the line where she sees fit. Or she can adopt the gradualist position. Or she can choose to make her decision according to quality-of-life factors as she interprets them. In any case we should let her be free to decide whether or not to have an abortion according to the dictates of her conscience.

Second, we should take seriously the reality of quality of life, in its various dimensions, for the woman, for the child, and for all of society, as in the various pro-choice quality-of-life arguments that we considered (chapters 2 and 3). These quality-of-life factors are real; the status of the BIW, whether or not it is a person, is highly uncertain. And we should take very seriously Thomson's claim that the woman has no duty to sustain the being inside her, that she may have it removed by an abortion; and that she may do so even if it is already a person (chapter 5). Her desire to be free from the burden of sustaining this being is real, and this is what should be the determining factor.

Underlying both these pro-choice approaches, and lending them strength, is what we might call the agnostic factor. Who knows when human life begins, when a person first comes into existence? Who knows whether something like the gradualist position may or may not be true? Who can untangle all these knotty questions surrounding the coming into being of a person like the rest of us? What is real, what is certain and beyond any doubt, is the actuality of the woman, her body, her life; and the many quality-of-life concerns that surround the woman and society in general.

THE PSYCHOLOGY OF PRO-CHOICE AND PRO-LIFE

Why are certain people pro-choice? Why are others pro-life? Perhaps we can get a clue here for resolving or at least better understanding the matter of doubt.

How do the pro-choice arguments work? Is it (A) or (B)?

(A) A person is already committed to the pro-choice position. "What arguments can I find that will justify this position?" That is, one *decides ahead of time* that abortion is morally justified or neutral; then one finds something that can be put forward to support this.

(B) A person is *genuinely unsure* whether or not abortion is morally right or wrong. He then examines the pro-choice arguments and is convinced by one or more of them that they are valid arguments and that their conclusion is correct.

How do the pro-life arguments work? Is it (C) or (D)?

(C) A person is already committed to the pro-life position. "What arguments can I find that will justify this position?" That is, one *decides ahead of time* that abortion is morally wrong; then one finds something that can be put forward to support this.

(D) A person is *genuinely unsure* whether or not abortion is morally right or wrong. He then examines the pro-life arguments and is convinced by one or more of them that they are valid arguments and that their conclusion is correct.

Let me suggest the following. Approaches (A) and (C) are not reasonable and honest. One should not *decide ahead of time*, but rather after, and because, the evidence is in. That leaves us with (B) and (D). Here the question is: which one is more likely? I invite the reader to re-examine the pro-choice arguments in part one, chapters 2–5; then the pro-life arguments in part two, chapters 6–9; then the pro-choice replies in part three, chapter 10. And to do so each time from the point of view of which is more likely, the pro-choice side being correct or the pro-life side being correct. In addition it might be useful to review the suggested lines and discussion in chapter 11, and the various approaches discussed in chapter 12 (agnostic and gradualist positions and the future-like-ours argument). Again, which is more likely, the pro-life side being correct or the pro-choice side being correct?

THE SCOPE OF DOUBT: EARLY VERSUS LATE ABORTIONS

Here is a position one might consider. It makes sense to doubt that a tiny zygote, the BIW just after conception-fertilization, is a human person in the same sense as one of us, with the same right to life. But when we go to the other end of the spectrum of the time in the womb, the third trimester, the BIW in the seventh to ninth month, it is very hard not to see a baby, a small child; a baby who is essentially like a newborn baby, only a bit smaller, a bit less developed, more dependent and in a different environment. What this would mean is that the benefit of doubt arguments—pro-life and pro-choice—really apply only at the very beginning. As one moves further along, the reality of the child becomes more and more apparent. This can be seen by considering the facts about the being in the womb presented in chapter 1; and by looking at the pictures on the website given earlier (chapters 7 and 8): www.100abortionpictures.com.

Of course one can avoid this conclusion by adopting the not-a-person argument. But now a two-fold difficulty arises. First, this argument as noted rests essentially on the achievement view: you don't become a person until you achieve certain things. What things? How much of them? How do we decide? Who decides? Any set of answers one might give these questions must be fraught with doubt. What if we're wrong, and deny personhood to a being who is in fact a person? Or attribute it to a being who is in fact not a person? The achievement view approach is hardly helpful if we are concerned with attaining the truth, with getting it right, and start from the question, what we should do if we are in doubt. Far from helping settle the troublesome matter of doubt, this approach only makes it worse.

The first difficulty arises when we assume the basic approach of the not-a-person argument, try to see how it would work, and do not question its validity or its conclusion, that the BIW is not a person. A second difficulty arises when we raise the question: what if this argument is not valid? Perhaps its conclusion is not correct. Perhaps the BIW is a person. Isn't this possible? If we take this possibility seriously, we are again left in a state of doubt. And once again, far from helping settle the troublesome matter of doubt the achievement view approach only makes it worse.

There is still another option: the no-duty-to sustain argument, Thomson and her famous violinist. But can anyone seriously maintain that we can *know* that this argument is valid and that it applies effectively to the case of a pregnant woman who wants to get rid of the BIW inside her body? Does the analogy really fit? Who is the violinist? He is a stranger; but abortion has to do with the woman's own child, for whom she is surely responsible after birth. Can we be sure she is not also responsible before birth? And can we really be confident that abortion is like withdrawing support, rather than outright, direct, intentional killing? If a man stabs another man with a knife, that is surely killing, and not merely withdrawing support. Isn't abortion really like that? The no-duty-to-sustain argument is at best fraught with difficulties and doubts. Once again we have yet another instance where, far from helping settle the troublesome matter of doubt, this approach only makes it worse.

We have already noted, at the beginning of the current chapter, that the gradualist position and the agnostic position are themselves laden with doubt, and so cannot by their very nature help us in resolving the matter of doubt.

This leaves us with one final and hopefully decisive way of approaching the doubt question, and that is by asking: which way of going wrong is worse?

WHICH WAY OF GOING WRONG IS WORSE?

Consider the two basic possibilities:

- PL IS REALLY CORRECT.
- PC IS REALLY CORRECT.

What should we do?

- If PL IS REALLY CORRECT: We should adopt the PL position.
- If PC IS REALLY CORRECT: We should adopt the PC position.

But we may be in doubt about which position is really correct. Then we should reckon with the possibility of going wrong. There are two ways of going wrong:

A. We adopt the pro-life position, but in reality the pro-choice position is correct. Result: the woman is wronged: she is forced to carry an unwanted pregnancy for nine months; and then either take care of the child, or place him for adoption.
B. We adopt the pro-choice position, but in reality the pro-life position is correct. Result: the child is wronged: he is killed, by abortion methods that cause him horrible pain, and he is deprived of his entire future.

Which of these, (A) or (B), is worse? A diagram may help us think about this:

THE MORAL DIAGONALS

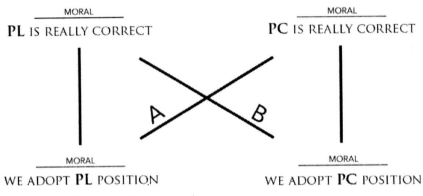

Figure 13.1. The Moral Diagonals

Which of these, (A) or (B), is worse? Consider:

A. We defend the right of the child to live and *deny the woman her right to choose.* In reality the woman has this right.

B. We defend the right of the woman to choose and *deny the child his right to live.* In reality the child has this right.

IV

hợp pháp

THE LEGAL QUESTION

đạo đức

So far we have examined the moral question of abortion: is abortion *morally* right or wrong? Let us turn now to the legal question: should abortion be *legal* or not?

14

The Legal Status:
Pro-Choice and Pro-Life

CAN WE LEGISLATE MORALITY?

make law

It is often said: "We cannot legislate morality." For some parts of morality this is certainly true. Being ungrateful is a moral failure that falls outside the domain of law. We cannot legislate morality when it comes to virtues such as gratitude and compassion. But now consider the virtue of justice. Should our laws be just? The answer is obvious. Thus when we try to make our laws embody justice, we are "legislating morality." We are trying to legislate what is morally called for.

 One of the most important functions of law, of what we legislate, is the protection of human persons and their basic rights. Thus laws against murder, slavery, and assault constitute legislating morality, the morality of respecting persons. Our laws protect our right to choose in countless ways. We can choose our religion or lack thereof, our life careers, whether or not to marry and if so whom to marry, and much else. Does the right to choose abortion also come under this heading? Pro-choice says yes, pro-life says no. We protect our born children from being killed. Should this protection also be applied to the BIW? Pro-life says yes, pro-choice says no. Let us now examine each of these.

THE PRO-CHOICE LEGAL POSITION

If women have a *moral* right to abortion, then surely this right should be enshrined in the law; they should then also have the *legal* right to abortion. Like every other basic moral right—such as the right to life, freedom

133

of expression, and property—the right to end an unwanted pregnancy by abortion should be protected by law. We may view a woman's legal right to abortion under four key headings:

1. *Autonomy.* We must respect a woman's autonomy, her right to make her own decisions about her life; and especially her right over her body.
2. *Don't impose.* It is wrong for some people to impose their personal views on others. Those opposed to abortion on moral grounds have a right to their opinion; not the right to impose it on others. The woman must be free from all coercion, free to make her own decision. The legal right to abortion guarantees that.
3. *Difficult situations.* As we saw in examining the feminist pro-choice quality of life argument (chapter 2), women often face difficult and even agonizing situations in their lives that involve pregnancy. They must be free to choose whatever course of action they see as best for themselves in their own unique situation.
4. *Safe and legal.* We must ensure that abortion remains safe for women; that they are not forced to seek illegal abortions from back-alley butchers. Only if abortion remains legal can we be assured that it will remain safe for women.

The pro-choice legal position builds on the pro-choice moral position and the arguments that support it. Let us briefly recall these arguments.

- The feminist pro-choice quality-of-life arguments of Susan Sherwin and Alison Jaggar (chapter 2).
- The general pro-choice quality-of-life argument for an unwanted child, a severely handicapped child, the woman's quality of life, and over-population (chapter 3).
- The Warren-Tooley-Boonin and the Maguire-Morgan not-a-person arguments and the achievement view (chapter 4).
- The no-duty-to-sustain argument of Thomson and her violinist (chapter 5).

Table 14.1. PC: Keep Abortion Safe and Legal

Keep abortion safe and legal
Women should have the right to choose
The government should protect this right

The pro-choice legal position is basically the thesis that the government must protect a woman's moral right to choose abortion by making this a legal right and then enforcing it just like every other legal right. Notice that this means the government cannot be neutral on this issue. It must take its stand on the side of women's rights.

THE PRO-LIFE LEGAL POSITION

If the child in the womb has a *moral* right to live, then surely this right should be enshrined in the law; he should then also have the *legal* right to live. Like every other basic moral right—such as the right to equal treatment, freedom of expression, and property—the right to live should be protected by law. We may view the child's legal right to live under four key headings:

1. *Protect the child's right to live.* The small person in the womb is "one of us," a member of our human community. He should be given the same respect and the same legal protection for his right to live as the rest of us.
2. *Don't impose.* Abortion imposes a cruel death on a small, innocent child. Recall the methods, how the child is cut to pieces, and the terrible pain this causes.
3. *No one should have the legal power of life or death over another.* Giving women the right to have their pre-born babies killed, in difficult situations or otherwise, gives some the power to choose death for others.
4. *Safe and legal.* This should apply to the child in the womb. Only with legal protection for his moral right to live will he be safe in the womb. We should not legalize one form of killing (abortion in general) in order to try to minimize another form of killing (back-alley abortion).

The pro-life legal position builds on the pro-life moral position and the arguments that support it. Let us briefly recall these arguments.

- The reality of the child in the womb; continuum and SLED (chapter 6).
- The terrible evil of deliberately killing this child (chapter 7).
- The fact, or at least the great risk, of causing terrible pain to the child (chapter 8).
- The fact that abortion-killing denies the BIW his entire future (chapter 12).

The pro-life legal position is basically the thesis that the government must protect a child's moral right to live by making this a legal right and then enforcing it just like every other legal right. Notice that this means the government cannot be neutral on this issue. It must take its stand on the side of pre-born persons' rights.

Table 14.2.   PL: The Child in the Womb Is a Real Person

The child in the womb is a real person
The child in the womb should have the right to live
The government should protect this right

15

The Role of Government

THE GOVERNMENT CANNOT BE
NEUTRAL: IT MUST TAKE A STAND

Many people think the government should remain neutral on the abortion issue. They say it is a private matter and so the government "should stay out of it." They do not want the government to prohibit women from having abortions. They want women to be free to choose abortion, to have the right to do so. And so they say the government should stay out. But a little further thought makes it clear that what they really want is that the government should protect this "right of choice." And if the government does that, then of course it steps into the fray and is not neutral. The same logic applies on the pro-life side. Defenders of the pro-life position also do not want the government to be neutral; they want it to step in on the side of the child in the womb and protect his right to live. What this means is that the government *cannot* be neutral; it is necessarily involved. The question is then *not whether* the government should be involved, *but how* it should be involved. The government has only two options:

1. It rules that women have a legal right to choose abortion and to be protected by the law. It protects this right by ensuring that women have free access to abortion clinics. This includes and implies that the BIW does not have a legal right to life and to be protected by the law.
2. It rules that the BIW has a legal right to life and to be protected by the law. It protects this right by ensuring that abortion clinics are not allowed to operate. This includes and implies that women do not have

a legal right to choose abortion and should not be protected by the law to have an abortion.

Each position the government can take is a stand. Pro-life is a stand: that the BIW is a small *person*, a human being like the rest of us, "one of us." It is the stand that we must protect this child against being killed; that there should be no legally protected choice to kill any human beings. Pro-choice is a stand: that the BIW is not a person to whom the rights of a person apply. It is the position of the U.S. Supreme Court in *Roe v. Wade*, January 22, 1973, that a woman has a constitutional right to abortion. The ruling held that the woman is the only *person* involved.

Table 15.1.   Government Must Take a Stand

The government must take a stand:
- It either protects the woman's right to choose.
- Or it protects the child's right to live.
- It cannot do both. Neutrality is impossible.

THE GOVERNMENT CANNOT BE NEUTRAL: IT MUST DRAW THE LINE SOMEWHERE

The government must draw the line somewhere. In present-day America it has done so: at birth. As we saw briefly in chapter 1, it has taken this stand in *Roe v. Wade*. This is essentially the position of Mary Ann Warren. The Court indicated its agreement with "the view that life does not begin until live birth." It summarized its position by saying, "In short, the unborn have never been recognized in the law as persons in the whole sense." It ruled that in the first two trimesters the abortion decision is entirely up to the woman and her doctor. In the third trimester, after the time of viability, the state "may, if it chooses, regulate, and even proscribe [forbid] abortion, except where it is necessary, in appropriate medical judgment, for the preservation of the life or health of the mother."[1] If the term "health" is taken broadly enough, it means that according to *Roe v. Wade*, abortion is de facto allowed until birth, when the "fetus" becomes a "child," a "person in the whole sense." This is a definite stand the government has taken: before birth, abortion is allowed, after birth, killing it is illegal.

Table 15.2.   The Government Must Draw a Line Somewhere

WEEKS					MONTHS				
0 6 13 19 26			32 39		1 2 3				

BIRTH = Current law

Drawing a line at any place after conception-fertilization means separating the terrain governed by pro-choice from the terrain governed by pro-life. Before the line, abortion is allowed as pro-choice wants, and after the line, abortion is prohibited as pro-life wants. Before the line, the government protects the woman's right to choose; after the line, it protects the child's right to live. The key point is that to draw such a line is to take a stand.

phan đối

"I'M PERSONALLY OPPOSED TO ABORTION, BUT I THINK IT SHOULD BE LEGAL"

Many people hold what they take to be a kind of middle position that tries to be both "pro-life" and also "pro-choice." *I think abortion is morally wrong; I'm personally opposed to it. But I think it should be legal; I should not impose my personal moral beliefs on others. Every woman should be able to decide for herself whether or not to have an abortion.* This is one way of expressing the idea that the government has no legitimate role to play in the abortion issue. Is it a reasonable and coherent position? Let us examine this matter carefully from a strictly logical, philosophical viewpoint.

Those who adopt this view say that abortion is morally wrong. *Why* do they say that abortion is morally wrong? Is it because they believe that the BIW is a real baby and that abortion kills this little baby? But if one believes that there is a small baby, a real person in the womb, shouldn't that person be protected from being killed just like the rest of us? Shouldn't his *moral* right to life be protected by law, and thus recognized as a valid *legal* right? But then isn't it a strange confusion of beliefs to add: *I think abortion should be legal*? Doesn't it amount to saying "I wouldn't kill my baby as that is morally wrong, but I want the law to protect your right to kill your baby?"

Whether you are pro-life or pro-choice, it should be obvious that something is wrong here. You cannot have it both ways! Either you are really *pro-life* and take a moral stand for the reality and intrinsic value of the child, and a corresponding legal stand to ensure that the law defends the right of that child to live. Or you do not take such a stand, but rather a stand for the woman's legal right to choose, and then you are of course *pro-choice*. In the first case you are not pro-choice; in the second case you are not pro-life. You can't be both. Logically you must choose the one side or the other.

But abortion is a hot topic where emotions often rule the discussion and logic runs amok. Therefore, let us consider some comparison cases. First, imagine the time when slavery was a controversial issue in America. Someone says, *I think slavery is morally wrong; I'm personally opposed to it. But I think it should be legal; I should not impose my personal moral beliefs on others. Everyone should be able to decide for himself whether or not to own slaves.* Isn't this absurd? If one is opposed to slavery, isn't it because treating persons in this way is a moral outrage? Isn't it because persons have a right not to be so treated? But if so, shouldn't this right be legally protected? Doesn't it then follow that once a moral stand for the personhood of blacks is taken, one cannot be "personally opposed" to slavery and at the same time say that others should be allowed to decide for themselves whether or not to own slaves?

Second, imagine someone saying, *I think child abuse is morally wrong; I'm personally opposed to it. But I think it should be legal; I should not impose my personal moral beliefs on other. Everyone should decide for himself whether or not to engage in this practice.* Again, isn't it clear that this cannot work? But isn't this precisely what the *pro-life-personally-opposed-but-pro-choice-keep-it-legal* position does in the realm of abortion? "I would never kill my own pre-born baby. But it's all right with me if you kill yours; and I favor laws that allow you the choice to do that, and so I'm pro-choice on pre-born baby killing."

True pro-life says that slavery, child abuse, and abortion are all perfectly parallel: all three are horrible moral evils, terrible violations of human rights and human dignity; and all three must be outlawed to protect innocent human beings. In none of the three cases should the decision of how the subjects are to be treated, what is to be allowed and what is to be forbidden by law, be left up to other individuals. None of them fall under the umbrella of *I think it should be legal, everyone should decide for himself.* Thus pro-life says there is a parallel—but of course it never claims to be pro-choice. It doesn't say *it should be legal*; it only says *I'm opposed*, leaving out the *personally*, which seems like a foot in the door to pro-choice.

True pro-choice says that while slavery and child abuse are all perfectly parallel, abortion is most definitely *not* parallel with them. Slavery and child abuse are horrible moral evils, terrible violations of human rights and human dignity; and must therefore be outlawed to protect innocent human beings. In the case of abortion the innocent human beings who must be protected by law are the women and their right to choose. In the case of abortion it is precisely the decision of how the matter is to be treated that must be left up to other individuals, a decision protected by the force of the law. Abortion is the classic case of something that falls under the umbrella of *I think it should be legal, everyone should decide for himself.* Thus pro-choice says there is no parallel—but of course it never claims to be pro-life. Pro-choice doesn't say *I think abortion is morally wrong as the killing of a small child*; it only says *it should be legal.*

Perhaps some who say *I'm personally opposed* and also say *it should be legal* do so because they have negative *feelings* about abortion. Their stand is on the level of feelings. They feel negatively about abortion, but they also realize others have different feelings. They very rightly say they do not want to impose their own "mixed feelings" on others. Of course, if you are "personally opposed" to slavery—opposed *not* because you believe that blacks are persons and slavery is an outrageous affront to human dignity, but merely because owning slaves makes you personally uncomfortable and this discomfort is only a matter of your personal mixed feelings—then it would follow that letting others decide for themselves is the reasonable position. But once a deeper moral stand is taken, this emotional loophole is no longer available. Once one goes beyond the level of feelings to a recognition of the moral reality itself, then it can only be either the full pro-life stand or the full pro-choice stand that is logically coherent.

Once again, it should be stated emphatically that as long as one is dealing only on the level of feelings, none of the arguments, distinctions, theories, and other philosophical matters discussed here apply with any real and objective logical force. And this applies equally to pro-choice and to pro-life. Both the pro-choice not-a-person argument and the pro-life continuum argument, for example, make claims about reality; the reality of the being in the womb, claims that goes beyond the realm of feelings. They make opposing claims, so that they cannot be both correct. Herein lies the conflict, and the challenge to move beyond our mixed feelings to an understanding of the deeper moral issue.

No doubt there are cases where it makes perfectly good sense to say, *I'm personally opposed but I think it should be legal.* That is, it makes good logical and ethical sense, with a claim that so it really is, as opposed to a mere emotional reaction. An example would be smoking. A person may believe that smoking is morally wrong because it seriously harms one's body, and thus never practice it himself or herself—and at the same time recognize that other people see this very differently, and therefore hold that "everyone should decide this for himself"; and that it must therefore of course remain legal. There are many examples of such things. They all have one crucial element in common: none of them involve assaults on other persons, violating their fundamental rights; especially the right to life, the right to freedom, and the right to not be physically abused. They are all matters that concern the personal lives of individuals.

Slavery and child abuse clearly fall outside the realm of the personal in this sense. On pro-life the protection of the child in the womb does too, and in exactly the same way. On pro-choice the protection of a women's right to choose does too, and in exactly the same way.

16

Other Significant Legal Aspects

THE QUESTION OF DISCRIMINATION

Both sides of the legal issue are concerned with avoiding discrimination. Each side claims the other represents a form of discrimination. Assuming that each side has a plausible case, which form of discrimination is more serious?

The pro-choice side says making abortion illegal means discrimination against women. Men don't have the burden of pregnancy; women shouldn't either. The availability of legal abortion is necessary to *ensure equality between men and women*. This was the key point made by Alison Jaggar in chapter 2.

The pro-life side says making abortion legal means discrimination against the child in the womb. It means that we protect the born child but not the pre-born child. Legal abortion means saying to child in the womb, *you don't count, you're too small.*

THE QUESTION OF IMPOSING

In the abortion debate we often hear talk about not imposing something on others. Normally this stems from a spirit of consideration for the rights and beliefs of others. When faced with the question of abortion, however, some imposing is inevitable. The pro-choice side contends that we should not impose an unwanted pregnancy on the woman. We should respect her freedom and let her choose for herself. The pro-life side replies by saying that no one should impose death on the child. We should give the child his right to live. Thus pro-life wants to impose a duty on the woman to carry the BIW to term and thus take away her option of ending her pregnancy. And pro-choice wants to give the woman her option of ending her pregnancy and thus impose death on the BIW.

The key point is that *there is some imposing in any case.* Supporting the pro-choice side does not avoid imposing; rather, it means allowing a particular imposing, namely death on the BIW. So too, supporting the pro-life side does not avoid imposing; rather, it means allowing a particular imposing, namely continuation of an unwanted pregnancy on the woman. The question remains: which imposing is justified?

- Pro-choice: "Don't impose *continuing pregnancy on the woman*; let her choose."
- Pro-choice: "Don't impose *other people's values and beliefs* on the woman."
- Pro-life: "Don't impose *death on the child*; let the child live."
- Pro-life: "Don't impose *horrible pain on the child*; have compassion for the child."
- Therefore, there is some imposing in any case.

Which imposing is justified? The pro-choice quality-of-life arguments, the thesis that the BIW is not a person, and the idea that the woman has no duty to sustain the BIW; all these strongly imply that the pro-choice imposing is justified. But the pro-life thesis that the BIW is a real person and that abortion is the direct killing of this person strongly implies that the pro-life imposing is justified.

Does the pain factor complicate matters? Even if the BIW is not a person, and even if the woman does not have a duty to sustain it, does the fact that mid- and late-term abortions cause horrible pain to the BIW tip the balance? Perhaps it does. But already we hear the pro-choice cry out and call our attention to the emotional pain of the woman. Which pain has the final say? And which corresponding imposing must we avoid?

THE QUESTION OF PRIVACY

Is abortion a private matter? Pro-choice says yes. This was made clear in the January 22, 1973, *Roe v. Wade* decision of the U.S. Supreme Court which ruled that women have a fundamental, constitutional right to terminate their pregnancies. This right is largely based on a person's right to privacy. Clearly abortion *is* a private matter. The court held:

> The Constitution does not explicitly mention any right to privacy. In a line of decisions, however . . . the Court has recognized that a right of personal privacy, or a guarantee of certain areas or zones of privacy, does exist under the

Constitution. . . . These decisions make it clear that only personal rights that can be deemed "fundamental" or "implicit in the concept of ordered liberty" . . . are included in this guarantee of personal privacy. . . .This right of privacy . . . is broad enough to encompass a woman's decision whether or not to terminate her pregnancy. The detriment that the State would impose upon the pregnant woman by denying this choice altogether is apparent.[1]

Is abortion a private matter? Pro-life says no. Abortion involves not only the woman but the BIW as well. Is the BIW a person? If it is, and if abortion means killing this person, then abortion is not a private matter, but a deadly assault on another person, a classic case of something that is *not* a private matter. Indeed the Court itself in the *Roe* decision acknowledged that the question of personhood is crucial. It said:

> The appellee and certain *amici* argue that the fetus is a "person" within the language and meaning of the Fourteenth Amendment. . . . If this suggestion of personhood is established, the appellant's case of course collapses, for the fetus' right to life would then be guaranteed specifically by the Amendment.[2]

This means that the issue of privacy is really a reflection of other and more fundamental issues; those with which we have been concerned in this book. If the one or more of the pro-choice moral arguments in part one is correct, then abortion is indeed a private matter, something that must be left to the woman's own personal decision. On the other hand, if the pro-life position as given in part two is correct, then abortion is not a private matter, but a deadly assault on another person, something that should definitely not be left up to any other person's decision.

THE QUESTION OF POWER-FREEDOM-CONTROL FOR WOMEN: A PRO-CHOICE VIEW

Legalized abortion is necessary to ensure that women are truly free, that they are properly empowered to have control over their lives. A basic statement of this is from Ronald Dworkin:

> Laws that prohibit abortion or make it difficult or expensive to procure one deprive pregnant women of a freedom or opportunity that is crucial to many of them. A woman who is forced to bear a child she does not want because she cannot have an early or safe abortion is no longer in charge of her own body: the law has imposed a kind of slavery on her.[3]

A further defense of this position is offered by Susan Sherwin:

> Even without patriarchy, bearing a child would be a very important event in a woman's life, because it involves significant physical, emotional, social, and

(usually) economic changes for her. The ability to exert control over the incidence, timing, and frequency of childbearing is often tied to a woman's ability to control most other things she values. Because we live in a patriarchal society, it is especially important to ensure that women have the authority to control their own reproduction. Despite the diversity of opinion among feminists on most other matters, most feminists agree that women must gain full control over their own reproductive lives if they are to free themselves from male dominance.

Moreover, women's freedom to choose abortion is linked to their ability to control their own sexuality. Woman's subordinate status often prevents them from refusing men sexual access to their bodies. If women cannot end the unwanted pregnancies that result from male sexual dominance, then their sexual vulnerability to particular men may increase, because caring for an(other) infant involves greater financial needs and reduced economic opportunities for women. As a result, pregnancy often forces women to become dependent on particular men. Because a woman's dependence on a man is assumed to entail her continued sexual loyalty to him, restriction of abortion serves to commit women to remaining sexually accessible to particular men and thus helps to perpetuate the cycle of oppression.

In contrast to most nonfeminist accounts, feminist analyses of abortion direct attention to how women get pregnant. Those who reject abortion seem to believe that women can avoid unwanted pregnancies "simply" by avoiding sexual intercourse. These views show little appreciation for the power of sexual politics in a culture that oppresses women. Existing patterns of sexual dominance mean that women often have little control over their sexual lives. They may be subject to rape by their husbands, boyfriends, colleagues, employers, customers, fathers, brothers, uncles, and dates, as well as by strangers. Often the sexual coercion is not even recognized as such by the participants but is the price of continued "good will"—popularity, economic survival, peace, or simply acceptance. Many women have found themselves in circumstances where they do not feel free to refuse a man's demands for intercourse, either because he is holding a gun to her head or because he threatens to be emotionally hurt if she refuses (or both). Women are socialized to be compliant and accommodating, sensitive to the feelings of others, and frightened of physical power; men are socialized to take advantage of every opportunity to engage in sexual intercourse and to use sex to express dominance and power. Under such circumstances, it is difficult to argue that women could simply "choose" to avoid heterosexual activity if they wish to avoid pregnancy. Catherine MacKinnon neatly sums it up: "The logic by which women are supposed to consent to sex [is]: preclude the alternatives, then call the remaining option 'her choice'" (MacKinnon 1989, 192).[4]

THE QUESTION OF POWER-FREEDOM-CONTROL FOR WOMEN: A PRO-LIFE VIEW

The idea that legalized abortion empowers women surely seems logical. But an opposing view is offered by Richard Stith. His claim is that:

Legalized abortion was supposed to grant enormous freedom to women, but it has had the perverse result of freeing men and trapping women.

The likelihood of this cultural development was foreseen by the radical feminist Catherine MacKinnon . . . [in] an essay called "Privacy vs. Equality,":

"Abortion facilitates women's heterosexual availability," MacKinnon pointed out: "In other words, under conditions of gender inequality [abortion] does not liberate women; it frees male aggression. The availability of abortion removes the one remaining legitimized reason that women have for refusing sex besides the headache.". . . In the end, MacKinnon pronounced, *Roe's* "right to privacy looks like an injury got up as a gift," for "virtually every ounce of control that women won" from legalized abortion "has gone directly into the hands of men."[5]. . .

When birth was the result of passion and bad luck, some people could sympathize with a young woman who was going to need help with her baby. . . .

But once continuing pregnancy to birth is the result neither of passion nor of luck but only of her deliberate choice, sympathy weakens. After all, the pregnant woman can avoid all her problems by choosing abortion. So if she decides to take those difficulties on, she must think she can handle them.

Birth itself may be followed by blame rather than support. Since only the mother has the right to decide whether to let the child be born, the father may easily conclude that she bears sole responsibility for caring for the child. The baby is her fault. . . .

Throughout human history children have been the consequence of natural sexual relations between men and women. Both sexes knew they were equally responsible for their children, and society had somehow to facilitate their upbringing. Even the advent of birth control did not fundamentally change this dynamic, for all forms of contraception are fallible.

Elective abortion changes everything. Abortion absolutely prevents the birth of a child. A woman's choice for or against abortion breaks the causal link between conception and birth. It matters little what or who caused conception or whether the male insisted on having unprotected intercourse. It is she alone who finally decides whether the child comes into the world. She is the responsible one. For the first time in history, the father and the doctor and the health-insurance actuary can point a finger at her as the person who allowed an inconvenient human being to come into the world.

The deepest tragedy may be that there is no way out. By granting to the pregnant woman an unrestrained choice over who will be born, we make her alone to blame for how she exercises her power.[6]

WHICH WAY OF GOING WRONG IS WORSE?

What should be our stand as a society? What is the proper role of government in this issue? What should the government protect? Pro-choice claims the government should protect the woman and her right to choose and her quality of life. Pro-life claims the government should protect the child and his right to life, and protect him from the pain that is inflicted by abortion. Because the government can only protect one right—either the right of the woman to choose or the right of the child to live—it is important to ask: which way of going wrong is worse?

Suppose we make abortion illegal and deny the woman her right to choose to have the BIW killed. But in reality the BIW is *not* a small person; it is only a biological organism. In this case, we would make a mistake by denying a woman a right that she really has (call this A). The other scenario is that we make abortion legal and give the woman her right to choose to have the BIW removed and killed. But in reality the BIW *is* a small person, the same person all the way through the course of the pregnancy. Then our mistake is denying the child the right to live that she really has (call this B).

The crucial question is: *Which way of going wrong is worse?* A or B? Let us use the same diagonals as we did before in chapter 13 with the PC-PL moral question:

THE LEGAL DIAGONALS

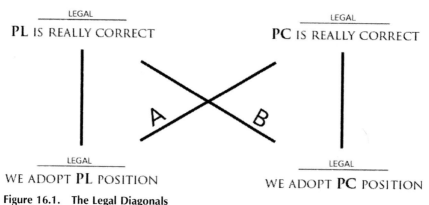

Figure 16.1.　The Legal Diagonals

Which of these, (A) or (B), is worse? Consider:

(A) We make abortion illegal. Pro-life wins. In reality the BIW is not a person, only a biological organism, with no right to life.
WE DENY THE WOMAN THE RIGHT TO CHOOSE.

(B) We make abortion legal; we affirm women's right to choose. Pro-choice wins. In reality the BIW is a real person with the same right to life as the rest of us.
WE DENY THE CHILD THE RIGHT TO LIVE.

17

The Hard Cases: Rape, Life of the Woman, Severe Deformities

TWO POSITIONS ON THE HARD CASES

In the abortion debate, there are people who describe themselves as pro-life but with exceptions for the so-called hard cases (rape, incest, deformed child, and the life of the woman). They will say, "I believe abortion is usually wrong; it is wrong except in cases of rape, incest, and the other hard cases." When faced with the hard cases (besides pro-choice), there are two "pro-life" positions that may be taken:

1. *Pro-life with exceptions*: no abortions except in the hard cases.
2. *Total pro-life*: no abortions; no exceptions; protect every child.

Let us begin with the case of pregnancy resulting from rape. Some rape cases are, to make matters worse, also cases of incest. Those who justify abortion for pregnancy due to rape also justify it for incest, and vice versa; and for similar reasons. Therefore we will not discuss abortion for incest cases as a separate topic; what is said about rape cases applies to incest as well. This practical equivalence is noted by Lawrence Tribe: "Most cases of incest involve an older relative and a young child, and so in most people's experience, incest is really a particular kind of rape."[1]

Fortunately, cases of pregnancy resulting from rape are rare; the usual figure given is 1 percent or less of rape cases result in pregnancy. But the emotional, moral, and legal issues are very important and far-reaching, and deserve careful attention. When such a devastating pregnancy does occur:

- Should the government protect *the woman's choice,* her right to seek an abortion if she conceives by rape? Pro-choice and pro-life-with-exceptions says the government must protect this right, so that the woman is free to get rid of every last vestige of the horror that was done to her by the rape.
- Or should the government protect *the innocent child?* Total-pro-life says the government must protect this person; specifically his right to live, despite the horror of the situation.

THE CASE OF RAPE: PROTECTING THE WOMAN'S CHOICE

This is the position held in common by the standard pro-choice view and the pro-life-with-exceptions view. The former obviously holds that every woman always has the right to end her pregnancy, regardless of how it came about. This is a fundamental right. Pro-choice defends a woman's moral right and legal right to choose abortion in all cases. The rape case is an especially clear and dramatic example of these rights. The latter, the pro-life-with-exceptions view, holds that abortion is as such wrong, but in this case an exception should be made because of the extraordinary, horrible circumstances of the conception. It acknowledges that the BIW is a child, and that abortion means killing this child, but claims that abortion is morally justified in cases of rape and should be allowed by law.

Whether pro-choice or pro-life-with-exceptions, those who say that abortion is morally allowable in rape cases, and should be legal, make several key points:

- We should have compassion on the woman. The crime she has suffered is horrible, unspeakable.
- She has suffered enough. She has been degraded enough! Don't compound the situation with a pregnancy.
- The child will be a constant reminder of the rape and of the rapist himself.
- We shouldn't punish her by forcing her to continue with pregnancy.
- We should help her move on with her life, and forget everything associated with the rape.
- Thomson's Violinist Argument can be used here: since she didn't consent to the intercourse that led to the pregnancy, she should not be required to continue it.

This view is also defended in the pro-choice literature. Let us consider a few typical examples. Recall the words of Susan Sherwin, quoted in chapter 2:

> If the fetus is a result of rape or incest, then the psychological pain of carrying it may be unbearable, and the woman may recognize that her attitude to the child after birth will be tinged with bitterness.[2]

Another defense of abortion for rape cases is from Laurence Tribe:

> Nothing is more devastating than a life without liberty. A life in which one can be forced into parenthood is just such a life. Rape is among the most profound denials of liberty, and compelling a woman to bear a rapist's child is an assault on her humanity.[3]

In a similar vein, speaking of the assault of rape, Ronald Dworkin argues that:

> Requiring a woman to bear a child conceived in such an assault is especially destructive to her self-realization because it frustrates her creative choice not only in sex but in reproduction as well.[4]

Following the general pattern of Thomson's no-duty-to-sustain argument, and noting its special force and cogency in the rape case, F. M. Kamm argues for the "moral permissibility of killing the fetus" in cases of pregnancy due to rape. In the case of rape, the following conditions apply:

1a. A fetus that you are not responsible for creating needs to begin to use your body in the manner of pregnancy for nine months. You need not allow it to do this.

1b. A fetus that you are not responsible for creating is in your body. The fact that it needs your body to survive does not, alone, justify your having to continue aiding it. For example, if the fetus drops out, you need not return it to your body.

2a. Assume that someone deliberately intrudes on your body and as a side effect acquires your genetic material. The material happens to fall into a test tube and develops into a fetus growing in a laboratory. He (this someone) then calls you up and tells you that the fetus will die unless you put it into your body for nine months, all the while enduring the burdens, changes, and risks of pregnancy and labor. In this case you have no obligation to support this fetus that someone else created. You are not causally responsible for creating this fetus or for its needing your aid. In addition, I believe, its genetic connection to you would not make it impermissible for you to let the fetus die. Even a genetically related fetus does not have an inherent right to your bodily support simply because it needs it, nor do you have a duty to provide it.

2b. In the case of rape, where a forced sex act begins the fetus in your body, you have made no commitment to continue support already begun, and no special obligations exist (e.g., because of genetic connection) which require you to continue your support of the fetus.[5]

Another statement defending abortion for rape cases is from Caroline Whitbeck:

The woman who is pregnant by rape and is struggling to come to terms with and recover from the experience of rape, faces a special dilemma that exists in some form for all pregnant women, that of coming to terms with the experience of pregnancy. One author of a well-known pregnancy manual describes the early fetus in the following terms: "It is already alive, a human being, although its movements are still too feeble to be felt. And it has immense power. It can make a person take care of it, and adjust her whole organism to serve it." Small wonder that a woman pregnant by rape frequently experiences her pregnancy as a nine-month continuation of that rape. Not only does she, like many raped women, wake up at night screaming, but when she does, she finds that her body is still possessed by another. . . .

Being taken over by another being is an idea that has evoked both wonder and horror through the ages. It evokes wonder where it represents a desired union with God or some divine force (for example, being filled with the Holy Spirit, or being inspired by a muse). It evokes horror where it represents being taken over unwillingly by some human or demonic force (for example, being possessed by a troubled spirit or the ghost of a person who has died, or by a demon, witch or sorcerer). Possession and inspiration provide the closest analogy to the ultimately unique experience of pregnancy. The experience of a wanted pregnancy is as different from that of an unwanted pregnancy as the two experiences of inspiration and possession.[6]

What lies behind the *pro-life with exceptions* view as it applies to the rape case? Tribe offers an answer. Setting pregnancy in the Thomson-violinist context, he says:

The pregnant woman, at least in most cases, "volunteered" in the sense that she chose to have sex and ran the risk of getting pregnant. Thus she is not in the same position with regard to the fetus as she would have been with regard to the uninvited violinist.

This feeling probably plays a significant role in shaping people's view about abortion rights. What the feeling suggests is not an argument that because the fetus is an "innocent human life," *all* abortions must be prohibited. Rather, it suggests an argument, or at least a sentiment, that, when the woman is "responsible" for the pregnancy, she loses at least her moral right to claim that its continuation interferes with her autonomy.

This sentiment might in turn explain the widespread sense that abortion must be allowed in cases of rape. With rape, of course, the sexual intercourse resulting in pregnancy occurred without the woman's consent.[7]

What does this mean for those who claim to be pro-life but take the *pro-life with exceptions* view for the rape case? It seems that they have implicitly accepted Thomson's no-duty-to-sustain argument, an argument for the general pro-choice position. For as Thomson presents it, it is an argument not limited to the rape case but meant to apply to all cases of unwanted pregnancy. But if advocates of the *pro-life with exceptions* position base their stand on Thomson's argument for the general pro-choice position, can they then deny its application to other cases? For the core of the argument is that abortion is not a case of unjust killing, but only the exercise of the right not to sustain the BIW. Once the argument is accepted, it is hard to see how this right cannot be extended to other cases as well. And if this is so, if acceptance of the force of Thomson's argument for the rape case logically commits one to accepting it as such and therefore in other cases as well, the *pro-life with exceptions* view for rape cases falls into the general pro-choice view. It thus ceases to be what it was originally meant to be, namely a version of the "pro-life" view. This leads us to our next section.

THE CASE OF RAPE: PROTECTING THE INNOCENT CHILD

Let us turn now to the position held by the total pro-life view, that there should be no abortions at all, since there can be no exceptions to the moral rule against killing an innocent person. Even for the horrible rape case it says abortion is still morally wrong, and the government must still protect the innocent child. Let us note three reasons for holding this position.

First, abortion is morally wrong because it is the direct, intentional killing of an innocent human person. It remains wrong even if it would be of great benefit to the woman. One cannot kill A to benefit B, or kill B to benefit A. Compassion for the woman should not translate into lack of compassion for the pre-born child. One can have total compassion for the woman and recognize rape for the horrendous crime that it is, and still hold that this crime and its effects on the woman do not justify another horrendous crime against an innocent small child. And such a crime must be prohibited in the law; the law must protect the child and his right to live.

Second, does abortion for a rape-induced pregnancy really benefit the woman? A strong case can be made that it does not, *that it actually hurts the woman*. It is then entirely counterproductive. David Reardon (as we will see in the quotation below) claims that "most women describe the negative effects of abortion on their lives as even more devastating than the sexual assault." And so he rejects abortion as a helpful response to the rape victim because it only "adds to and accentuates the traumatic feelings associated with sexual assault." The crucial fact is that "rather than easing the psychological burdens of the sexual assault victim, abortion adds to them."

Third, there is the matter of principle. It is an illusion to believe one can have a basically pro-life stand but then make an exception for rape. The exception establishes a principle which will destroy the desired pro-life setting in which it is placed.

Let us now examine each of these in more detail. First, abortion is morally wrong and should be illegal because it is the direct, intentional killing of an innocent human person. It violates the rights and the dignity of the small person in the womb. We must always remember that the child is absolutely innocent. Specifically:

1. Every child deserves respect and protection; every child without exception. It is not the child's fault that conception was through rape.
2. We should not discriminate against this innocent child.
3. Total pro-life asks: Would you kill the rapist? Most people would say *no*. But those who adopt the pro-life with exceptions view are saying it is right to kill this child—who is absolutely innocent—but not right to kill the rapist, who is clearly not innocent but rather terribly guilty. Isn't this rather ironic?
4. Total pro-life asks: Would you kill a born child for similar reasons? Suppose the woman carried the child to term and then discovered that he bore a resemblance to the rapist and thus caused her great pain. Would it then be right to kill the born child to spare the woman that pain? Most people would say *no*. But now we should ask: Is there a real difference? That is, if it would be wrong to kill a *born* baby because he reminded his mother of the rape, why would killing a *pre-born* baby for this reason be any different?

Second, abortion after rape is not a benefit to the woman. Worse, it may actually hurt the woman. It is therefore possibly entirely counterproductive.

- A woman who is victimized by rape needs love, acceptance, and healing.
- Not participation in more violence by killing her child through abortion.
- Abortion is a quick fix solution that doesn't really help the woman.
- Having the abortion will not heal the memories of the rape.
- Abortion does not make the rape go away; it never goes away.
- Abortion is always dangerous for women, physically and psychologically. It is especially dangerous for women in the "hard cases," as we will see below.

- The terribly painful choice of adoption should be considered as an alternative to the even more painful and more detrimental choice of abortion. Clearly in a pregnancy following rape there are no simple, pain-free solutions; only the hope of less pain in the long run.

Reardon makes a strong case against abortion for rape victims:

It is a little known fact that the vast majority of sexual assault victims do not want abortions. In addition, when sexual assault victims *do* have abortions, the long term, and even short term, psychological effects are devastating. Most of these women describe the negative effects of abortion on their lives as even more devastating than the sexual assault.[8]

Many women report that their abortions felt like a degrading form of "medical rape.". . . Abortion involves a painful intrusion into a woman's sexual organs by a masked stranger who is invading her body. Once she is on the operating table, she loses control over her body. . . . And while she lies there tense and helpless, the life hidden within her is literally sucked out of her womb. In both sexual and medical rape, a woman is violated and robbed. In the case of sexual rape she is robbed of her purity. In the case of medical rape via abortion, she is robbed of her maternity. . . .

Abortion, then only adds to and accentuates the traumatic feelings associated with sexual assault. Rather than easing the psychological burdens of the sexual assault victim, abortion adds to them.[9]

In his earlier book he states his case against abortion for rape victims and the other "hard cases": "*The more difficult the circumstances prompting abortion, the more likely it is that the woman will suffer severe post-abortion sequelae [consequences].*"[10]

It is surely understandable that many people believe abortion is morally justified in the case of rape, and should be legally available. But if, besides the woman, there is another human person present; and if abortion means the direct, intentional killing of this person, then what has been presented here goes in the opposite direction. It says that abortion even for rape cases is morally wrong, and should not be legally allowed. Certainly we must have compassion. But what does this mean? Two factors are crucial:

- Compassion on the child. Do not kill the child.
- Abortion for rape is not true compassion for the woman: it hurts her!

If this is so, denying abortion for rape cases is not being heartless. It is sensitivity to the real nature of the case, to all those concerned. Christopher Kaczor puts it well:

Obviously pregnancy due to rape is horrendously difficult. The just rage felt by those who have been sexually assaulted needs to be fittingly discharged. But is abortion a proper outlet? Abortion cannot undo what has been done in rape. Abortion doesn't even punish the rapist for what he did. Instead it harms an innocent human being, and, given the health and psychological risks described . . . [above] puts the woman again in harm's way.

Unfortunately, nothing, including having an abortion, can undo a rape. However, to bear a child in these most difficult of circumstances is to perform an act that is in complete contradiction of what takes place in rape. In rape, a man assaults an innocent human being; in nurturing life, a woman protects an innocent human being. In rape a man undermines the freedom of another; in nurturing life, a woman grants freedom to another. In rape, a man imposes himself to the great detriment of another; in nurturing life a woman makes a gift of herself to the great benefit of another.[11]

Third, there is the matter of principle. It is an illusion to believe one can have a basically pro-life stand (moral and legal) but then make an exception for rape. The exception establishes a principle which will destroy the desired pro-life setting in which it is placed. That is, if you allow abortion in the case of rape, can you really forbid it in others? Allowing it here establishes a principle: "Some abortions are right if the need is great enough." Who then decides if the need is great enough? Obviously it is the woman. This brings us back to the standard pro-choice view, and thereby destroys the attempted middle view, pro-life-with-exceptions. It leaves the abortion decision basically up to the choice of the woman.

THE CASE OF RAPE: THE TESTIMONY
OF A PERSON CONCEIVED IN RAPE

Rebecca Kiessling describes herself as "conceived in rape" and "product of rape." She provides an interesting perspective:

We've all heard someone say: "I'm pro-life, well, *except* in cases of rape." Or "I'm pro-choice *especially* in cases of rape!"

Have you ever considered how really insulting it is to say to someone, "I think your mother should have been able to abort you"? It's like saying, "If I had my way, you'd be dead right now." And that is the reality with which I live every time someone says they are pro-choice or pro-life "except in cases of rape" because I absolutely would have been aborted if it had been legal in Michigan when I was an unborn child, and I can tell you that it hurts. But I know that most people don't put a face on this issue—for them abortion is just a concept—with a quick cliché, they sweep it under the rug and forget about it. I do hope that, as a child conceived in rape, I can help put a face, a voice, and a story to this issue.[12]

THE CASE OF RAPE: SOME FINAL THOUGHTS

Instinctively, many people, perhaps most people, will say that abortion is morally justified in the case of rape, and should be legally allowed. This is certainly understandable as an expression of compassion for the woman, something she surely deserves. But if we look further and probe more deeply, we begin to question this and see another possibility as well. Is there another human person present? Does abortion kill an innocent child? Or is it simply the erasing of the impersonal residue of a monstrous crime? Does abortion help the woman victimized by this horrendous evil? Or does it involve her in another evil? And hurt her further? So we must ask: how many lives hang in the balance when we consider abortion in the case of rape? And whether you answer one or two, is abortion an answer to the horror of rape?

THE LIFE OF THE WOMAN

It goes without saying that all who are pro-choice in general allow abortion to save the life of the woman. If abortion is justified as a woman's choice, and where there are personal reasons to terminate a pregnancy, all the more is abortion justified, morally and legally, when it is the woman's very life that is a stake. What is of interest in life-of-the-woman cases concerns those who say they are pro-life. It is here that the issue lies.

> Such cases are extremely rare, or perhaps even non-existent. Consider: Abortion is never necessary to save a woman's life. Four hundred and eighty physicians have signed a public declaration stating: "I agree that there is never a situation in the law or in the ethical practice of medicine where a preborn child's life need be intentionally destroyed by procured abortion for the purpose of saving the life of the mother."[13]

Despite the rarity or nonexistence of such cases, the question of abortion as it pertains to them is worth pursuing as there are crucial principles involved. Such cases, though extremely rare or nonexistent in practice, are not so rare in discussions of the abortion issue. Hence an understanding of the principles involved is of great importance.

As in the rape case, many people who see themselves as basically pro-life make an exception for the life of the woman. This means that among all those who call themselves pro-life, there are two main views:

The pro-life-with-exceptions view: it is right to kill the child in the womb in order to save the life of the woman.

The total pro-life view (no exceptions; protect every child): it counters this claim by applying the principle that it is wrong to kill one person in order to benefit another, even to save the life of another. Consider:

- It would be wrong to kill the woman in order to save the child.
- It would be wrong to kill the child in order to save the woman.

The two are perfectly parallel. That is: *We must treat pre-born persons and born persons in the same way.* What this means in practice is that if complications arise during the course of the pregnancy, where either the mother or the child or both are in danger of death, we must do everything we possibly can to *try to save both* the mother and the child. But we must *never kill one to save the other.*

What should we do in the case of an ectopic pregnancy or a cancerous womb? An ectopic pregnancy means that implantation occurs in the Fallopian tube instead of the uterus. In both these situations, if nothing is done both the woman and the small human being will die. The total pro-life view holds that it is permissible to remove a part of the Fallopian tube or the womb in order to save the life of the woman. The intention is to *remove* the small human being, not to *kill* him; *it is not an abortion.* It is a medical procedure necessary to save the life of the woman in a case where, no matter what is done, the small human being cannot be saved. The procedure saves the life of the woman, and has the death of the small human being as a foreseen but unintended consequence. It is not a case of killing one to save the other. In cases other than ectopic pregnancies, after removal, every attempt is made to save the life of the tiny baby, if at all possible. Removal is held off as long as possible to increase chances of saving the baby as balanced with maternal survival.

If *the total pro-life view* explained here seems extreme consider the following. First, let me suggest that those who claim to be truly pro-life but say that they "would of course make an exception for the life of the woman" have in mind the kind of cases described above for ectopic pregnancy and a cancerous womb. They do not mean that one can directly and intentionally kill the child to save the mother; just as they would say quite generally that one cannot intentionally kill one person to save another.

Second, if abortion as direct killing of the child is to be allowed in this case, a principle will have been established, that it is sometimes right to kill one person to benefit another; this was noted earlier in discussing the rape case.

Third, *the pro-life-with-exceptions view* contains an inherent inconsistency, which *the total pro-life view* avoids. As pro-choice advocate Ronald Dworkin argues,

It is a very common view, for example, that abortion should be permitted when necessary to save the mother's life. Yet this exception is also inconsistent with any belief that the fetus is a person with a right to life.[14]

Fourth, couldn't one justify abortion to save the life of the woman by appeal to the right to self-defense? After all the BIW can be seen as an attacker threatening the woman's life, even if this is not its intention. Dworkin replies to this:

> Some people say that in this case a mother is justified in aborting a fetus as a matter of self-defense; but any safe abortion is carried out by someone else—a doctor—and very few people believe that it is morally justifiable for a third party, even a doctor, to kill one innocent person to save another.[15]

THE CHILD WITH SEVERE DEFORMITIES

As before in the rape case and the case of the life of the woman, it goes without saying that all who are pro-choice in general allow abortion in the case of child with a severe deformity. So, what is of interest here concerns those who say they are pro-life but allow this exception. As in the previous cases, let us consider the two main views:

1. *The pro-life-with-exceptions view:* it is right to kill the child in the womb in order to save him from a life of misery.
2. *The total-pro-life view:* abortion is wrong because it is the direct, intentional killing of a child; the desire to save the child from a life of misery is a noble end, but it does not justify the means used to obtain it, the killing of an innocent person.

The prediction that a child will be born with a severe disability may be mistaken. Suppose it is mistaken and the mother goes through with the abortion. Then a healthy child has been needlessly killed! Why not wait until birth to see if the child is healthy or deformed? If he is born with a disability, would those who hold to the pro-life-with-exceptions view favor killing the child then? Most people, including those who hold the pro-life-with-exceptions view, would strongly oppose killing a born child, even if he were deformed. But if it is wrong to kill a deformed child *after* birth, why would it be right to kill him *before* birth? It's the same child, whether in the womb or outside it.

One might ask those who favor ending the life of a child because of his deformity: *If* the child is to be killed because of this deformity, wouldn't it be better to do so painlessly with anesthesia after birth and thereby spare the child the pain that he would suffer in the abortion, rather than inflicting this terrible pain on him (or the great risk of it) in utero?

In general one can ask: Is it right to kill a *born* child for such a reason? If not, why a *pre-born* child? What's the difference? That is, can one consistently oppose the killing of a born child and also approve the killing of a pre-born child? *The total pro-life view* says one cannot. Peter Singer, a noted and highly influential pro-choice advocate, agrees with pro-life on this point. He says that "the *intrinsic* wrongness of killing the late fetus and the *intrinsic* wrongness of killing the newborn infant are not markedly different."[16] By "*intrinsic* wrongness" he means what is wrong in itself, in its very nature as an act; as opposed to what is wrong because of its adverse consequences, for example, "in most cases, to kill an infant is to inflict a terrible loss on those who love and cherish the child."[17] Thus pro-life, while strongly disagreeing with Singer's stand, credits him with being consistent. One cannot draw a reasonable line between infanticide, the killing of a born child, and abortion, the killing of a pre-born child.

Then there is the matter of principle. As noted in the case of rape, if we allow some abortions we set a precedent. *Allowing abortion for a child with deformities means establishing the principle that some abortions are justified.* By doing so we as a society are saying in essence, "Killing an innocent person is sometimes justified." Saying this is very dangerous. Which innocent persons may be killed? Who makes the decision? Who else but the woman? To say the decision is up to the woman is simply the pro-choice position, and the destruction of an attempted middle position, pro-life with exceptions.

In addition to these matters we would do well to take into consideration the thoughts of Dorothy Roberts, Professor of Law at Northwestern University:

> The reasons why some parents do not want a disabled child are varied. While some women may use genetic selection in an upwardly mobile quest for the "perfect child," others want to prevent their children from suffering the pain, illness, and physical limitations that accompany disabilities or worry that they are not capable of dealing with disability's social consequences. Yet given medical professionals' implicit directive favoring genetic selection and powerful stereotypes that negatively depict disabled people, many women are left with a false impression of the nature of parenting a disabled child and the quality of disabled people's lives (which genetic testing cannot predict). Pregnant women are rarely able to make truly informed decisions about what to do with test results because they, obstetricians, and counselors typically have little information about the lives of disabled people and their families. Moreover, some of the undesirable events likely to happen to a child with a serious disability that parents may reasonably wish to prevent, such as limited educational and employment opportunities are caused by social as much as physical impediments. Unable to count on societal acceptance or support, many women feel compelled to turn to genetic testing to ensure their chil-

dren's welfare. Without judging the morality of individual women's decisions, we must critically evaluate the social, political, and legal incentives for genetic testing as well as consequences of genetic testing for people with disabilities. Building on the disability critique, we must also question the role that the eugenic approach to disability plays in neoliberal governance.[18]

A GENERAL ANALYSIS OF THE PRO-LIFE-WITH-EXCEPTIONS VIEW

Table 17.1. Three Basic Views

I. *Total pro-choice.* No exceptions: Total commitment to a Woman's choice.	II. Pro-life-with-exceptions for the "hard cases." *The middle position.*	III. *Total pro-life.* No exceptions: Total commitment to child.

The middle position II is sharply criticized from both the other views:

I. The total pro-choice view says to the middle position: Why allow a woman to choose *only* in these cases? Why must it be the extreme need of the rape case, or her life, or a severely deformed child, to establish what is already the fundamental moral and legal right of a woman, choice? She has that right in every case, not just rape or the other difficult cases. No exceptions.

II. The total pro-life view says to the middle position: How can you claim you are "pro-life" when you are ready to sacrifice the child in the womb to the woman's "right" to have him killed? To be pro-life means a full commitment to every child. Every child is precious. Every child should be respected and protected. No exceptions.

An important feature of the abortion issue is that there seems to be no reasonable middle ground. In this way it is just like the civil rights issue. We would not be satisfied with granting some blacks some rights some of the time. Rather we insist that *all* civil rights are due to *all* of them *all* of the time, with no exceptions. Similarly, total pro-choice demands full abortion rights for all women all the time; and total pro-life demands full protection for every child in the womb all the time.

Table 17.2. Total Pro-Choice and Total Pro-Life

PC: Full commitment to *woman.* Her right over her body, always!	PL: Full commitment to *child.* Equal value, dignity of every child!

As a final point, let us note that abortions for the "hard cases" are extremely rare. The three most frequently cited "hard cases" in which some argue abortion might be justified are rape, incest, and protecting the life of the mother. However, women rarely report that they are seeking an abortion for any of these reasons. Here are the figures:

Rape: 0.3 percent

Incest: 0.03 percent

Protection of mother's life: 0.2 percent

In other words, out of one thousand women procuring abortion, only three cite rape as the primary reason, and only two cite protecting her life as the reason for the abortion. Out of ten thousand women procuring abortion, only three cite incest as a reason.[19]

V

CONCLUDING TOPICS

18

Safety Issues

PRO-CHOICE: KEEP ABORTION SAFE AND LEGAL

Some abortions will always occur, and no law can stop them. If a woman feels that she cannot continue with her pregnancy or feels this is not the right time, or any number of other similar reasons, she will usually opt to terminate that pregnancy; and she will do so regardless of whether or not abortion is legal. And so what we must do is keep abortion safe and legal. We must tell women that they have the right to choose, to do what they feel they must do, including terminating their pregnancy. And we must protect this right by keeping abortion legal.

We must remember the horror of back-alley abortions. Making abortion illegal means forcing desperate women to resort to horrible back-alley abortion butchers or to a self-induced abortion with a coat hanger, as in the days before *Roe v. Wade*. Both of these forms of abortion often result in the woman's death or maiming. The consequences of making abortion illegal would be truly disastrous. We should remind ourselves of what the abortion scene looked like before abortion was legalized and realize that we will return to that horror scene if abortion is once again made illegal. Susan Sherwin speaks to this point:

> The need for abortion can be very intense; no matter how appalling and dangerous the conditions, women from widely diverse cultures and historical periods have pursued abortions. No one denies that if abortion is not made legal, safe, and accessible in our society, women will seek out illegal and life-threatening abortions to terminate pregnancies they cannot accept. Anti-abortion activists seem willing to accept this cost, although liberals definitely

are not; feminists, who explicitly value women, judge the inevitable loss of women's lives that result from restrictive abortion policies to be a matter of fundamental concern.[1]

All this is fully supported by data from the National Abortion Federation:

Surgical abortion is one of the safest types of medical procedures. Complications from having a first-trimester aspiration abortion are considerably less frequent and less serious than those associated with giving birth. Early medical abortion (using medications to end a pregnancy) has a similar safety profile.

Abortion has not always been so safe. Between the 1880s and 1973, abortion was illegal in all or most U.S. states, and many women died or had serious medical problems as a result. Women often made desperate and dangerous attempts to induce their own abortions or resorted to untrained practitioners who performed abortions with primitive instruments or in unsanitary conditions. Women streamed into emergency rooms with serious complications—perforations of the uterus, retained placentas, severe bleeding, cervical wounds, rampant infections, poisoning, shock, and gangrene.

Around the world, in countries where abortion is illegal, it remains a leading cause of maternal death. An estimated 68,000 women worldwide die each year from unsafe abortions.

Many of the doctors who provide abortions in the United States today are committed to providing this service under medically safe conditions because they witnessed and still remember the tragic cases of women who appeared in hospitals after botched, illegal abortions. . . .

Generally, the earlier the abortion, the less complicated and safer it is. . . . Early medical abortions are limited to the first 9 weeks of pregnancy. Medical abortions have an excellent safety profile, with serious complications occurring in less than 0.5 percent of cases. . . . Complication rates are somewhat higher for surgical abortions provided between 13 and 24 weeks than for the first-trimester procedures. General anesthesia, which is sometimes used in surgical abortion procedures of any gestation, carries its own risks. . . .

There are some things women can do to lower their risks of complications. One way to reduce risk of complications is to have the abortion procedure early. Generally, the earlier the abortion, the safer it is. Asking questions is also important. Just as with any medical procedure, the more relaxed a person is and the more she understands what to expect, the better and safer her experience usually will be.

For more information, and for specific sources for the above material, please go to National Abortion Federation website, from which this was taken, www.prochoice.org. This website also contains a section entitled, "Women's Feelings after Abortion":

Women have abortions for a variety of reasons, but in general they choose abortion because a pregnancy at that time is in some way wrong for them. Such situations can cause a great deal of distress, and although abortion may be the best available option, the circumstances that led to the problem pregnancy may continue to be upsetting. Some women may find it helpful to talk about their feelings with a family member, friend, or counselor. Feelings of loss or of disappointment, resulting, for example, from a lack of support from the spouse or partner, should not be confused with regret about the abortion. Women who experience guilt or sadness after an abortion usually report that their feelings are manageable.

The American Psychological Association has concluded that there is no scientifically valid support or evidence for the so-called "post-abortion syndrome" of psychological trauma or deep depression. The most frequent response women report after having ended a problem pregnancy is relief, and the majority of women are satisfied that they made the right decision for themselves. See Abortion Myths: Post-Abortion Syndrome.

PRO-LIFE: LEGAL ABORTION IS NOT SAFE

The first thing we should remember is that legal abortion is *not safe for the child*. It kills the child. We should not legalize the killing of innocent persons.

But just as important, legal abortion is *not safe for the woman*. And so another reason for making abortion illegal is *for the sake of women*. Let us consider some of the specific points:

1. Women who have abortions risk physical damage such as a perforated uterus.
2. And psychological damage such as depression and guilt. "I killed my baby!"
3. *Legal abortion can kill.* Here are some examples: In 1978, *The Chicago Sun-Times* uncovered twelve legal abortion deaths that had never been reported.[2] Kimberly K. Neil died on May 22, 2000, as the result of an abortion performed on her by Dr. Kenneth Wright of the Family Planning Associates Medical Group in Fresno, California. This makes at least twelve dead abortion patients for FPA. Nicey Washington, 26, underwent an abortion at Ambulatory Surgery Center in Brooklyn, NY, June 6, 2000, and died shortly thereafter. L'Echelle Head, 21, died October 11, 2000, after an abortion at Dayton Women's Health Services. Diana Lopez, 25, and nineteen weeks pregnant, went to a Planned Parenthood clinic for an abortion, and died later on that same day. Leigh Ann Stephens Alford underwent an abortion at the hands of Dr. Malachy DeHenre at Summit Medical Center of Alabama on November 25, 2003. She died about eighteen hours after the clinic sent her home. Tamilia Russell, 15, died January 8, 2004, after a second trimester abortion at Woman Care Clinic in Lanthrup Village near

Detroit. Christin Gilbert, 19, was taken to Dr. George Tiller's Wichita abortion facility January 10, 2005, for a late-term abortion, one that takes several days [most likely a D&X or "partial birth" abortion]. She died of complications January 12. Laura Hope Smith, 22, died on the abortion table in Hyannis, Massachusetts, September 13, 2007. The abortionist was Dr. Rapin Osathanondh; he later pleaded guilty to involuntary manslaughter and sentenced to six months in jail.[3] Karnamaya Mongar died November 12, 2009, overdosed by an unlicensed teen, employed by Dr. Kermit Gosnell in his Philadelphia clinic.[4]

4. The zone of privacy: an additional factor that explains why legal abortion now is not safe for women is that abortion clinics operate under a zone of privacy: there is no legal requirement to report abortion complications.[5]

5. *Making abortion legal has actually made it more dangerous for women.* Since legalization, more women have died from abortion than before. Abortion is safer for the individual woman, but because there has been a huge increase in the number of abortions, there have actually been more deaths by abortion than before legalization.[6]

6. If women had known the effects of abortion beforehand, 95 percent would not have chosen it.[7]

7. If abortion is illegal, it protects those women who don't want an abortion, who want to keep their baby. It protects them against those who pressure them into having an abortion. They can appeal to the law and the need to follow it if there is such pressure. This is in line with the Richard Stith thesis examined earlier in chapter 16: "Legalized abortion was supposed to grant enormous freedom to women, but it has had the perverse result of freeing men and trapping women." And, quoting pro-choice advocate Catherine MacKinnon, "abortion does not liberate women; it frees male aggression."

8. We now have legal abortion in America. But what actually happens can be a nightmare. Consider the case of Kermit B. Gosnell, MD, of Philadelphia, as reported by Michelle Malkin:

> It's time to talk about the climate of death, in which the abortion industry thrives unchecked. Dehumanizing rhetoric, rationalizing language and a callous disregard for life have numbed America to its monstrous consequences. Consider the Philadelphia Horror. . . .
>
> The 281-page grand jury report released Wednesday [January 29, 2011] provides a bone-chilling account of how Gosnell's "Women's Medical Society" systematically preyed on poor, minority pregnant women and their live, viable babies. The report's introduction lays out the criminal enterprise that claimed the lives of untold numbers of babies—and their mothers.

"This case is about a doctor who killed babies and endangered women. What we mean is that he regularly and illegally delivered live, viable babies in the third trimester of pregnancy—and then murdered these newborns by severing their spinal cords with scissors. The medical practice by which he carried out this business was a filthy fraud in which he overdosed his patients with dangerous drugs, spread venereal disease among them with infected instruments, perforated their wombs and bowels—and, on at least two occasions, caused their deaths. Over the years, many people came to know that something was going on here. But no one put a stop to it."[8]

Malkin's report tells us who didn't put a stop to it:

- The Pennsylvania Department of Health.
- The Pennsylvania Department of State was "repeatedly confronted with evidence about Gosnell—including the clinic's unclean, unsterile conditions, unlicensed workers, unsupervised sedation, underage abortion patients."
- The Philadelphia Department of Public Health.

PRO-CHOICE: BACK-ALLEY ABORTIONS

One of the strongest pro-choice arguments for making or keeping abortion legal is that if abortions are made illegal, some women will try to get them anyway, and resort to back-alley abortion butchers. Many will die who would have lived if they had been allowed to obtain a safe legal abortion. Let us not return to the days of such horrors.

The statement "Nine Reasons Why Abortions Are Legal" spells this out clearly and convincingly. The first six are particularly significant for the horror of back-alley abortions.

Abortion is never an easy decision, but women have been making that choice for thousands of years, for many good reasons. Whenever a society has sought to outlaw abortions, it has only driven them into back alleys, where they became dangerous, expensive, and humiliating. Amazingly, this was the case in the United States until 1973, when abortion was legalized nationwide.

Thousands of American women died and thousands more were maimed before abortion was legal. For this reason and others, women and men fought for and achieved women's legal right to make their own decisions about abortion.

However, there are people in our society who still won't accept this. Some argue that even victims of rape or incest should be forced to bear the child. And now, having failed to convince the public or the lawmakers, certain of these people have become violent extremists, engaging in a campaign of intimidation and terror aimed at women seeking abortions and health professionals who work at clinics.

Some say these acts will stop abortions, but that is ridiculous. When the smoke clears, the same urgent reasons will exist for safe, legal abortions as have always existed. No nation committed to individual liberty could seriously consider returning to the days of back-alley abortions—to the revolting specter of a government forcing women to bear children against their will. Still, amid such attacks, it is worthwhile to repeat a few of the reasons why our society trusts each woman to make the abortion decision herself.

1. Laws against abortion kill women. To prohibit abortions does not stop them. When women feel it is absolutely necessary, they will choose to have abortions—even in secret, without medical care, in dangerous circumstances. In the two decades before abortion was legal in the United States, it's been estimated that nearly one million women per year sought out illegal abortions. Thousands died. Tens of thousands were mutilated. All were forced to behave as if they were criminals.

2. Legal abortions protect women's health. Legal abortion not only protects women's lives, it also protects their health. For tens of thousands of women with heart disease, kidney disease, severe hypertension, sickle-cell anemia, and severe diabetes and other illnesses that can be life-threatening, the availability of legal abortion has helped avert serious medical complications that could have resulted from childbirth. Before legal abortion, such women's choices were limited to dangerous illegal abortion or dangerous childbirth.

3. A woman is more than a fetus. There's an argument these days that a fetus is a "person" that is "indistinguishable from the rest of us," and that it deserves rights equal to women's. On this question, there is a tremendous spectrum of religious, philosophical, scientific, and medical opinion. It's been argued for centuries. Fortunately, our society has recognized that each woman must be able to make this decision, based on her own conscience. To impose a law defining a fetus as a "person," granting it rights equal to or superior to a woman's—a thinking, feeling, conscious human being—is arrogant and absurd. It only serves to diminish women.

4. Being a mother is just one option for women. Many hard battles have been fought to win political and economic equality for women. These gains will not be worth much if reproductive choice is denied. To be

able to choose a safe, legal abortion makes many other options possible. Otherwise an accident or a rape can end a woman's economic and personal freedom.

5. Outlawing abortion is discriminatory. Anti-abortion laws discriminate against low-income women, who are driven to dangerous self-induced or back-alley abortions. That is all they can afford. But the rich can travel wherever necessary to obtain a safe abortion.

6. Compulsory pregnancy laws are incompatible with a free society. If there is any matter which is personal and private, then pregnancy is it. There can be no more extreme invasion of privacy than requiring a woman to carry an unwanted pregnancy to term. If government is permitted to compel a woman to bear a child, where will government stop? The concept is morally repugnant. It violates traditional American ideas of individual rights and freedoms.[9]

The basic message can perhaps be best summed up in a challenging question, addressed to all "pro-lifers" who oppose legal abortion: *Do you want to return to the butchery of self-induced or back-alley abortions?*[10]

PRO-LIFE: BACK-ALLEY ABORTIONS

Pro-life responds with three main arguments:

First, it cannot be stressed enough that *nobody wants to return to back-alley abortions*. Both sides equally abhor the death of the woman as a horrible tragedy. Pro-choice says: the solution is to make abortion legal. Pro-life says: *every abortion*, legal or illegal, is a terrible tragedy. It is the death of an innocent person, a small child who is killed because he cannot protect himself. The solution is not to say that abortion—which is the killing of a small child—is all right, by legalizing it. The solution must aim at stopping *all* killing, not just some killing. To acclaim "safe, legal abortion" as the answer to the threat of back-alley abortions is to fail to recognize the abortion procedure as one that *always* results in the death of an innocent person. Mary Anne Warren, a supporter of a woman's right to abortion, acknowledges this when she says "the fact that restricting access to abortion has tragic side-effects does not, in itself, show that the restrictions are unjustified, since murder is wrong regardless of the consequences of prohibiting it."[11]

Second, there are several practical matters that clearly show why legalizing abortion is not the solution to the horror of back-alley abortions.

1. Abortionists working in a legal-abortion setting can be back-alley butchers. We have only to recall the case of Kermit B. Gosnell, MD,

discussed above. Such cases can occur in large part because of lack of sufficient oversight by government officials. And that in turn can be traced in part to the legal "zone of privacy" noted above, which is part of the confidentiality of legalized abortion. "Abortion is a private matter."

2. The flip side of this coin is that the historical record shows that when abortion was illegal in the United States, most abortions were not performed by "back-alley" butchers but by regular doctors. "Mary Calderone (then Medical Director of Planned Parenthood) and Nancy Howell Lee (a pro-choice researcher) both investigated the practice of criminal abortion in the pre-legalization era." They "estimated that 90 percent of all illegal abortions in the early 1960s were being done by physicians . . . either illegally or through loopholes in the law." The other 10 percent: "5 percent performed by trained non-physicians (medical and lay) [and] 5 percent performed by amateurs, either the woman herself or somebody else."[12] The pro-choice picture of massive deaths of women from back-alley abortionists does not square with the facts. There were of course deaths from illegal abortion back then, as there are deaths from legal abortion now, as we have seen. Both are scenes of horror. The answer is to stop abortion, which kills women; not to legalize it, which encourages killing.

3. Making abortion legal makes it more socially acceptable, and more easily attainable. The result is obvious: more women will seek abortions. Since a certain number of these abortions result in the death of the woman, the more abortions the greater the number of woman who die from them. So, legalizing abortion *increases* women's deaths; it does not decrease it, despite the pro-choice rhetoric. This was David Reardon's point noted above: *making abortion legal has actually made it more dangerous for women.* Since legalization, more women have died from abortion than before. Abortion is safer for the individual woman but because there has been a huge increase in the number of abortions, there have actually been more deaths by abortion than before legalization.

4. Finally, the way to stop back-alley abortionists such as Kermit B. Gosnell, MD, is not by legalizing abortion, which didn't stop him; but by the threat of financially ruinous civil lawsuits. A woman could sue an abortionist who attempted or completed an abortion resulting in physical or psychological damages. By making civil liability available women could take matters into their own hands, and not be dependent on the zeal and efforts of local police and prosecutors.[13] Civil lawsuits are difficult now because the abortion industry is protected by a legal shield, a zone of privacy, as noted above.

Third, there are several more fundamental points that should be noted:

- *The challenging question.* Are you against the killing of human beings? "Yes of course, that's why I oppose back-alley abortions." But to try to achieve this goal by saying that abortion should be legal and therefore allowed is to give the opposite answer. "No, I do not oppose the killing of a small pre-born human being; that's all right." This is what favoring legal abortion means. If we are against killing human beings, we must be against abortion, for abortion is the killing of a human being. If we are not, we have no basis for the pro-choice back-alley argument. Thus we have:
- *The self-contradiction.* The pro-choice back-alley argument is for life and for death at the same time: for the life of the woman and the death of the child. "Kill the child so the woman can live." Does it make any sense to say that? What we have is:
- *The double standard.* The pro-choice back-alley argument works by saying "the woman counts, but the child doesn't count." As the true alternative let me suggest:
- *The reality of the child destroyed in every abortion.* Abby Johnson was the Director of the Planned Parenthood Clinic in Bryan, Texas, when she was called in to assist at an ultrasound-guided abortion. "I could see the entire, perfect profile of a baby." Then the suction machine was put into place. "As the cannula [instrument attached to the end of the suction tube] pressed in, the baby began struggling to twist and turn away." Later: "The image of that tiny baby twisting and struggling kept replaying in my mind." In those few minutes her whole life changed. Coming into the procedure she was pro-choice; she wanted to save the lives of women who otherwise "might resort to some back-alley butcher."[14] Then she saw firsthand the reality of the child. And she saw that child sucked into a machine and destroyed. Legal abortion is not the answer.

IS ABORTION SAFER THAN CHILDBIRTH?

The history of this question is rather interesting. The Supreme Court considered it in its *Roe v. Wade* decision when it gave as a reason why the states might want to proscribe or regulate abortion as, "to protect the pregnant woman from submitting to a procedure that placed her life in serious jeopardy." However the Court also noted that, due to medical advances "abortion in early pregnancy . . . is now relatively safe. Mortality rates for women undergoing early abortions, where the procedure is legal, appear

to be as low as or lower than the rates for normal childbirth." (See www
.lifeissues.net.)

Since these words were issued from the Supreme Court both pro-life and
pro-choice have discussed this question, with their respective answers of *no*
and *yes;* each one to its own advantage in the raging abortion debate. What
is the truth of the matter?

Pro-life says no. Abortion is not safer than childbirth. It begins by pointing out that for the unborn child abortion is most definitely not safe; it has
a 100 percent mortality rate. It emphasizes a point of the greatest importance: childbirth is a natural process, one that a woman's body is designed
for—while abortion is an intrusive procedure that goes against the natural
order. Pro-life holds that the statistics on abortion deaths are unreliable in
the direction of under-reporting. After all, when a woman dies from abortion, no one puts that as the reason on the death certificate. She died from
"hemorrhaging." This is less socially abhorrent.

In an article in *The New England Journal of Medicine* David Reardon
documents the newest record-based research showing that the risk of death
from abortion is actually higher than death from childbirth. This research
is based on studies that examine pregnancy-associated mortality related to
abortion and to childbirth using a common standard and methodology. He
also documents that women face higher risk of psychiatric illness following
an abortion.[15]

Another study concluded: "Compared to women who carry to term,
women who abort are 3.5 times more likely to die within a year."

Now a recent, unimpeachable study of pregnancy-associated deaths in
Finland has shown that the risk of dying within a year after an abortion is
several times higher than the risk of dying after miscarriage or childbirth.
This well-designed record-based study is from STAKES, the statistical analysis unit of Finland's National Research and Development Center for Welfare and Health. Since Finland has socialized medical care, these records are
very accurate and complete.

Figure 18.1 shows that the age-adjusted odds ratio of women dying in
the year they give birth as being half that of women who are not pregnant,
whereas women who have abortions are 76 percent more likely to die in
the year following abortion compared to nonpregnant women. Compared
to women who carry to term, women who abort are 3.5 times more likely
to die within a year. Such figures are always subject to statistical variation
from year to year, country to country, study to study. For this reason, the researchers also reported what is known as "95 percent confidence intervals."
This means that the available data indicates that 95 percent of all similar
studies would report a finding within a specified range around the actual
reported figure.[16]

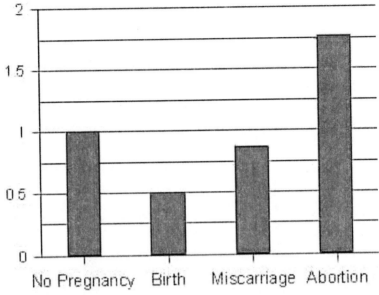

Figure 18.1. Total Deaths

Pro-choice says yes. Abortion is safer than childbirth. And it is not just safer but much safer! The Guttmacher Institute tells us, "The risk of abortion complications is minimal when the procedure is performed by a trained professional in a hygienic setting: Fewer than 1 percent of all U.S. abortion patients experience a major complication. The risk of death associated with abortion in the United States is less than 0.6 per 100,000 procedures, which is less than one-tenth as large as the risk associated with childbirth." (See www.guttmacher.org.)

However, the various pro-choice sources are not in agreement as to just how much safer abortion is than childbirth, as one can see from the following statistics. How much safer is abortion is than giving birth? We are told:

- Eleven times safer (www.gateway.org)
- Twelve times safer (www.sightline.org)
- Thirteen times safer (en.allexperts.com)
- Twenty times safer (www.pregnancyoptions.org)
- "Hundreds of times safer" according to Dr. LeRoy Carhart, a colleague of Dr. Tiller (www.old.harringtonreport.com)

There is obviously a problem here. Perhaps the problem lies in the gathering of the relevant data. That is, claims that abortion mortality rates are lower than maternal mortality rates related to childbirth, are based on comparing two sets of statistics: (1) Maternal mortality rates compiled by the National Center for Health Statistics (NCHS) through its National Vital Statistics System; and (2) the number of deaths reported to be abortion related by the Centers for Disease Control (CDC). This comparison is problematic for two general reasons. First, NCHS and CDC employ different standards and means of data collection. Second, both systems are prone to missing a large percentage of deaths associated with childbirth and abortion.

Death certificates are the primary source of data used by NCHS to compile mortality statistics through its National Vital Statistics System. In the United States, cause of death on death certificates is normally reported by the attending physician. In some cases, particularly when the cause of death is due to violent or unknown causes, medical examiners or coroners will make the final classification of causes. In either case, a recent pregnancy may not be recorded due to error or lack of knowledge on the part of the attending physician or coroner. More careful analyses in individual states reveal that 50 percent or more of death certificates for pregnant or recently pregnant women failed to note the pregnancy.

In many cases, the physician filing the death certificate may not know about a recent birth unless told by relatives. The physician is even less likely to know about a recent abortion, since most American women obtain abortions from specialists, not their own personal physicians. Similarly, interviews with relatives are less likely to be revealing in regard to abortion than they are in regard to childbirth, or even miscarriage. The deceased may not have told relatives about her abortion. Even if they are aware of it, relatives might refrain from telling the physician completing the death certificate about the abortion simply because they would not want it noted on this public record. There is also the risk that persons involved in reporting the death may deliberately obscure the underlying cause in cases of abortion-related death. This may be done either to protect families from potential embarrassment or to avoid the implication of malpractice against the abortion providers, who in some cases may also be the attending physician who is completing the death certificate.

Additional ambiguities arise in regard to efforts to accurately identify deaths that are related to pregnancy. The International Classification of Diseases ninth revision (ICD-9) defined "maternal death" as one which occurs while a woman is pregnant or within forty-two days of the termination of the pregnancy, regardless of the outcome (abortion, miscarriage, or delivery) and anatomical site of the pregnancy, where the death is judged to be caused by a disease related to or aggravated by the pregnancy or its management, excluding incidental deaths (www.lifeissues.net).

19

Going Beyond Abortion: The Unity Way

THE UNITY WAY: WOMAN AND CHILD GO TOGETHER

The pro-choice position focuses on the woman. The pro-life position focuses on the child. Is there a way to bring these two points of focus together? The unity way says there is. Let us now examine it.

The basic idea is that woman and child go together: help one and you help the other, harm one and you harm the other. Many women, probably most, choose abortion only reluctantly. Many do not really "choose" it but have their abortion because they feel they have no choice. They feel coerced. After working for twenty years in a pregnancy support community that helped women through unwanted pregnancies, executive director Kiki Latimer says that most women said, "I have to have an abortion; I have no choice." For most women facing an unwanted pregnancy "pro-choice" is a cruel lie: they feel they have no genuine choice. They feel coerced by other people, parents, boyfriends, college peers, and well-meaning friends; by circumstances such as lack of money; and by lack of support for what they really want to do, namely keep their baby. The unity way is dedicated to stopping this. There are several aspects.

It wants to provide a network of support for women who want to keep their baby but find it difficult to do so. It wants to re-educate society away from assuming that abortion is a natural and positive solution to difficult pregnancies. It wants to work towards a social climate where pregnancy is fully accepted in those types of cases where it is now frowned on. It opposes legalized abortion as providing what seems like an easy fix, but which really harms women in the long run. It also opposes it for the reason given above, that making abortion illegal affords women protection from

177

coercion. It opposes the abortion industry as a for-profit organization that exploits women.

THE UNITY WAY: ABORTION IS HARMFUL TO WOMEN

David Reardon is a major player in the unity way. One of his central themes is that abortion harms not only the child but the woman as well. As he puts it, "Abortion is inherently harmful to women. It is simply impossible to rip a child from the womb of a mother without tearing out a part of the woman herself."[1]

Reardon quotes Dr. Julius Fogel, a psychiatrist and obstetrician, and a long-time advocate of abortion, who has himself performed over twenty thousand abortions:

Every woman . . . has a trauma at destroying a pregnancy. A level of humanness is touched. This is a part of her own life. When she destroys a pregnancy, she is destroying herself. There is no way it can be innocuous. . . . Often the trauma may sink into the unconscious. . . . But it is not as harmless and casual an event as many in the pro-abortion crowd insist. A psychological price is paid. It may be alienation; it may be pushing away from human warmth, perhaps a hardening of the maternal instinct. Something happens on the deepest levels of a woman's consciousness when she destroys a pregnancy. I know that as a psychiatrist.[2]

Judge Edith H. Jones, of the Fifth Circuit Court of Appeals, in her opinion in *McCorvey v. Hill*, September 14, 2004, noted that:

there are about a thousand affidavits of women who have had abortions and claim to have suffered long-term emotional damage and impaired relationships from their decisions. Studies by scientists . . . suggest that women may be affected emotionally and physically for years afterward and may be more prone to engage in high-risk, self-destructive conduct as a result of having had abortions.[3]

According to a survey conducted by Reardon's Elliot Institute, the reactions of women who have had an abortion were as follows:

- Guilt—61.3 percent
- Sorrow—55.3 percent
- Depression—52.5 percent
- Unworthiness—52.4 percent
- Regret—52.1 percent
- Loneliness—45.2 percent
- Inner peace—3.0 percent

- Liberation—2.1 percent
- Happiness—2.1 percent

For more information, see the Elliot Institute's web page: www .afterabortion.org. Click on the research tab.

Once again we see that the woman and her child go together. Reardon says, "We are both pro-woman and pro-child. We . . . should help both the mother and her child. We believe that the legalization of abortion was not an advance for women's rights."[4]

As we have seen in chapter 18 at the end of the section, "Keep Abortion Safe and Legal," the idea that abortion is harmful to women is denied by the pro-choice side.

UNWANTED PREGNANCY VERSUS UNWANTED CHILD

It is usually assumed that an unwanted pregnancy means an unwanted child. Women with unwanted pregnancies are often heard to say: *I have to have an abortion because if I carry this baby to term I will love it too much to ever give it up for adoption.*

Women make a clear distinction between what is happening *to* their bodies (the pregnancy) and what is happening *in* their bodies (the baby). The pregnancy is unwanted and a burden for one reason or another; the child is not. They choose abortion before getting too attached to the child rather than having to face the pain of adoption or the difficulty of keeping a much loved child. The statement above is very telling of the state of mind in which many women choose abortion, a pain-filled decision that involves little or no choice.[5]

ABORTION IS ABOUT FAMILY RELATIONSHIPS

It is usually assumed that abortion is a matter of constitutional law. Perhaps this should be reconsidered. Helen Alvaré suggests it is family law rather than constitutional law that provides the best means of understanding the issue of abortion. She explains:

> It is becoming increasingly apparent that abortion is about family relationships, not simply a contest between the state and a woman who happens to be pregnant. Scientific discoveries about human development and the testimonies of women who have had or have considered an abortion suggest that it is family law rather than constitutional law that provides the best means of understanding the issue of abortion.

A person who spends even a little time in the company of post-aborted women and clients of crisis pregnancy centers will come away convinced that these women experienced their pregnancies as motherhood dilemmas. Their internal debates about abortion did not revolve around the question: "Should I kill?" Rather, they wondered, "Should I, can I, be a mother now?"

Abortion is a family issue in other ways as well, as explained in the affidavits of 180 women filed with the U.S. Supreme Court in the second partial-birth abortion case, *Gonzales v. Carhart*. They described how abortion affected their mothering, how siblings of aborted children experienced repercussions of the abortion, and how they became pregnant again quickly after the abortion in order to have a "replacement baby."

Justice Kennedy's majority opinion in *Gonzales v. Carhart* indicated that the Court itself was beginning to understand abortion in a family context. The opinion states outright that a bond exists between a woman and her biological offspring and that the severance of this bond via abortion might cause significant suffering for the woman. The majority wrote that "respect for human life finds an ultimate expression in the bond of love the mother has for her child." The Court's use of language like "mother" and "child" also indicates a family law context. So does the majority's choice of labels for the unborn including "a living organism while within the womb," "unborn child," "infant life," and "child assuming the human form." The Court continued: "Some women come to regret their choice to abort the infant life they once created and sustained."[6]

AN ALTERNATIVE TO ABORTION: ADOPTION

There is a positive, life-affirming, and dreadfully difficult alternative to abortion. If the mother cannot take care of the child herself, she can place him for adoption. Isn't it better to give the child the opportunity to live than to kill him? There are many couples who would love to have a child but cannot. How tragic that while some people desperately want a child but cannot have one, others destroy a child that could have been given to those who wanted him or her! Isn't it better to let the child live and then give her to a loving family to adopt, than to choose to have her killed by abortion? Certainly there is pain here in either case. But some kinds of pain are more bearable than others.

A woman faces a painful dilemma here. On the one hand, she does not want to have her child destroyed. On the other hand, it is terribly difficult and agonizing for her to give up her child after she has bonded with him for nine months. She knows her baby is out there somewhere, but she cannot have him. Still, is this not a worthy price to pay in order to allow the child to live, to make the couple who adopts him immensely happy, and to save oneself from the guilt and grief of having destroyed one's own child through abortion? Or at least the risk of that?

There is no painless way of resolving the adoption-abortion dilemma; to suggest otherwise would be untrue. Given an unwanted pregnancy, no matter which avenue is chosen— keep, give up for adoption, or abort—life as before is gone forever.

A FINAL NOTE

Sexual values and associated sexual behavior in our society range from committed sex with only one partner within the context of marriage to recreational sex with multiple partners. Pregnancy followed by abortion is clearly one among many possible consequences of sexual behavior. This shows us that, regardless of our values about sex, the sex act remains a deeply serious human choice with potentially painful consequences, especially for women, but for men as well. Therefore all of us, whether pro-life or pro-choice, would be well advised to think carefully and responsibly before engaging in sexual behaviors that can lead to a pregnancy.

20

Ultimate Issues

FIRST SET OF ULTIMATE ISSUES: WHAT IS ABORTION?

(1) The pro-life position is that abortion is *an unspeakable crime.*

For it is the killing of an innocent child, who cannot defend himself or speak for himself; and doing so by horrible, brutal methods that cause terrible pain.

The pro-choice position is that abortion is the legitimate exercise of a woman's right over her body! For the right to abortion is basically the right of a woman to control her life, and achieve personal and social equality with men.

(2) Pro-choice no-duty-to-sustain versus pro-life active-intentional killing.

Pro-choice, using Thomson's Violinist Argument, supports a woman's right to end her pregnancy by claiming she has *no duty to sustain* the fetus and to allow it to remain in her body, even if it is a person; and thus she *may have it removed by abortion.*

Pro-life claims abortion is not a mere withholding of support. It is the *active killing* of a small child by brutal, painful methods, not merely allowing the child to die; it is the *intentional killing* of the child, not merely foreseeing that the child will die.

For pro-choice: Boonin defends the Violinist Argument against these pro-life objections by his analogies: the trolley driver may actively run over the person on the tracks and the bomber may intentionally kill the innocent people on the roof of the ammunition factory. In a morally significant parallel way, abortion as actively and intentionally killing the child is permissible.

For pro-life: First, abortion is not like Boonin's fanciful cases. Thus even if running over a person on the tracks and bombing the innocent people are morally permissible, it does not follow that abortion as the active killing of a child is morally permissible. Second, is it really permissible for the trolley driver and the bomber to actively and intentionally kill these innocent persons? If not, the parallel to abortion breaks down and with it the Violinist Argument.

(3) Does a woman have the duty to sustain the BIW because it is her own?

Pro-choice says no. Thomson in her Violinist Argument and Boonin in his defense of Thomson claim that the mere fact of biological relatedness does not generate a duty for the woman to sustain the child; she would have this duty only on the basis of some voluntary action. That is, what makes a woman morally responsible for a child is not that she is in fact his biological mother but rather that she has chosen to accept this child.

Pro-life says yes. The biological bond is the basis of parental responsibility. "Are all children adopted?" Surely they are not. But Andrew Peach argues that this is what logically follows from these pro-choice claims: "All children, even those who are cared for by their biological parents, are in essence adopted."[1] Furthermore, if one comes upon a child in need of assistance, accidently and through no fault of one's own, one would be morally responsible for taking care of that child until other help arrived.

(4) The question of pain.

Pro-life claims that abortion is also wrong because it causes pain to the BIW, especially in the later stages; and that it is wrong for this reason regardless of whether the BIW is a person or not; and regardless of Violinist Argument considerations. And that this is clear when we consider the methods of abortion, especially late-term, such as "partial-birth" abortion.

Pro-choice counters that the matter of fetal pain is still a controversial question; and that we should not let it distract us from what is mainly at stake in the abortion issue: the woman, her well-being, her autonomy, her right to control her life, her right to her body; and of course the prevention of harm and pain for her.

SECOND SET OF ULTIMATE ISSUES:
WHAT IS A HUMAN PERSON?

(5) Pro-life person-from-the-very-beginning versus pro-choice not-a-person thesis.

The pro-life view is that a human being is a full person from the very beginning, a person all the way through his or her existence. He or she does not become a full person gradually as his or her physical development progresses. He or she does not become a full person at some particular point in his or her development (being a mere half or quarter of a person at an earlier stage), such as viability or higher brain functions or birth, so that this would be a line marking his or her beginning as a full person. Being a person is not an achievement; rather it is our very essence as human beings. We *are* persons. We do not become persons.

We can see this clearly by considering personal identity. I am now the same person I was five minutes ago, five years ago, and so on, to the moment of my birth. This process can be continued backwards through all the phases of my development in the womb. All this development represents changes happening to *me*, the same person all the way through this development; and, the same person who is now me. If I am now a person, with the right to live, I was a person at all these earlier phases of my existence after my birth; but equally all the times before my birth, the times I was in my mother's womb, when that BIW was me. This is the continuum argument, that a human person's existence is a single continuum, whose first phase is the time in the womb. Abortion is wrong for the same reason as killing a born person: it ends the life of a human person during an earlier phase of her existence along the continuum of life, when she is pre-born.

We can also see this through the SLED argument: the only differences between pre-born and born human beings are Size, Level of development, Environment and degree of Dependency. The pro-life view is that these are all morally irrelevant.

The pro-choice view is the not-a-person thesis. A human being is not a person from the very beginning; he is not a person all the way through his existence. Rather, he either becomes a person gradually as his physical development progresses. Or he becomes a person at some particular point in his development, such as viability or higher brain functions or birth, so that this is a line marking the beginning of a person. Being a person is an achievement; we are not persons simply because we are human.

What calls for respect are not simply human beings in the biological sense, members of the species *Homo sapiens*, but persons understood in a strict and proper philosophical sense. Thus Michael Tooley argues, first, that an entity is not a person and therefore cannot have a right to life unless it is capable of having an interest in its own continued existence; and, second, that an entity is not capable of having an interest in its own continued existence unless it possesses, at some time, the concept of a continuing self, or subject of experiences and other mental states. That is, self-consciousness is needed for being a person with a right to continued existence.

Clearly these do not apply to the fetus. There is indeed a continuum in human existence, but it is not the continuum of personal life; it is merely a biological continuum. One and the same biological organism grows and develops in the womb. After a time it achieves personhood, and then it calls for respect. Before that the right of the woman over her body is the only morally decisive matter. Abortion is justified because it is not the killing of a person.

From this we see the pro-choice view: level of development is morally relevant. Only when the fetus reaches sufficient development do we see the features essential to being a person indicated by Michael Tooley.

Which of these two views is correct? If we are purely physical beings, merely complicated biological organisms with highly developed brains, then the pro-choice view is probably correct. On the purely physical level a zygote or early embryo can hardly be seen as a person. It has none of the features we commonly associate with being a person. It is only if we see this zygote or early embryo as already the same being who will later clearly be a person that we can say this early being is already a person; the same person who will later be born and grow up. "I was once a tiny baby in my mother's womb." That is, we see human beings—all human beings, born and pre-born—as not merely physical beings, biological organisms, but as persons, as beings who have a spiritual element, a soul. Indeed a human person in the core of his being, in his essence, is a spiritual reality as we can see from the reality of consciousness. I am a conscious being, and my consciousness, though it depends on my body, especially my brain, is not as such something physical. It has no physical features such as length, weight, or color. I am a corporeal person, where "person" refers to my spiritual being and "corporeal" to my bodily being. Spiritual here does not imply anything religious, but only something beyond a material existence: mind, soul, spirit, essence, nonmaterial core.

Summary of Ultimate Question 5

Pro-life continuum view. A pre-born human being:

- Is a real person: the same person, the same "I" all the way through.
- Has the being of a person even though he cannot yet function as a person.
- Has the same value, dignity, and rights as a born human being.
- Is only smaller, less developed, in a different environment and more dependent.

Pro-choice achievement view. A pre-born human being:

- Is not a real person, only a potential person, a mere biological organism.
- Does not have the being of a person because it cannot function as a person.

- Has none of the value, dignity, or rights of a born human being.
- Achieves being a real person only after sufficient development.

(6) Pro-choice denial of strong personal identity versus pro-life strong personal identity.

Pro-life rests on strong personal identity: I was once a baby in my mother's womb; I am a person now, and I was equally a person then. The pro-choice achievement view is a direct denial of this. In its place the continued existence of a human being is merely a continuity of various psychological states, which do not reach back to an early beginning of the person that is now me. I am now so different from the baby that was "me" as a newborn baby that it is inaccurate and misleading to say that that baby was really me, the same person I am now. There are a series of psychological states that follow each other like phases of the weather in a particular place, all associated with my body. They are largely but of course not entirely connected by memory. Therefore the fact that I am now a person does not entail that all of these phases connected with my body were really phases of one and the same continuous person; the earliest phases were not phases of me, the person who exists now.

For pro-life the continuum argument is basic to its case. For pro-choice the not-a-person thesis and the arguments supporting it are offered as countering the pro-life continuum argument that the BIW is a person. With Parfit we have a direct attack on the continuum argument by a denial of its core tenet: strong personal identity. Strong personal identity, as we saw, means that whether a given future person is me or not me is an all-or-nothing affair: any future person is either me or he is not me, there is no in-between or gray area. It means that I am a persisting subject of experiences, which make all these experiences *my* experiences, tied together as the experiences of one and the *same* person.

For pro-choice: Parfit denies all this. On his view each of us is not a persisting subject of experiences, but rather a series of entities existing over time, tied together by psychological continuities, where memories are passed from earlier phase to later ones like a baton in a relay race. Persons are like clubs or political parties: there is no single, correct answer to the question "is it now the same club, or political party?" It is basically a matter of "take your pick." A future person may be partly me and partly not me. But all this doesn't matter; it is not (strong) personal identity that matters, but only some degree of psychological continuity. And, Parfit argues, that is just as good as old-fashioned survival, survival as the *same* person, the *same* me.

For pro-life: All this surely runs counter to what we all believe about ourselves and others; what we intuitively assume in daily life. Surely the kind, elderly gentleman who looks very much like the Nazi war criminal either really is the same person or really is not the same person. We may not know which it is, or we may believe falsely in either direction; but surely there is an absolute fact of the matter. It cannot possibly be a matter of degree or a case of take-your-pick. That is why we can demand personal responsibility for past actions. The same is true when we consider our own lives. I have changed considerably during the sixty or so years since I started college. But there can be absolutely no doubt that it was *me*, the *same person*, who changed over these years, and that I am now that same person as I was then. In fact the changes make sense and are significant only as changes occurring in the life of one and the same person.

Countless other examples and applications could be cited here. Marital fidelity means that each person is committed for the rest of his or her life to *the same person* as the one he or she originally married. Holding a person accountable now for doing x makes sense only if he or she is *the same person* as the one who did x in the past. If I am grateful to you now, that can only be because you now are *the same person* as the one who favored me in the past; and because I now am *the same person* as the one who received this favor in the past. This does not mean that we, as persons, do not change. Of course we change! But those changes happen to us, in us.

Parfit raises some interesting questions and confronts us with some fascinating puzzles. What would happen if I were to divide, my left brain going into one body and my right brain going into another? What would happen to *me*? And suppose my brain were to be significantly modified so as to break down the usual psychological continuity that I have with my past, so that I retain only a small portion of my current memories and personality traits. Again, what would happen to *me*? In reply let us look at the following considerations:

First, no one really knows what would happen in such cases; or indeed if such bizarre things could even happen. So much of what Parfit claims seems to be pure speculation.

Second, given this, the fact that we may not have clear and compelling answers to Parfit's challenges to strong personal identity doesn't destroy the reality of this identity. There are somewhat comparable puzzles about time. If the past is gone and therefore no longer real, and the future is not yet here and so also not real, and the present moment vanishes as soon as it arrives, it could be said that there is nothing left, and that therefore time is unreal. Yet it clearly isn't unreal; it is undeniably real, as when you are rushing to get to work on time. That we cannot solve challenging and intriguing puzzles about certain fundamental items in our immediate experience does not mean these items are not fully real. Personal identity is like time in this respect. For each there are puzzles that may stump us. But each one is so much part of our daily existence that it is impossible and senseless to deny it. Even Parfit puts his name on his books, implying that he is the same person now as the one who wrote the books in the past. And he probably considers his mother as the woman who gave birth to him. These all testify to the reality of the strong personal identity which he denies.

Third, if we now conclude that Parfit has not destroyed strong personal identity with his far-out cases, we can also conclude that the continuum argument for pro-life, for establishing the reality of the child in the womb, has not lost its foundation, strong personal identity.

As a final point, it is interesting to note that Parfit himself occasionally has misgivings about his view. He asks: "Do I find it impossible to believe this View?"

> What I find is this. I can believe this view on the intellectual or reflective level. I am convinced by the arguments in favor of this view. But I think it is likely that, at some other level, I shall always have doubts. . . . But I expect that I would never completely lose my intuitive belief in the Non-Reductionist View [strong personal identity].[2]

(7) Pro-life the being-functioning distinction versus pro-choice the achievement view.

If the pro-choice achievement view is correct, then *functioning* as a person must be the operative term, with being a person reducible to "that which now functions as a person or has done so in the past." If the pro-life person-from-the-beginning view is correct then *being* a person is the operative term, and functioning is seen as what a person essentially can do after sufficient development. That is, the ultimate issue between pro-choice and pro-life can be seen in terms of the being-functioning distinction and the achievement view. Pro-choice denies the moral relevance of the being-functioning distinction as it is used by pro-life. That is, pro-choice simply defines being as able to function; that is, as having achieved the capacity to function, and it thereby adopts the achievement view. Pro-life is a denial of the achievement view. We are persons in our very nature as human beings; we do not achieve being a person sometime during our physical or psychological development. Contrary to pro-choice, pro-life says that being a person does not depend on achieving anything. Thus the BIW counts as a person simply because it has the being of a person even though it cannot yet function as a person.

In brief: On the pro-choice achievement view you count as person when you achieve *functioning* as a person. On the pro-life view you do not need to be able to function as a person; *being* a person is sufficient to count as a person.

THIRD SET OF ULTIMATE ISSUES:
FURTHER MORAL CONSIDERATIONS

The ultimate issue between pro-life and pro-choice as formulated in terms of the being-functioning distinction and its relation to the achievement view can be used to throw light on other topics. Let us now review some of the topics discussed earlier, mainly in part III.

(8) *Drawing Lines.*

We examined ten suggested places to draw the line to mark the beginning of a human person. Setting aside conception-fertilization, which is an issue of its own, each of the other lines presents difficulties: why is *that* the place to draw the line and not some other? Is the difference really significant enough to mark the radical contrast between a nonperson and a person? Pro-life says no. It claims that for each of these lines the same being is present on both sides of it. This means that no line marks any real difference with regard to *being* a person: the person is there before as well as after. He does not achieve his being a person by acquiring something represented by any of the lines; he has this being in his very nature. Pro-choice claims that there is a real beginning to *being* a person, marked by one of these lines; the one that represents achieving personhood by the attaining of the feature necessary for being a person, such as self-consciousness. The contrast in the two views also turns on functioning as a person:

Clearly these lines have a bearing on *functioning* as a person. A baby after birth interacts with others in a way not possible before birth. The presence of organized cortical brain activity is a significant milestone in the child's development as a functioning person. Sentience is basic to functioning as a person. Pro-choice claims that *functioning* as a person is primary: being a person must be defined in terms of functioning as a person; to have the being of a person one must be able to function as a person, either now or at some time in the past. Being a person is an achievement, and it is attained by being able to function as a person. Pro-life claims that *being* a person is primary: you have the being of a person before you can actually function as a person. Your capacity to function as a person depends on the more basic reality that you have the being of a person. A tiny human being in the womb, near the beginning of his existence, has the being of a person and with this the basic inherent capacity to function as a person, which will gradually develop into the capacity to actually function as a person. The tiny human already has his being as a person; it is not an achievement attained later.

In short: For pro-life *being* a person is primary, and the various lines have no significance in terms of being a person. They are of interest only in terms of the development necessary for acquiring the capacity to function as a person. For pro-choice *functioning* as a person is primary, and the lines are significant precisely in the latter way: as marking possible places where the development necessary for acquiring the capacity to function as a person takes place, thus indicating that personhood has been achieved.

(9) *The Agnostic Position.*

If it is concluded that these lines do not work, it might be natural to say that it is simply not known when a human person begins to exist. This represents one option, and it is probably employed by many people. But it is not without its difficulties and limitations. Perhaps what we should say is that it is not known when *functioning* as a person begins. Pro-life will say that this doesn't matter, since *being* a person is what counts and that is there all along; the development of functioning is what it is because the being of the person is already there. Pro-choice says that *being* is achieved only through sufficient *functioning*; and if we do not know when functioning as a person begins, we also do not know when being a person begins.

(10) *The Gradualist Position.*

This represents another option employed by some people. Pro-lifers will say that gradualism is false when applied to the *being* of a person, but valid when applied to *functioning* as a person. There is no single place in the development of human life where functioning begins. It is a continuous and gradual development all the way through: we gradually develop our basic inherent capacities to function as persons. Pro-choicers who adopt the gradualist position will say that gradualism does apply to *being* a person; and that consequently later abortions should be taken more seriously than earlier ones. Early ones are morally justified, some later ones are not justified, with a gray area in between.

(11) *The Notion of Potential Person.*

Pro-choice will typically maintain that the BIW is not an actual person deserving our respect and protection but merely a potential person. For it has not yet achieved what is necessary for being an actual person. Until that achievement is attained, in terms of the capacity to actually function as a person, there is no real, actual person. Potentiality for something is not equivalent to actuality. Pro-life will say that the BIW is an actual person. The notion of potential, false when applied to *being* a person, is perfectly valid when applied to *functioning* as a person. If "person" is taken as "functioning person," then clearly a child in the womb or just born is only potentially such a person. That is, what is potential about the child is not her *being* as a person but rather her *functioning* as a person. She is not a potential person, but rather a *potentially functioning* actual person. To be a potentially functioning person already ensures that one is an actual, full person, for a potentially functioning person must necessarily be a person.

FOURTH SET OF ULTIMATE ISSUES: OTHER ITEMS

(12) The pro-choice feminist quality-of-life argument says abortion is justified to preserve and further the quality of life of women, and to ensure the basic equality of men and women in society. Pro-life counters that these are undoubtedly worthy goals but that it is wrong to kill a baby in order to achieve them.

(13) The pro-choice general quality-of-life argument says abortion is justified to preserve and further the quality of life of people in general, including the insurance that every child will be a wanted child, and a healthy child; and to ensure that humankind is not overwhelmed by overpopulation. Pro-life again counters that these are surely worthy goals but that it is wrong to kill a baby in order to achieve them.

(14) Should abortion be legal or illegal? If the pro-life position is correct, abortion should be illegal so that we protect the child's right to live. Killing pre-born babies should be seen in the same way as killing born babies: morally wrong and illegal. If the pro-choice position is correct, abortion should be legal so that we protect a woman's right to choose. Abortion is not like killing a baby; it is either the destroying of a biological organism or the exercise of a woman's right over her body, her right to not sustain the life of the being inside her body.

(15) Does rape justify abortion? Total pro-choice and the "pro-life with exceptions" middle position say yes. We must have *compassion* on the woman. Even if one says abortion is generally wrong, one must be flexible and allow reasonable exceptions. Total pro-life says no: *every* child must be respected and protected, with no exceptions. Abortion does not really help women; it even hurts them more. And allowing abortion for some cases where it is felt to be needed opens the door to all cases where it may be felt to be needed, as decided by the woman; and thus leads logically to the standard pro-choice position, and thus the abandoning of the attempted middle position.

(16) Keep abortion safe and legal? Pro-choice says yes. Let us not make it illegal and return to the days of back-alley abortion butchers. Legal abortion is a safe medical procedure that benefits women by allowing them to take control of their lives. Women feel a sense of relief when they can end an unwanted pregnancy. Pro-life says no: legal abortion is not safe. It is not safe for the child; it kills the child. It is not safe for the woman either. It is an invasive procedure that can harm the woman physically; in some cases legal abortion even kills the woman. Abortion can also hurt women emotionally. Many women later come to regret their decision: "I have killed my baby!" Abortion is destructive, not safe; it should not be legally allowed.

FINAL SET OF ULTIMATE ISSUES:
IDENTIFYING WITH THOSE INVOLVED

Pro-Choice: Identify with the Woman

1. The BIW is not a real person, it is not a child. It is a mere biological organism. It has not yet achieved the level of development necessary to give it the status of being a person.
2. Therefore it does not have the right to life that the rest of us have.
3. The woman has no duty to sustain the fetus. Therefore, she has the right to abort it.
4. Golden Rule: If I were in the woman's position, I would want the right to choose a safe and legal abortion. Do this for the woman.

Pro-Life: Identify with the Child

1. The BIW is a real person, a child, the same baby who will later be a born baby.
2. Therefore he has the same right to life as the rest of us.
3. Abortion is killing the child by horrible, painful methods.
4. Golden Rule: If I were a child in danger of being killed, I would want you to try to save me, to stand up for me. Do this for the child in womb.

Unity Way: Identify with Both the Woman and the Child

1. Identify with the child, support the child—and you will also support the woman.
2. Identify with the woman, support the woman—and you will also support the child.
3. Harm the child—and you will also harm the woman.

Notes

CHAPTER 1: INTRODUCTION

1. Ian Shapiro (ed.), *Abortion: The Supreme Court Decisions, 1965–2000* (Indianapolis: Hackett, 2001), Roe v. Wade, section IX, 40 and 42.

2. Based on a statement presented to the U.S. Supreme Court by over two hundred doctors before the court handed down its famous *Roe v. Wade* decision, January 22, 1973. *Motion and Brief Amicus Curiae of Certain Physicians, Professor and Fellows of the American College of Obstetrics and Gynecology in Support of Appellees*, 8–29.

3. Landrum B. Shettles and Robert Rugh, *From Conception to Birth: The Drama of Life's Beginnings* (New York: Harper and Row, 1971), 54.

CHAPTER 2: THE FEMINIST QUALITY OF LIFE ARGUMENT

1. Susan Sherwin, *No Longer Patient: Feminist Ethics and Health Care* (Philadelphia: Temple University Press, 1992), 101–2. Numbers have been added; capital letters at the beginning of items 2, 8, and 11 have been added.

2. Based on Sherwin, 102.

3. Based on Sherwin, 102–3.

4. Based on Sherwin, 104.

5. Based on Sherwin, 111.

6. Alison M. Jaggar, "Abortion Rights and Gender Justice Worldwide: An Essay in Political Philosophy," in Michael Tooley, Celia Wolf-Devine, Philip E. Divine, and Alison M. Jaggar, *Abortion: Three Perspectives* (New York and Oxford: Oxford University Press, 2009), 144.

7. Ibid., 147–49.

CHAPTER 3: THE GENERAL QUALITY OF LIFE ARGUMENT

1. Quoted in K. B. Welton, "An Unwanted Child Justifies Abortion," in Charles P. Cozic and Stacey L. Tipp (eds.), *Abortion: Opposing Viewpoints* (San Diego: Greenhaven Press, 1991), 127.

2. Constance Robertson, *The Religious Case for Abortion*, 1983. Quoted in *Abortion: Opposing Viewpoints*, 126.

3. Peter Singer, *Practical Ethics*, 2nd ed. (Cambridge: Cambridge University Press, 1993), 184.

4. Welton, 127. For a development of the general Quality of Life position, see Peter Singer, *Practical Ethics*; and *Rethinking Life and Death: The Collapse of Our Traditional Ethics* (New York: St. Martin's Griffin, 1994); and Jonathan Glover, *Causing Death and Saving Lives* (Penguin Books, 1977).

CHAPTER 4: THE NOT-A-PERSON ARGUMENT

1. Based on Sherwin, 108–11.

2. Based on Sherwin, 111.

3. Mary Anne Warren, "On the Moral and Legal Status of Abortion." *The Monist*, vol. 57 (1973). Reprinted in Joel Feinberg (ed.), *The Problem of Abortion*, 2nd ed. (Belmont, CA: Wadsworth Publishing Co., 1984), 111.

4. Ibid., 111–12. Italics in original. Capital letters at the beginning of each numbered item have been added.

5. Michael Tooley, "In Defense of Abortion and Infanticide," in Feinberg, 132.

6. Ibid.

7. Tooley, "Why a Liberal View Is Correct," in *Abortion: Three Perspectives*, 9.

8. Ibid., 10.

9. Ibid.

10. Feinberg, 132–33.

11. Tooley, *Abortion: Three Perspectives*, 61-62.

12. David Boonin, *A Defense of Abortion* (New York: Cambridge University Press, 2003), 19–90. The specific theme, and the title, of chapter 2 is "The Conception Criterion." But what he says there applies not only to the question whether conception marks the beginning of a human person's existence but also to the status of the fetus in all its phases, whether or not it is a human person.

13. The first of these three arguments is in sections 2.1–2.4 of this chapter, 20–33. The second is in section 2.5, 33–45. The third is in sections 2.6–2.7, 45–56. There is an overview of these arguments on pages 45–46.

14. Ibid., 23.

15. Ibid., 24. The species essence argument is on pages 23–25.

16. See page 25.

17. Ibid., 27. The kindred species argument is on pages 26–27.

18. Ibid., 40. The slippery slope argument is discussed on pages 33–45. The reference to "Thomson" is to Judith Jarvis Thomson whose essay we will discuss in our next chapter. In the remaining part of this section Boonin defends his rebuttal to the slippery slope argument by answering various objections.

19. Ibid., 48.

20. Boonin's analysis and refutation of the potentiality argument as summarized here is on pages 45-56.

21. Marjorie Reiley Maguire, "Symbiosis, Biology, and Personalization" and Lynn M. Morgan, "When Does Life Begin? A Cross-Cultural Perspective on the Personhood of Fetuses and Young Children" in Edd Doerr and James W. Prescott, *Abortion Rights and Fetal 'Personhood'* (Long Beach, CA: Centerline Press, 1989), 11–19 and 97–114 respectively. As we shall see later in chapter 11 Mary Anne Warren holds an essentially similar view when it comes to drawing the line marking the beginning of a person's existence, namely at birth. It is her not-a-person argument in terms of the five features listed above in this chapter that places her in the same category as Tooley and Boonin. Susan Sherwin's version of the not-a-person argument has significant similarities to the version we are considering here.

22. Ibid., 11.

23. Ibid., 13.

24. Ibid., 14.

25. Ibid., 15.

26. Ibid., 97–101. The first three are on pages 97–99, one on each page; the last two are on page 101. Numbers have been added; a footnote reference has been omitted.

27. Joel Feinberg, "Potentiality, Development, and Rights," in Feinberg, 147–48. In his rejection of potentiality as sufficient for personhood, Feinberg echoes Boonin's argument above.

28. Boonin, 115–29.

29. See "The Moral Significance of Birth," in *Hypathia* vol. 4, 3 (Fall 1989). Reprinted in Louis P. Pojman and Francis J. Beckwith (eds.), *The Abortion Controversy: A Reader* (Boston and London: Jones and Bartlett, 1994), 425–43.

30. Michael Tooley, *Abortion and Infanticide* (Oxford: Clarendon Press, 1983), 407–25.

31. Ibid., 411–12.

32. Ibid., 424.

33. Singer, *Practical Ethics*, 169.

34. Ibid., 173. Italics in original. See also Singer's *Rethinking Life and Death*, 210 ff.

CHAPTER 5: THE NO-DUTY-TO-SUSTAIN ARGUMENT

1. Martha Brandt Bolton, "Responsible Women and Abortion Decisions," in Onora O'Neill and William Ruddick (eds.), *Having Children: Philosophical and Legal Reflections on Parenthood* (New York: Oxford University Press, 1979), 42.

2. Judith Jarvis Thomson, "A Defense of Abortion," *Philosophy & Public Affairs*, vol. 1, no. 1, 1971. Reprinted in Feinberg, 173–87. Page references are to Feinberg.

3. Ibid., 175.

4. Ibid., 182.

5. Ibid., 179.

6. Ibid., 180.

7. Ibid., 87.

8. Ibid.

9. Taken from the Planned Parenthood website.

10. The Free Dictionary. Partial birth abortion. See www.medical-dictionary.thefreedictionary.com. September 15, 2011.

11. "*Statement on So-Called 'Partial Birth Abortion' Laws by the American College of Obstetricians and Gynecologists,* " 2002-FEB-13, at: http:/www.acog.org/.

12. Taken from the website, prochoiceactionnetwork-canada.org.

13. Ibid.

14. Richard Smith, *Obstetrics, Gynecology & Reproductive Medicine.* Volume 19, Issue 4, April 2009, 115–16.

CHAPTER 6: THE REALITY OF THE CHILD IN THE WOMB

1. Arnold Gesell, MD, *The Embryology of Behavior* (New York: Harper & Brothers, 1945), 172.

2. H. M. I. Liley, MD, *Modern Motherhood*, rev. ed. (New York: Random House, 1969), 50.

3. Andrew Peach, "Pro-Choice 'Personhood': An Abortive Concept." *Life and Learning XIII: Proceedings of the Thirteenth University Faculty for Life Conference at Georgetown University, 2003,* 190–91.

4. Ibid., see page 192.

5. Ibid., 193–94. Italics in original.

CHAPTER 7: ABORTION MEANS KILLING THIS CHILD

1. Websites, www.abortiontv.com/methods/themanyways.htm; www.lifesitenews.com/abortiontypes/; and brochure, "Life or Death" (Cincinnati, OH: Hayes Publishing, 1993, 2009).

2. Websites, www.godandscience.org/doctrine/abortion.html and www.lifesightnews.com.

3. Samuel W. Calhoun, "'Partial-Birth Abortion' Is Not Abortion: *Carhart II's* Fundamental Misapplication of *Roe." Life and Learning XVII: Proceedings of the Eighteenth University Faculty for Life Conference at Marquette University, 2008,* 87–88.

4. Laila Williamson, "Infanticide: An Anthropological Analysis," in Marvin Kohl (ed.), *Infanticide and the Value of Life* (Buffalo, NY: Prometheus Books, 1978), 62.

5. Patrick Lee, *Abortion and Unborn Human Life* (Washington, DC: The Catholic University of America Press, 1996), 115.

6. Thomson, in Feinberg, 175.

CHAPTER 8: ABORTION CAUSES PAIN TO THE CHILD

1. LifeNews.com, June 1, 2006.

2. Ibid.

3. Ibid.

4. Vincent J. Collins, MD, Steven R. Zielinski, MD, and Thomas J. Marzen, Esq., *Fetal Pain and Abortion: The Medical Evidence* (Chicago: Americans United for Life, 1984), 7.

5. Doctorsonfetalpain.com, June 25, 2005.

6. Ibid.

7. LifeSiteNews.com

8. Partial-Birth Abortion Ban Act, Public Law 108–288. Please see next note.

9. Ruling by Judge Richard C. Casey, U.S. District Court for the Southern District of New York, August 26, 2004. This and the previous quote are from *National Right to Life News*, September 2004, 18.

10. International Association for the Study of Pain, Volume XIV, No. 2, June 2006.

CHAPTER 9: THE DIGNITY OF THE HUMAN PERSON

1. "One of the first acts of war: Make killing seem honorable." *The Providence Journal*, May 5, 2004, A-9.

CHAPTER 10: SOME PRO-CHOICE REPLIES TO PRO-LIFE CLAIMS

1. Thomas Reid, *Essays on the Intellectual Powers of Man*, Essay III, Chapter IV, "Of Identity."

2. Derek Parfit, *Reasons and Persons* (Oxford: Clarendon Press, 1984, 1987), 245.

3. Ibid., 254–55.

4. Ibid., 255–56.

5. Ibid., 211.

6. Ibid., 223.

7. Ibid., 276.

8. Ibid., 214.

9. Ibid., 215. Parfit adds: "In an account of what matters, the right kind of cause could be any cause."

10. Ibid., 206.

11. Ibid., 279.

12. Boonin, *A Defense of Abortion*, 193. Section 4.5 is a detailed reply to "The Killing versus Letting Die Objection."

13. Ibid., 200. Separate paragraphs for each of the three items, (a)–(c), have been added.

14. Ibid., 202. Separate paragraphs for each of the three items, (a)–(c), have been added.

15. Ibid.

16. Ibid., 214.

17. Ibid.

18. Ibid., 223. Section 4.6 is a detailed reply to "The Intending versus Foreseeing Objection."

19. Ibid.

20. Ibid., 225.

21. Ibid., 229.

22. Ibid., 232.

23. Ibid., 232–33.

24. Boonin discusses this pro-life objection in section 4.15 of his book (266–72), "The Duty to Save the Violinist Objection."

25. Peter Singer, *Rethinking Life and Death: The Collapse of Our Traditional Ethics*, 189.

26. Ibid., 189–200. Italics in original.

CHAPTER 11: WHEN DOES A PERSON BEGIN TO EXIST

1. Boonin, 39–40.

2. Ibid., 39.

3. Ibid., 255.

4. Samuel L. Blumenfeld, *The Retreat from Motherhood* (New Rochelle, NY: Arlington House, 1975), 150.

5. "The Moral Significance of Birth," in Pojman and Beckwith, 441.

6. Ibid.

7. Ibid., 435.

8. Bernard N. Nathanson, MD. *The Abortion Papers: Inside the Abortion Mentality* (New York: Frederick Fell, 1983), 132.

CHAPTER 12: OTHER APPROACHES

1. Parfit, 322.

2. These points are taken from Andrew Peach, "Late- vs. Early-Term Abortion: A Thomistic Analysis," *The Thomist*, January 2007.

3. *The Journal of Philosophy* 86 (April 1989). Reprinted in Pojman and Beckwith, 320–38.

4. *The Journal of Philosophy* 87 (May 1990). Reprinted in Pojman and Beckwith, 339–42.

5. Ibid., 341.

6. Published in Pojman and Beckwith, 343–53.

7. Ibid., 345.

8. Ibid., 347.

CHAPTER 15: THE ROLE OF GOVERNMENT

1. *Roe v. Wade*, section XI; Shapiro, 43.

CHAPTER 16: OTHER SIGNIFICANT LEGAL ASPECTS

1. *Roe v. Wade*, section VIII; Shapiro, 35–36.
2. Ibid., section IX, 38.
3. Ronald Dworkin, *Life's Dominion: An Argument about Abortion, Euthanasia, and Individual Freedom* (New York: Vintage Books, 1994), 103.
4. Sherwin, 102–4. Footnotes have been deleted.
5. See MacKinnon's *Feminism Unmodified* (1987), 93–102, for a similar expression of her views. Cited in Stith's original paper of which the above is an abridged version. See also her essay in Pojman and Beckwith, "*Roe v. Wade*: A Study in Male Ideology," 109–18.
6. Richard Stith, "Her Choice, Her Problem: How Abortion Empowers Men," in *First Things*, Number 195, August/September 2009, 7–9.

CHAPTER 17: THE HARD CASES: RAPE, LIFE OF THE WOMAN, SEVERE DEFORMITIES

1. Laurence H. Tribe, *Abortion: The Clash of Absolutes* (New York: W. W. Norton, 1992), 231.
2. Sherwin, 101.
3. Tribe, 3.
4. Dworkin, 96.
5. F. M. Kamm, *Creation and Abortion: A Study in Moral and Legal Philosophy* (New York: Oxford University Press, 1992), pp. 83–84. Kamm discusses five conditions in all, on pages 83–92.
6. Caroline Whitbeck, "Taking Women Seriously as People: The Moral Implications for Abortion," in Pojman and Beckwith, 399.
7. Tribe, 131–32. Italics in original.
8. David C. Reardon, Julie Makimaa, and Amy Sobie (eds.), *Victims and Victors: Speaking Out about Their Pregnancies, Abortions, and Children Resulting from Sexual Assault* (Springfield, IL: Acorn Books, 2000), ix–x.
9. Ibid., 15.
10. David C. Reardon, *Aborted Women: Silent No More* (Chicago: Loyola, 1987), 163. Emphasis added.
11. Christopher Kaczor, *The Ethics of Abortion: Women's Rights, Human Life, and the Question of Justice* (New York and London: Routledge, 2011), 184.
12. Rebecca Kiessling, website, www.rebeccakiessling.com.
13. American Life League. Declaration: Protecting the Life of the Mother. www.whyprolife.com/abortion-facts/
14. Dworkin, *Life's Dominion*, 32.
15. Ibid.
16. Peter Singer, *Practical Ethics*, 173. Italics in original.
17. Ibid.
18. *Signs: Journal of Women in Culture and Society*, Summer 2009, 795.
19. William Robert Johnston, "Reasons Given for Having Abortions in the United States." See www.johnstonsarchive.net/policy/abortion/abreasons.html.

CHAPTER 18: SAFETY ISSUES

1. Sherwin, 101.

2. David C. Reardon, *Aborted Women*, 109.

3. Taken from the website, realchoice.0catch.com/library. The jail sentencing in the last item is from *The Providence Journal*, September 15, 2010, A-2.

4. Doug Patten, January 24, 2011. From the website, www.gopusa.com.

5. David C. Reardon, *Aborted Women*, 90–91.

6. Ibid., 292.

7. Ibid., 25.

8. Michelle Malkin, "The Philadelphia Horror: How Mass Murder Gets a Pass." January 22, 2011. From the website, www.creators.com.

9. From the website, http://www.cafemom.com. November 11, 2011.

10. This is the title and theme of a brochure published by NARAL, National Abortion Rights Action League, n.d.

11. Warren, "On the Moral and Legal Status of Abortion," Feinberg, 103.

12. From the website, http://realchoice.blogspot.com/2005/05/bad-old-days .html.

13. *The Post-Abortion Review*, Vol. 12, No. 4, October–December 2004, 2.

14. Abby Johnson with Cindy Lambert, *Unplanned: The Dramatic True Story of a Former Planned Parenthood Leader's Eye-Opening Journey across the Life Line* (San Francisco: Ignatius Press, 2010. In association with Tyndale House and Focus on the Family). Quotations are from pages 3, 5, 8, and 4 respectively. The event described was in September 2009.

15. David C. Reardon, N. J. Hoeldtke, P. Marchetti M. F. Greene, and J. L. Ecker, "Abortion, Health, and the Law," *New England Journal of Medicine 2004*, 350:1908– 1910, April 29, 2004. Correspondence.

16. From the website, www.abortiontv.com/Glitch/AbortionMoreDangerous .htm.

CHAPTER 19: GOING BEYOND ABORTION: THE UNITY WAY

1. David C. Reardon, *Making Abortion Rare: A Healing Strategy for a Divided Nation* (Springfield, IL: Acorn Books, 1996), 5.

2. Dr. Julius Fogel in an interview with Colman McCarthy, "A Psychological View of Abortion," *The Washington Post*, March 7, 1971. Quoted in Reardon, *Making Abortion Rare*, 5.

3. *The Post-Abortion Review*, Vol. 12, No. 4, October–December 2004, 2.

4. David C. Reardon, *Making Abortion Rare*, 11.

5. This was Kiki Latimer's repeated experience when she worked as a counselor at Woman-to-Woman, a pregnancy advising agency, for twenty years.

6. Helen Alvaré, "Abortion Is Family Law." The Witherspoon Institute. Public Discourse, Ethics, Law and the Common Good, 2010, http://www.thepublicdiscourse .com/2010/11/2055. Helen Alvaré is Associate Professor at George Mason University School of Law and Senior Fellow at The Witherspoon Institute, where she serves

as chair of the Task Force on Conscience Protection. These remarks are based on her presentation at the Conference on Life and Choice, Princeton University, October 2010.

CHAPTER 20: ULTIMATE ISSUES

1. Andrew Peach, "Are All Children Adopted?," unpublished paper. See his "Abortion and Parental Obligation," *Life and Learning XIV: Proceedings of the Fourteenth University Faculty for Life Conference at the University of St. Thomas Law School 2004*, 193–218. The latter is a revised and expanded version of the former.

2. Parfit, Section 94, "Is the True View Believable," 279–80.

Works Cited

Alvaré, Helen. "Abortion Is Family Law." The Witherspoon Institute. Public Discourse, Ethics, Law and the Common Good, 2010. http://www.the publicdiscourse.com/2010/11/2055.

American Life League. Declaration: Protecting the Life of the Mother.

Blumenfield, Samuel L. The Retreat from Motherhood. New Rochelle, NY: Arlington House, 1975.

Bolton, Martha Brandt. "Responsible Women and Abortion Decisions." In O'Neill and Ruddick, Having Children, 40–51.

Boonin, David. A Defense of Abortion. New York: Cambridge University Press, 2003.

Calhoun, Samuel W. "'Partial-Birth Abortion' Is Not Abortion: Carhart II's Fundamental Misapplication of Roe." Life and Learning: Proceedings of the Eighteenth University Faculty for Life Conference at Marquette University, 2008, 83–149.

Collins, Vincent J., MD, Steven R. Zielinski, MD, and Thomas J. Marzen, Esq. Fetal Pain and Abortion: The Medical Evidence. Chicago: Americans United for Life, 1984.

Cozic, Charles P., and Stacey L. Tipp, eds. Abortion: Opposing Viewpoints. San Diego: Greenhaven Press, 1991.

Doerr, Edd, and James W. Prescott, eds. Abortion Rights and Fetal 'Personhood.' Long Beach, CA: Centerline Press, 1989.

Dworkin, Ronald. Life's Dominion: An Argument about Abortion, Euthanasia, and Individual Freedom. New York: Vintage Books, 1994.

Feinberg, Joel, ed. The Problem of Abortion, Second Edition. Belmont, CA: Wadsworth, 1984.

———. "Potentiality, Development, and Rights." In Feinberg, The Problem of Abortion, 145–50.

———. First Things. No. 195, August/September 2009.

Fogel, Julius. "A Psychological View of Abortion." The Washington Post, March 7, 1971. Quoted in David Reardon, Making Abortion Rare, 5.

The Free Dictionary. Partial birth abortion. See www.medical-dictionary.thefree dictionary.com. September 15, 2011.

Gesell, Arnold, MD. *The Embryology of Behavior.* New York: Harper & Brothers, 1945.

Jaggar, Alison M. "Abortion Rights and Gender Justice Worldwide: An Essay in Political Philosophy." In Tooley, et al., *Abortion: Three Perspectives,* 120–79.

Johnson, Abby, with Cindy Lambert. *Unplanned: The Dramatic True Story of a Former Planned Parenthood Leader's Eye-Opening Journey across the Life Line.* San Francisco: Ignatius Press, 2010. In association with Tyndale House and Focus on the Family.

Johnston, William Robert. "Reasons Given for Having Abortions in the United States." See www.johnstonarchive.net/policy/abortion./abreasons.html.

Kaczor, Christopher. *The Ethics of Abortion: Women's Rights, Human Life, and the Question of Justice.* New York and London: Routledge, 2011.

Kamm, F. M. *Creation and Abortion: A Study in Moral and Legal Philosophy.* New York: Oxford University Press, 1992.

Kohl, Marvin, ed. *Infanticide and the Value of Life.* Buffalo: Prometheus Books, 1978.

Lee, Patrick. *Abortion and Unborn Human Life.* Washington, DC: The Catholic University of America Press, 1996.

———. *Life and Learning XIII: Proceedings of the Thirteenth University Faculty for Life Conference at Georgetown University, 2003.*

———. *Life and Learning XIV: Proceedings of the Fourteenth University Faculty for Life Conference at the University of St. Thomas Law School, 2004.*

———. *Life and Learning XVIII: Proceedings of the Eighteenth University Faculty for Life Conference at Marquette University, 2008.*

"Life or Death." Brochure. Cincinnati: Hayes Publishing, 1993, 2009.

Liley, H. M. I. *Modern Motherhood,* Revised Edition. New York: Random House, 1969.

MacKinnon, Catherine A. *Feminism Unmodified: Discourses on Life and Law.* Cambridge: Harvard University Press, 1987.

———. "*Roe v. Wade:* A Study in Male Ideology." In Pojman and Beckwith, *The Abortion Controversy,* 109–18.

Maguire, Marjorie Reiley. "Symbiosis, Biology, and Personalization." In Doerr and Prescott, *Abortion Rights and Fetal 'Personhood,'* 11–19.

Malkin, Michelle. "The Philadelphia Horror: How Mass Murder gets a Pass." January 22, 2011. From the website, www.creators.com

Marquis, Don. "Why Abortion Is Immoral." *The Journal of Philosophy* 86, April 1989. Reprinted in Pojman and Beckwith, *The Abortion Controversy,* 320–38.

McInerney, Peter K. "Does a Fetus Already Have a Future-Like Ours?" *The Journal of Philosophy* 87, May 1990. Reprinted in Pojman and Beckwith, *The Abortion Controversy,* 339–42.

Morgan, Lynn M. "When Does Life Begin? A Cross-Cultural Perspective on the Personhood of Fetuses and Young Children." In Doerr and Prescott, *Abortion Rights and Fetal 'Personhood,'* 97–114.

Motion and Brief Amicus Curiae of Certain Physicians, Professors and Fellows of the American College of Obstetrics and Gynecology in Support of Appellees, 8–29. Submitted to the U.S. Supreme Court, October Term, 1971.

Nathanson, Bernard N., MD. *The Abortion Papers: Inside the Abortion Mentality.* New York: Frederick Fell, 1983.

National Abortion Rights Action League. Brochure on back-alley abortions, n.d.

National Right to Life News, September 2004.

O'Neill, Onora, and William Ruddick, eds. *Having Children: Philosophical and Legal Reflections on Parenthood.* New York: Oxford University Press, 1979.

Parfit, Derek. *Reasons and Persons.* Oxford: Clarendon Press, 1984, 1987.

Partial-Birth Abortion Ban Act, Public Law 108-288.

Paske, Gerald H. "Abortion and the Neo-Natal Right to Life: A Critique of Marquis's Futurist Argument." In Pojman and Beckwith, *The Abortion Controversy,* 343–53.

Patten, Doug. January 24, 2011. www.gopusa.com.

Peach, Andrew J. "Pro-Choice 'Personhood': An Abortive Concept." *Life and Learning XIII: Proceedings of the Thirteenth University Faculty for Life Conference at Georgetown University, 2003,* 187–210.

———. "Are All Children Adopted?" Unpublished paper. See his "Abortion and Parental Obligation." *Life and Learning XIV: Proceedings of the Fourteenth University Faculty for Life Conference at the University of St. Thomas Law School 2004,* 193–218. The latter is a revised and expanded version of the former.

———. "Late- vs. Early-Term Abortion: A Thomistic Analysis." In *The Thomist* 71, 2007, 113–42.

Pojman, Louis P., and Francis J. Beckwith, eds. *The Abortion Controversy: A Reader.* Boston and London: Jones and Bartlett, 1994.

The Post-Abortion Review, Vol. 12, No. 4, October–December 2004.

The Providence Journal, May 5, 2004.

———, September 15, 2010.

Reardon, David. *Aborted Women: Silent No More.* Chicago: Loyola Press, 1987.

———. *Making Abortion Rare: A Healing Strategy for a Divided Nation.* Springfield, IL: Acorn Books, 1996.

Reardon, David, Julie Makimaa, and Amy Sobie, eds. *Victims and Victors: Speaking Out about Their Pregnancies, Abortions, and Children Resulting from Sexual Assault.* Springfield, IL: Acorn Books, 2000.

Reardon, David, N. J. Hoeldtke, P. Marchetti, M. F. Greene, and J. L. Ecker. "Abortion, Health, and the Law." *New England Journal of Medicine 2004,* 350:1908–1910, April 29, 2004. Correspondence.

Reid, Thomas. *Essays on the Intellectual Powers of Man,* 1785. The Edinburgh Edition of Thomas Reid, Volume 3. Edited by Derek R. Brookes. University Park, PA: Pennsylvania State University Press, 2002.

Robertson, Constance. *The Religious Case for Abortion.* 1983. Quoted in Cozic and Tipp, *Abortion: Opposing Viewpoints.* 126.

Shapiro, Ian, ed. *Abortion: The Supreme Court Decisions, 1965–2000,* Second Edition. Indianapolis and Cambridge: Hackett, 2000.

Sherwin, Susan. *No Longer Patient: Feminist Ethics and Health Care.* Philadelphia: Temple University Press, 1992.

Shettles, Landrum B., and Robert Rugh. *From Conception to Birth: The Drama of Life's Beginnings.* New York: Harper and Row, 1971.

Signs: Journal of Women in Culture and Society, Summer 2009.

Singer, Peter. *Practical Ethics,* Second Edition. Cambridge: Cambridge University Press, 1993.

———. *Rethinking Life and Death: The Collapse of Our Traditional Ethics.* New York: St. Martin's Griffin, 1994.

Smith, Richard. *Obstetrics, Gynecology & Reproductive Medicine*. Volume 19, Issue 4, April 2009.

Stith, Richard. "Her Choice, Her Problem: How Abortion Empowers Men." In *First Things*, Number 195, August/ September 2009, 7–9.

Thomson, Judith Jarvis. "A Defense of Abortion." *Philosophy & Public Affairs*, Vol. 1, No. 1, 1971, 47–66. Reprinted in Feinberg, *The Problem of Abortion*, 173–87.

Tooley, Michael. *Abortion and Infanticide*. Oxford: Clarendon Press, 1983.

———. "In Defense of Abortion and Infanticide." 1984. In Feinberg, *The Problem of Abortion*, 120–34.

———. "Why a Liberal View Is Correct." 2009. In Tooley, et al., *Abortion: Three Perspectives*, 3–64.

Tooley, Michael, Celia Wolf-Devine, Philip. E. Divine, and Alison M. Jaggar. *Abortion: Three Perspectives*. New York and Oxford: Oxford University Press, 2009

Tribe, Laurence H. *Abortion: The Clash of Absolutes*. New York: W. W. Norton, 1992.

U. S. District Court for the Southern District of New York, August 26, 2004.

Warren, Mary Anne. "On the Moral and Legal Status of Abortion." *The Monist*, Vol. 57, 1973. Reprinted in Feinberg, *The Problem of Abortion*, 102–19.

———. "The Moral Significance of Birth." *Hypathia* Vol. 4, 3. Fall 1989. Reprinted in Pojman and Beckwith, *The Abortion Controversy*, 425–44.

Welton, K. B. "An Unwanted Child Justifies Abortion." In Cozic and Tipp, *Abortion: Opposing Viewpoints*, 124–30.

Whitbeck, Caroline. "Taking Women Seriously as People: The Moral Implications for Abortion." In Pojman and Beckwith, *The Abortion Controversy*, 384–407.

Williamson, Laila. "Infanticide: An Anthropological Analysis." In Marvin Kohl, *Infanticide and the Value of Life*, 61–75.

Index

Abortion Pain Prevention Act, 76
abortion, a woman's right to. *See*
 woman's right to abortion
achievement view of persons. *See*
 person(s)
adoption, 18, 180–81
agnostic position on beginning of a
 person's existence, 117–18, 191
Allen, Anita, 18
Alvaré, Helen, 179–80
American Psychological Association,
 167
Anand, Kanwaljeet, 75–77

back-alley abortions: pro-choice
 perspective, 165–66, 169–71, 192;
 pro-life perspective, 171–73, 192
beginning of a person's existence,
 105–16
being a person. *See* person(s)
birth: after, when personhood is
 achieved, 31–33, 106, 114–15;
 when personhood is achieved at, in
 defense of, 6, 28, 31, 95, 112–13;
 when personhood is achieved at,
 in opposition to, 113–14; when
 personhood is achieved at, question

of or proposed, 31, 85, 106. *See also*
 infanticide; partial-birth abortion
being in the womb (BWI), 7
Blumenfeld, Samuel L., 112
Bolton, Martha Brandt, 36
Boonin, David: conception-fertilization,
 rejection of, 107–8; not-a-person
 argument, 25–27, 30, 58, 95;
 personhood, when achieved, 30–31;
 slippery slope argument, rejection
 of, 26–27, 49; violinist argument,
 defense of, 96–101, 183–84
brain activity, when person begins to
 exist, 31, 106

Calderone, Mary, 172
Calhoun, Samuel W., 64
cancerous womb, 158
childbirth, abortion and, 173–76
child in the womb: if in doubt,
 recognize, 124–25; reality of
 asserted, 47–59, 135, *136*, 173,
 183–85, 193; reality of denied,
 21–33, 134, 170, 185–87, 193; right
 to live denied if defend woman's
 right to abortion, 129, 148. *See also*
 under right(s)

Collins, Vincent, 76
conception-fertilization, 105–8, *108*, 116. *See also* agnostic position
continuum argument, 47–51, *51*, 89–94, 184–89

deaths, women and legal abortion: from abortion and childbirth compared, 173–76, *175*; pro-choice perspective, 165–66, 169–71; pro–life perspective, 167–69, 171–73
deformities, child with severe, 20, 82, 159–60
dignity of the human person, 81–86, 103–4
discrimination, 18, 143, 171

doubt: how it may arise, 123–24; pro-choice arguments regarding, 125–26; pro-life arguments regarding, 124–25; scope of, 127–28; and going wrong, which way is worse, 128–29, 147–48
Dworkin, Ronald, 145, 151, 158–59

early versus late abortions, 119–20, 127–28
ectopic pregnancy, 158
exceptions in pro-life views. *See* hard cases

facts about the being in the womb, 8–11
family law, relationships, 179–80
Feinberg, Joel, 30
feminist accounts of abortion and feminist quality of life argument. *See under* quality of life
fertilization. *See* conception-fertilization
"fertilized ovum," 8
fetus: has no absolute value, 21–22; and achievement view, 30–31; and "child," "baby," and being in the womb (BIW), 7; medically referred to as from six weeks on, 9; are not persons, 22, 33; is a potential person, not an actual one, 29–30; pro-choice view of, 21–22, 29–30, 33, 185–86; use as defensive, dehumanizing, prejudicial and manipulative, 86
Finnis, John, 86
Fogel, Julius, 178
future-like-ours argument, 120–22

gender equality. *See* Jaggar, Alison
Gesell, Arnold, 49–50
Gonzales v. Carhart, 180
Gosnell, Kermit B, 168–69, 171–72
government, role of, 137–41, *138*
gradualist position on beginning of a person's existence, 118–19, 191
Guttmacher Institute, 77

hard cases (rape, incest, deformed child, life of the woman), 149–62; pro-life with exceptions view of, 149–53, 156–61, *161*, 192; total pro-life, no exceptions view of, 149–50, 153–61, *161*, 192; two positions on, 149–50, 157–61
harmful to women, abortion as: affirmed by pro-life and unity way, 178–79, 192; denied by pro-choice, 167, 179, 192. *See also* safety issues
healthy child, 20, 82, 192
heartbeat, 8
human beings, and persons, 21, 57–58
human life, 105

identity. *See* personal identity
imposing, 143–44
incest, 16, 149, 162
infanticide: abortion as, 64–66; Kamchadal practice as, 65–66; Lynn M. Morgan's defense of, 29, 84; partial-birth abortion as, 64; the question of, 84–85, 115. *See also* Singer, Peter; Tooley, Michael
intruder argument. *See* Thomson, Judith Jarvis

Jaggar, Alison, 17–18, 84, 143
Johnson, Abby, 173
Jones, Edith H., 178

Kaczor, Christopher, 155–56
Kamchadal practice. *See* infanticide
Kamm, F. M., 151–52
Kiessling, Rebecca, 156
killing: the child in the womb, abortion
    as, 61–74, 183; and letting die,
    66–70, 96–100, 183; made to seem
    honorable, 85–86

late abortion. *See* early vs. late abortion
law: family, 179–80. *See also* legal
    question of abortion; legal status of
    abortion
Lee, Nancy Howell, 172
Lee, Patrick, 70
legal question of abortion, 5–6, 131–
    62, 192
legal status of abortion: government
    must take a stand, 137–39; pro-
    choice position, 133–35, *134*, 192;
    pro-life position, 135–36, *136*, 192
legislating morality, 133
Life and Choice conference, 76, 86
life of the woman, 157–59
Liley, A., 50
Liley, H. M. I., 50
line(s) marking when a person begins
    to exist: and achievement view and
    being-functioning distinction, 116,
    190–91; government must draw one
    somewhere, 138–39; an objection
    to almost all, 116; overview of,
    106; proposed, 31–32, 105–15. *See
    also* agnostic position; gradualist
    position

MacKinnon, Catherine, 146–47, 168
Maguire, Marjorie Reiley, 28–29, 31,
    83–84, 95
Malkin, Michelle, 168–69
Marquis, Don, 120–22
McInerney, Peter K, 121–22
McMahon, James T., 63

methods of abortion: dilation and
    curettage (D & C), 40, 62, 65, 69;
    dilation and evacuation (D & E), 40,
    62, 65, 69; dilation and extraction
    (D & X); hysterotomy, 62, 96–98;
    mifepristone–abortion pill (RU–
    486), 40–41, 62; prostaglandin, 62;
    suction aspiration, 39, 61, 69. *See
    also* partial–birth abortion
moral question of abortion, 5–6
Morgan, Lynn M., 28–29, 83–84

Nathanson, Bernard N., 113
National Abortion Federation, 166–67
Neerhof, Mark G., 64
no-duty-to-sustain argument, 35–43;
    Martha Brandt Bolton's view, 36;
    and a woman's right over her body,
    35. *See also* Thompson, Judith Jarvis
not-a-person argument, 21–33, 55–59,
    83–84, 89–96, 127, 185–87. *See also*
    person(s), achievement view

Obama, President, 4
obligation of parent to child, 70–72,
    100–101, 184
overpopulation, 20, 83, 134, 192

pain: abortion as cause of for child,
    75–79, 125, 144, 183–84, 193;
    abortion and women, 78, 144, 165,
    169, 184; argument applies even
    if the being in the womb (BIW) is
    not a person, 79, 144; controversy
    regarding, 77–78, 144, 184; fetal,
    question of, 43; Nebraska fetal law,
    76; pro-choice replies to pro-life
    claims regarding, 43, 77, 103, 184;
    risk factors concerning the child,
    78; special horror of partial-birth
    abortion, 76–77; weighing harms
    and benefits, 78
parental obligation. *See* obligation of
    parent to child
Parfit, Derek, 90–94, 118, 187–89
partial-birth abortion, 41–42, 63–65,
    69, 76–77, 180

Paske, Gerald H., 122

Peach, Andrew, 57–58, 184

person(s): when achieved, begin to exist, 31–33, 105–15; being in the womb affirmed as by pro-life, 47–59, 184–89; being in the womb denied as by pro-choice, 21–33, 184–89; dignity of the human, 81–86, 103–4; and human beings, 21; and human being distinction, engineered to try to justify abortion, 57–58; potential, 27, 29–30, 33, 120, 186, 191; question of regarding the being in the womb, 7; and *Roe v. Wade* Supreme Court decision, 6, 31, 138, 145. *See also* not-a-person argument; personal identity

person(s), achievement view of: gradualist position as resting on, 119; and lines marking the beginning of personhood, 116; as basis for pro-choice not-a-person argument, 30–31, 33; and ultimate issues, pro-choice and pro-life, 186, 189, 193

person(s), being and functioning distinction regarding: and gradualist view, 118–19; and lines marking the beginning of personhood, 116; pro-choice replies to pro-life argument regarding, 95–96; as part of pro-life argument that the being in the womb is a person, 55–59; and ultimate issues, pro-choice and pro-life, 186–87, 189–91

personal identity: affirmation of, 47–51, 89–90, 93, 184–89, 193; denial of, 90–94, 185–88, 193

Peterson, Scott and Laci, 66

Planned Parenthood, 173

population. *See* overpopulation

power-freedom-control for women: a pro-choice view, 145–46; a pro-life view, 146–47

pregnancy, 1–4, 17–18, 20, 151, 171. *See also* no-duty-to-sustain argument

privacy, 144–45, 171

pro-life with exceptions view. *See* hard cases

pro-life with no exceptions view (total pro-life). *See* hard cases

psychology of pro-choice and pro-life, 126–27

quality of life: of the child, 19–20, 81–82, 125, 192; overpopulation and, 20, 83, 192; of the woman, 15–18, 20, 82–84, 125, 145–47, 192

rape: whether abortion benefits women in case of, 153–57, 192; and innocent child, 153–57, 192; as reason to have an abortion, 16, 150–53, 157, 192; testimony of a person conceived in, 156; Thomson's violinist argument and the case of, 37, 71–72, 151–53

Reardon, David, 153–55, 172, 174, 178–79

Reid, Thomas, 90

religious issue, 6

results of abortion, 64–65

right(s): basic human, 17–18; a child's over his body, 69, 102–3; a child's to live, 124–25, 129, 135–38, 148, 183; to life, Thomson, on the meaning of, 38; to life, Tooley, on the meaning of, 23–24. *See also* woman's right to abortion; woman's right over her body

Roberts, Dorothy, 160–61

Robertson, Constance, 6, 19

Roe v. Wade, (U. S. Supreme Court decision legalizing abortion): ruling that birth is when personhood is achieved, 6, 31, 138; dangers of abortion before, 165, 169, 173–74; and partial–birth abortion, 64; ruling that right to privacy is basis for right to abortion, 144–45, 147

safety issues: abortion and childbirth compared, 173–76, *175*; pro-choice perspective, 165–67, 169–71, 192; pro-life perspective, 167–69, 171–73, 192. *See also* harmful to women, abortion as

Sanger, Margaret, 19

Schmidt, Richard T. F., 76

segmentation, when person begins to exist, 105, 108–10

sentience, when person begins to exist, 106

sexual values, 181

Sherwin, Susan: feminist quality of life argument, 15–17, 84; fetus has no absolute value argument, 21–22; and the need for legal abortion, 165–66; on power-freedom-control for women, 145–46; rape case, 16, 151

Singer, Peter: infanticide, defense of, 20, 32–33, 84, 115, 160; sanctity of human life, rejection of, 103–4

SLED argument, 51–55, 55, 95, 107, 185–86

slippery slope argument, 26–27, 49

Smith, Richard, 43

species membership argument, 25–26

Sprang, M. Leroy, 64

Stith, Richard, 146–47, 168

Thomson, Judith Jarvis: intruder argument, 37–38; on the right to life and to abortion, 38–39, 125; and slippery slope argument, 27; and defense of violinist argument, 36–39, 96–102, 183–84; and doubt about violinist argument, 127–28; pro-life reply to violinist argument, 66–73; violinist argument, and rape case, 37, 150–53

Tooley, Michael: defense of infanticide, 24–25, 31–33, 84–85, 114–15; not-a-person argument, 23–24, 30, 58, 95; on when personhood

is achieved, 30–33, 96, 114–15, 185–86

Tribe, Lawrence, 149, 151–53

ultimate issues, 183–93

unity way: abortion as harmful to women, 178–79, 193; woman and child go together, 177–78, 193

unwanted child, 19, 81–82, 179

unwanted pregnancy, 179

viability (when person begins to exist), 31, 106, 110–12, 185

violinist argument. *See* Thomson, Judith Jarvis

wanted child, 19, 81–82, 192

Warren, Mary Anne: birth, personhood achieved at, 31, 95, 106, 112–13; legal restrictions on abortion justified, 171; not-a-person argument, 22–23, 30, 56, 58, 95; relative to social acceptance view of being a person, 31, 95, 112–13

Welton, K. B., 20

Whitbeck, Caroline, 152

woman's right to abortion: based on fetus not being a person, 21–33, 89–96, 185–87; based on her right over her body, 35–39, 114, 183, 185–86; and birth, as marking when personhood is achieved, 114; denied if defend child's right to live, 129, 148; essential for gender equality, 17–18; legal, 133–35, 137–39. *See also under* quality of life

woman's right over her body: begins at conception, 69; if in doubt, recognize, 125–26. *See also* woman's right to abortion

Wright, Jean, 75

zygote, 8, 107, 121, 127, 186

About the Authors

Stephen D. Schwarz is professor emeritus of philosophy at the University of Rhode Island, where he started teaching in 1963. He continues teaching on a part-time basis, including ethics and the philosophy of the human person. The present book developed from lectures and discussions on abortion in his ethics classes over the last thirty years or so. Schwarz studied philosophy at Fordham University under Dietrich von Hildebrand and Balduin Schwarz, his father. He received his BA and MA at Fordham and his PhD at Harvard. He is the author of *The Moral Question of Abortion*.

Kiki Latimer collaborated with Stephen Schwarz in the production of this book. She wrote the opening section, *"Oh my God, I'm pregnant."* She has served as his teaching assistant in ethics and other classes over the last twenty-five years. She received her BA in speech communication and psychology, with a minor in philosophy from the University of Rhode Island; she graduated *summa cum laude*. Latimer is executive director emerilus at Woman-to-Woman, a pregnancy advising agency for twenty years. She is the author of three children's books: *Islands of Hope, The WaterFire Duck, Bubble Butt*, and and the upcoming *Heal of the Hand*. www.kikilatimer.com.